Three

A fan's eye-view of United's championship hat-trick

by Linda Harvey
& Paul Windridge

EMPIRE
PUBLICATIONS

EMPIRE PUBLICATIONS
1 Newton Street, Manchester M1 1HW

Copyright Paul Windridge & Linda Harvey 2001
ISBN 1 901 746 24 0
Photographs, cover and graphic design: Paul Windridge
Typeset by Ashley Shaw and Stuart Fish

Printed in Great Britain by
Cox and Wyman
Cardiff Road
Reading
RG1 8EX

Contents

About the Authors

Linda Harvey

Linda Harvey was born and bred in Salford. As a child, her footballing heroes were the Busby Babes, particularly Eddie Colman. Over the years she has occasionally had cause to stretch the umbilical cord which attaches her to Old Trafford, but thankfully it has never snapped and she has remained a 'local', now living in the hills surrounding Manchester, and working in the City Centre.

Paul Windridge

Paul Windridge was born in Warwickshire. Much to the dismay of his family of fanatical rugby supporters he had somehow been infected by a virulent form of the Red virus. When the family moved to Lancashire in the early sixties it gave him the opportunity to seek out fellow sufferers on the Stretford End. There was no turning back!

Introduction

If Only

At the end of a season when Manchester United won the Premier League title for the third year running there were still some who weren't satisfied. It is clearly not enough to come out so far ahead of the rest that we were more or less celebrating the League on New Year's Day. Were they 'avin' a larf or what?

On the other hand, the news that the gaffer was going to sever all ties after his final season left us with a sour taste. People were citing the Busby syndrome as the reason he should depart, but to us that is absolute nonsense. The fact is Alex Ferguson sought advice from Sir Matt whenever he felt it necessary. Sir Matt was the one with all the experience then, now it is Sir Alex. There is no substitute for that experience.

The gaffer has built a team which, on its day, is capable of beating any other in the world. It is not quite the culmination of his life's work as we still have one season left with the man who has guided us to so many trophies but it is easy to lose count. The trouble is — all this success has led to a certain amount of complacency among certain supporters.

Introduction

Though these are more than likely supporters who have been attracted to the club fairly recently and who have known little else but success.

Those of us who have been supporting for more years than we care to remember can recall several years when little reward came our way. It's not that we didn't grumble — of course we did — but if anyone had said to us that by the end of the 90s we would be basking in the sunshine of Barcelona having just won the biggest prize of the lot after winning the Premiership and the FA Cup as well, we'd have been phoning for a doctor.

So a season when we 'just' win the Premiership we can cope with, thank you! The fact that we have endured several trophy-less years, 26 years between championships and 31 years between European Cups, has made the past decade all the sweeter.

You cannot fully appreciate winning unless you have lost. So those who have been heard to say, "If only" would be best to remember that success tends to go in cycles and one day they will have to endure back-to-back trophy-less seasons. They may have to survive several years without success, or maybe by then they will have disappeared to pastures new and demonstrated that their support was not what it seemed in the first place but was mere infatuation instead.

In the meantime, we are in an era of rich reward. The players wear the shirt with pride and the loyalty and dedication to the cause is second to none. All these are virtues instilled into them by Alex Ferguson and for that we are forever in his debt.

The close season

Early on in June it was announced that not only had United won the Premiership in style, but they had also won it fairly by topping the FA Premiership Fair Play League, with 48 yellow cards and four red with relegated Sheffield Wednesday were in second spot — in retrospect, maybe Sheffield Wednesday should have considered not playing so fairly — they may not have gone down!

The silver polish had only just emerged from the Old Trafford cupboard when United made their first signing in readiness for the new season's assault — Fabien Barthez became the first to join us from Monaco. I couldn't help thinking it was going to be a bit of a meteorological shock for the man who'd been used to the Mediterranean sun beating down on his bald pate. There was also a bit of a shock in store for the less hirsute of us as well:

Fabien, Fabien, give us a wave

I just happened to be down at Old Trafford on the afternoon of the press conference. I had made it up the M6 with half an hour to spare so decided to call in and pay a brief visit to check on building work etc. I parked my car by the North Stand and walked over

The close season

towards the museum when a crowd of kids spotted me and ran over brandishing a variety of pens and autograph books.

"Blimey," I thought, "I only got a couple of copies of ,A Seat in the Crowd this week on approval, how the hell did they know?!" "Where are you off to?" they asked in unison. "I'm going to meet Linda in a bit," I said, "we're doing an interview on BBC GMR." "Linda?" they said, as the lads jumped from foot to foot, hardly able to contain themselves. "Thought you'd given up on her?" "No, I've not given up on her!" I replied and I'm thinking — blimey, fame spreads bloody quick!

The lads were becoming very animated and asked where Linda was and seemed disappointed when I told them that she would be meeting me at the BBC around 6 o'clock that evening. They eventually settled and the first book was thrust in my direction. I signed it and the recipient looked aghast.

"What's up?" I say, looking aggrieved. "What sort of signature is that?" he said. "You're not Fabien Barthez, you're just another baldy bastard — and anyway I thought it was strange you didn't have that fuzz on your chin. So, who's this Linda you're on about? Not Evangelista I don't suppose?!"

Whoops! Now there's a co-incidence! There was I at Old Trafford at the same time as the Barthez Press conference — looking baldy and eventually on my way to do a radio show chat thing with Linda (not Evangelista) to promote our book!

Mind you if Linda (not Evangelista) was actually Linda Evangelista, I suspect we may have sold a few more copies, n'est pas?

On June 10th Shay Brennan, one of United's 1968 European Cup heroes, died from a heart attack. Shay had been drafted into the first post- Munich game against Sheffield Wednesday in 1958 to make his debut on the left wing and scored twice. He only ever scored six goals for United in his whole career — 355 appearances altogether in the red shirt! Ironically he was deposed at full back for the 1963 FA Cup Final by Tony Dunne. The two of them went on to form a full-back partnership that served United for years. I had the privilege of meeting the man at the memorial service at Old Trafford for Dennis Viollet. He will be sadly missed.

At the end of June our new Season Tickets arrived, earlier than ever before, but then they'd had our money earlier than ever before as well! For those who were still harbouring fantasies about turning the so-called 'singing end' into an Italian type Curva, with Jonah perched precariously on the front barrier while conducting proceedings, the accompanying letter would have done little to offer optimism. And as Linda said at the time, "We'd heard it all before I suppose, but I'd still like to know why standing in front of your seat, as opposed to jumping up and down every few minutes is more dangerous. I can understand the argument about those wanting/needing to sit down not being able to see, although in the section where most so-called trouble had occurred during the last couple of seasons, it had been almost impossible to find anyone who had complained. But for some of us (i.e. people like me with arthritic knees) it is actually more uncomfortable to remain seated in seats with little leg room and it's certainly more uncomfortable to keep having to get up and down than to remain standing!

This was an issue that raised its head again in August when it was reported on Greater Manchester

The close season

Radio that Trafford Council had said that they were considering closing sections of Old Trafford in response to persistent standing. What wasn't reported at the time was that Trafford Borough Council would welcome a trial of limited safe standing and would be looking into standing arrangements at German grounds.

Back in mid-July a chance to see the King presented itself:

A Dream Cast with one Major Player

The mad Dane had been offered two free tickets for the Richmond Dreamcast beach football tournament, but as he was in Denmark, and not (quite) daft enough to have come over for the day, I was the lucky recipient. The fact that Eric would be playing was a deciding factor in me taking advantage of the offer and also the factor which persuaded Gina to come with me. So on the Saturday morning we set off for Surrey. Gina wore her Eric t-shirt and was intent on one thing — getting the great man's autograph.

The tournament consisted of seven games, with each team playing the other for eight minutes a half, a short break in between and then the final between the two most successful teams. The first game was United old boys against the Ancient Bin-dippers. Representing our illustrious past were Arthur Albiston, Clayton 'Sunbed' Blackmore, Paul Parker, Billy Garton, Colin 'K Stand' Gibson, Peter Barnes, Frank Stapleton, with Dave Ryan in goal. The crowd was mostly United, some Arse, some French, but very few Dirties — they had probably decided to stay back and visit all the houses vacated by those who

Three in a Row

had bothered to turn up!

Our first goal was scored by "Frankie, Frankie", but the Scousers were 2-1 up by half-time and it was all our fault for serenading them with "One-nil in your cup final" after Stapleton had scored, because they netted immediately afterwards. And then scored again as we were singing "1-1 in your cup final!" We shut up after that and let the lads take a half-time break. It did the trick as 'K Stand' scored the equaliser, Barnesy put us 3-2 and then 4-2 up and Frank made it 5-2. The Scousers did pull a goal back at the end but the game finished 5-3 and they were lined up for a photo-call with a giant beachball, and it seemed appropriate that the PA was blaring out the theme to the Benny Hill show at the same time!

Next up were the French against the Arse — a mis-match if ever there was one! The French were 3-0 up by half-time and two of the three had been scored by Eric. There was much rejoicing — many "ooh – aahs" and by the end of the half a full rendition of "What a friend we have in Jesus". Eric is still King and court jester rolled into one — slightly heavier than when he played in the red shirt, but he was looking good and the skill was still there in abundance. By the end of the game the French had strolled to a 6-1 victory and we were singing "You've only come to see Eric".

Then it was United's turn to smack the Arse, but not until they had given them a goal start — nothing new there then! By this time Gina had requested a move from behind the goal, as she had taken exception to the bunch of Gooners who had stationed themselves behind us. So we took temporary seats by the corner flag. Early on we were nearly taken out by a misdirected Stapleton missile which whistled

The close season

inches past our ears — it was obviously safer behind the goal!

It was Stapleton who eventually made the scores level, Parker who claimed the lead and Barnes who took us further ahead. The PA encouraged the Arse fans to get behind their team which only produced a response from the Reds of "You're supposed to be at home!" After the half-time break Barnes made it 4-1, Charlie Nicholas (apparently — but if that was really Charlie Nicholas he's taken up Sumo wrestling) pulled one back for the Gooners. Dave Ryan in our goal made a couple of good saves and was treated to, "Are you Barthez in disguise?" — mind you, the only similarity was the bald head — the girth was more reminiscent of a certain Ozzie! Billy Garton, running from almost his own goal line finally made the score 5-2.

On next it was the Scouse against the French which surprisingly stayed goalless until after the half-time break, but finished up 4-0 with Eric scoring twice again and one of them a superb scissors kick and us singing "Hello, hello, Eric is god, Eric is god". 'Supersub' David Fairclough came on and immediately missed a sitter while Grobbelaar was serenaded with "Brucie, Brucie what's the score?"

Then United were up against the French with Eric on the wrong side. Gina was in no doubt about who she was supporting — Eric! The rest of us were content either way and a good job too because the game had hardly started before the King had back-heeled a goal against us. Now where have I heard that before (1974 was it?). He then made it 2-0 and 4-0 for the first hat-trick. The score was made slightly more respectable by Billy Garton, but still ended 4-1 to the French.

Three in a Row

The Scousers and the Arse were next on, so we took time out to visit the Sega tent and the bar. Outside the main arena we wandered past several very unsuitably dressed young females advertising Sega. The abundance of naked flesh had attracted a huge crowd of males all pretending to be playing football with their offspring, but frequently misdirecting passes due to lack of attention to the 'beautiful game' and more attention to the beautiful body!

As soon as the final group game was over we went back to our original spot on the front row for the final which was between United and France. Apart from Gina, we all supported United, while singing Eric songs — she just sang Eric songs! It was inevitable the great man should score first — after all, he had controlled every game. But Sunbed was not to be upstaged and bagged his first soon after and his second soon after that to put the Reds into the lead. A header from an Eric corner made it 2-2 and an Eric scissors kick, 3-2 to the French by half-time.

The second half could have gone either way with both Stapleton and Parker missing sitters and the latter burying his head (literally) in the sand coming up with what looked a natty new bleached hairstyle! The French, however, took both their chances to stretch their lead, but Sunbed wasn't finished and slammed in his hat-trick from at least 200 yards to make the final score 3-5 to the French. Gina celebrated by blowing raspberries to us all as the King lifted the trophy.

The only thing left was the autograph hunt. Problem was, Eric had disappeared and security was very strict. We were on the wrong side of the fence so our first job was to get on to the pitch and from there

The close season

closer to the official tent. We slipped past security while their backs were turned and made it over to where the remaining press delegates were stood. There was a small, but persistent group, waiting patiently for the King to show, but the security guard eventually informed us that Eric had left. Not wanting to give up quite so soon, I took Gina by the hand and we made our way through to the back of the tents past the PA and right through security to where there were two parked vehicles. In a four-wheel drive passenger seat, no more than 50 feet away, sat Eric awaiting his driver. Trouble was, we had encountered our final obstacle and this one proved impossible to pass. The over-zealous security man took his job very seriously despite the fact we were but two people, one of whom was ten years old who desperately wanted her hero's autograph. It would have done little harm to be allowed through but the hard-faced security man was unmoved even by Gina's tears. So near, yet so far as we watched the great man driven away. Sometimes you just can't win.

Post-tournament comment ranged around the possibility of Eric succeeding Fergie based on "Of course I would like to end up at Old Trafford. I love Manchester United. I had a great time there and it would be difficult to follow Alex who, I think, is the best manager in the world. If I come back into football I shall do it in England." How many of us would like to see Eric back at the club in whatever capacity? Okay — all of us then!

Monday July 17th will go down in history as the day when Martin Edwards announced he would be stepping down from his position as Chief Executive. August 1st was the date set when Peter Kenyon would take over with David Gill his deputy. Edwards would remain as non-executive director of Manchester United plc and would continue the task of being the non-executive chairman of Manchester United FC. The City seemed to think the announcement was a good one as the share price rose by 36p!

Edwards made it clear enough that any ideas we had of him disappearing from Old Trafford and spending the rest of his life sunning himself on some tropical island far away from wet and windy Salford, were as far from his thoughts as taking out subscriptions to the United fanzines. "It is just not going to happen," he said.

The new man at the helm, Peter Kenyon, proposed a fans' charter and talked about working with groups that have tended to be most critical of Edwards. But whether Kenyon would pay any more than lip service to the hardcore supporters was open to debate.

Another issue was rumbling beneath the surface. Well, at least it was over here, but in Malaysia and South Africa, it was very much on the surface.

Overseas supporters — who needs 'em?

MUplc say they do, but do they understand the real meaning of the word support?

That Manchester United has a global following has never been in doubt — at least since the late fifties. Supporters' clubs all over the world were formed many years ago, but recently a couple of those clubs have fallen foul of the global 'brand'

The close season

extension so beloved of MUplc. The first to suffer the ignominious elbow were the Malaysians, followed swiftly by the South Africans. Both had been forced underground having had any 'official' privileges taken away from them. Be in no doubt that these two supporters' clubs were established, traditional clubs of some repute. They were run by supporters who cared deeply for the club and their fellow members. So, who would be next? Scandinavia? USA? Australia? Or perhaps even Malta?

In Singapore, the supporters had been campaigning for years for official recognition without success — suddenly they knew why. But, to rub salt in their wounds, the merchandising arm appointed a Liverpool supporter to run the new branch. In Malaysia, the club did have official status and was always prominent in the United Year Book — but, not any more! The Malaysian branch was run by supporters who received no financial aid from United whatsoever and survived by meagre subscription charges and sponsorship. They conducted themselves in accordance with the wishes of Manchester United and were afforded privileges when travelling to Manchester such as meeting players and management. Cantona, Best, the Lord Mayor of Manchester, Edwards and Charlton had all visited the Malaysian clubhouse along with the British High Commissioner. Even the Queen took the time to meet them in Kuala Lumpur at the end of the 1998 Commonwealth Games.

Now MU South East Asia supporters' club was been formed. A flagship merchandise store opened in Singapore in July and all the tradition of the former club had been discarded with the previous season's shirts. You may wonder why this would be of any concern to those of us over here, but the truth is, despite the fact they are thousands of miles away, the Malaysian supporters are just as daft about United as we are and many of them have been that daft as long as we have!

They do not object to the merchandising empire lumbering into the Far East though. If United can make money out of the vast local population, then all well and good. But they do object to the merchandising outfit running the supporters™ club and the fact that the former official club now has to bow to the new boys — another case of real supporters being trampled by the jackboots of the merchandising juggernaut. To add even more insult to injury, the lawyers of MUplc even wrote to the ex-official Malaysian supporters club telling them to cancel their anniversary luncheon! They went ahead anyway, with their Prime Minister's daughter, the British High Commissioner, and 250 supporters in attendance.

On another continent the South Africans suffered a similar fate. The South African branch was another official branch, full of long-term, loyal supporters, with supposedly good relations with the club. In short, Manchester United plc have sold the commercial and marketing rights to their 'brand' to FC Fortune and with it, control of the Manchester United Supporters' Club (South Africa), which enjoyed ten years under Gary Bailey's chairmanship was subsequently 'officially' dissolved.

The chairman of the new supporters' club based in Cape Town is allegedly a Chelsea supporter who is first and foremost a marketing man. Nothing wrong with that on the face of it, or is there? Isn't a supporters' club supposed to be run by supporters of

The close season

the club? But, just as in Malaysia, the new South African club seems to be run by an ardent fan of the opposition! This new man decreed that the membership of the old supporters' club be disbanded and their membership renewal cheques sent back. Fancy that — being told what to do by someone who probably supports the opposition and who was been put in charge of the new supporters' club by our caring, sharing MUplc!

However, the individual branches have vowed to continue. In Johannesburg, Port Elizabeth, Durban and Cape Town, they will still exist, because as Ethel Sleith said, "Manchester United is not a 'brand'. It is essentially a football club, but above all, it is an ideal; a spirit, and for most of us, a way of life. We will always be United, and the team, at least, will always have our support."

The question is — have you been at all surprised by any of this? Is this just the start of the end of Manchester United supporters' clubs actually run by supporters? It's another them and us, isn't it? Would the club instigate the promised 'fans' forums' and actually take notice of what we have to say? If they don't start to listen soon to how we define the word 'support' and how they should nurture that support, they may find it is too late.

Not long after, news came through from South Africa that real progress had been made. Six members of the original South African Supporters Club had met with Peter Draper in Cape Town. They were iearmed and readyld but there was no need. In his opening presentation, Peter Draper gave them virtually everything they had demanded. In short the privileges afforded to the original members would continue as before for as long as they renewed their annual membership through Cape Town.

The Fans' Forums were instigated and those who attended gave evidence that they were, and should continue to be, very useful. If nothing else, those who attended were very well fed!

As usual, by the start of the warm-ups, we were all glad to get back to football. The first two friendlies were in York and Shrewsbury — a far cry from the Far East — much to the relief of the players! Roy Keane scored twice at York in a 2-0 scoreline, but with the next game ending 8-1 at the Shrews the scorers were: Butt, Ole with two, Sheringham, Clegg, Fortune with two and Healy. The Shrews weren't that bothered though, as they had benefitted from a £40,000 pay-day as United had played for expenses only. Next was a friendly against Wrexham and fittingly, Ryan Giggs scored the only goal. Next up was the Bayern Munich Centenary Tournament where United won one and then lost the final to Bayern 3-1 with Quinton Fortune scoring a blinder for the Reds. The game against Real Madrid was won by a very late Solskjaer goal. And it was Solskjaer who also took the plaudits in Malta, scoring twice in the 5-1 victory over Maltese champions Birkirkara. The other goals were scored by Beckham, Yorke and Scholes.

Charity, what charity?

Chelsea 2 Manchester United 0
FA Charity Shield,
Sunday 13 August 2000, Wembley.

This was the 27th Charity Shield, and the last at

The close season

Wembley in its present guise as an ashtray. It was the third time Chelsea and United had met under the twin towers and United had won both previous games, but not so this time. United had featured in a record 19 Charity Shields and had won ten of them and as this was sponsored by One-to-One you'd have thought the omens were good for number 11 wouldn't you? Co-incidentally we even set off at 11.11 as well — not that it did us any good!

Chelsea had finished 26 points behind Manchester Utd the season before, after only being nine points behind at the start of March — a collapse of monumental proportions in anyone's language, or in the case of Chelsea — Italian. Since then, they had been playing catch-up by spending a cool £25 million — nearly a million pounds a point.

The day was cloudy but warm as we left the Midlands. Gina was with us, but whereas she has always been our lucky mascot at Old Trafford, her powers had waned at last year's Charity bash and unfortunately this time weren't any better! On the instructions of the Big Daft Sod we parked up at Hillingdon and caught the train to Wembley Park — it was easy — we even got a family ticket which saved us a few quid. All those times I've driven down to Wembley, parked at the ground at huge expense, waited for hours to get out after the match and then joined line upon line of excruciatingly slow moving traffic, when the alternative was there all the time. Ironic I should finally find the best route the year they're stubbing out the last cigarette!

We made our way straight to the Torch where the songmeister Boyle was holding court. Nice to see the area returned to its rightful colour — red. The only time I can remember it not being a United pub was

Three in a Row

when the Barcodes dinked into town in '99. Nasher the mastman was also hanging around — we'd missed his superior knowledge of telecommunications masts while he'd been dossing around in Europe. But now he was back we could resurrect our spotters guidebooks and fill in those annoying blanks! BDS finally arrived having stuffed himself with a cheap Sunday lunch and several pints of the local brew and we wandered down Wembley Way for the last time — calling into Lance's swaggerama for the latest t-shirt for a certain young lady.

We made our way round to the tunnel end where we'd been last year, but only after Gina had called in to the ladies to don her newly-purchased red shirt. Déjà vu filled the air and Nasher's prediction of a defeat loomed large. It was one of those days when things didn't seem quite right. Every time I've ever been to Wembley I've had a feeling about the result. Almost everyone I know who has experience of these occasions has the feeling too — there's an atmosphere that tells you what the outcome is going to be. We're either 'up for it' or not, and this time, it seemed we weren't.

We negotiated our way past the Wembley Response Team (I kid you not) and the stewards, and finally reached our seats down by the corner flag near the goal United were defending (if that's the right word) in the first half. The atmosphere was pretty good — encouraged by two small lads directly in front of us who will be potential song leaders once their voices have dropped. The place was packed with the usual trippers, many of whom left with 20 minutes to go, but the two directly behind us didn't even last that long — they disappeared at half-time!

The close season

Not that I was surprised as the young daughter was one of the most miserable children I've ever come across — charity — what charity?

We did our best to gee up the lads but, apart from Keano, who knows no other way to play, they didn't seem to be listening. After the first couple of minutes when a vague optimism filled the air, the game was more or less dominated by Chelsea and in fact they could have had three by the time they scored their first. And it had to be the ex-sheep Hasselbaink — the diving, conniving Jimmy-Floyd. So, 15 million quid well spent I suppose. We re- united and sang a few choruses of our favourite song of the afternoon: "And George Weah said, I thought you played in red — are you 'avin' a laugh?" in celebration of City's latest, but soon to be gone, signing.

The second half started a little better after a probable Fergie dust-down, but quickly deteriorated into a brawl. Riley, the ref, had failed miserably in his duty and should have been chucking yellow cards around long before, especially at Leboeuf, who had hacked Giggs waist high in the first half and Hasselbaink for his assault on Keane's ankles from behind. This is what sparked the major trouble and it seemed inevitable someone would see red. It was also plainly obvious who it would be — only we all thought it would be for clattering the aforementioned Jimmy-Floyd — but it wasn't. Poyet was the actual recipient of the retribution, and Keano walked off to a crescendo of noise from the red half. And the atmosphere became more heated both on and off the pitch. I actually thought we may just pull something out of the fire then, but it wasn't to be. We all ended up hoarse with trying though including Gina who was also dishing out some stick!

Three in a Row

From where we were, Barthez seemed to be unsighted as the ball flashed through Stam's legs, but whatever, they were still 2-0 up and Gina slumped in her seat. "I hate losing," she said, "I don't mind drawing — but I HATE losing." Despite me reminding her that it's never over till the final whistle goes, I didn't really believe we'd be taking this particular trophy back to OT. The game eventually petered out and we left as the baying mass of blue celebrated their victory, their collective birthday, Christmas and the second coming, all at the same time. We would see who had the last laugh when May came around.

Unbeknownst to us at the time, Chelsea chairman Ken Bates had tried to place a medal around the Wizard's neck as he went up to collect his losers one. Fergie had called Bates 'Chairman Mao' prior to the game and Bates had responded with the medal which was inscribed "Lord Fergie, the best thing since sliced bread" and was supposed to be a peace offering — oh really! The infamous Chelsea chairman should maybe start reading from Fergie's LITTLE RED BOOK.

That was the start of a new season — a season, despite the game and result, which was full of promise on the pitch. Off it I was far from sure and had a nagging feeling it was going to be a troublesome campaign full of incident and discontent. A pointer of things to come was manifest that day in the actions of the stewards — every time anyone stood, they were out beckoning everyone to sit down. To our left some were ejected early on, to our right one particular steward delighted in rushing to her feet and waving her arms about in a frantic fashion which looked as though she was attempting to become airborne — and I know of a few people who would

The close season

have gladly helped her on her way. Tempers were getting frayed.

These over-zealous guardians are doing their best to ruin the spectacle of live football — they are killing the game stone dead for spectators who want nothing more than to be able to encourage their team. Anybody who has ever been to the ashtray knows how difficult it is to see, so what do you do? You stand up so that you CAN see. And you don't need some uniformed moron jumping up every time and waving their arms about, ordering you to sit down, when you're trying to follow your team's fortunes down the other end of the pitch.

It is not against the local authority safety regulations to stand at a football match during moments of 'extreme excitement' so why don't the stadium authorities issue correct instructions to these automatons before they drive everyone insane.

A Fans' Charter

The Charity Shield might have been the high profile curtain raiser for the season as far as the rest of the country was concerned, but this particular year there was a game a few days later that had the nerves tingling all over Manchester. Manchester City had somehow managed to wangle their way back into the Premiership and were to be the oppo- nents at Denis Irwin's testimonial. In the intervening period, however, we fans were informed that our lives were to be improved beyond measure as 'greedy clubs' were going to be 'called to account' with the introduction of a new Premier League clubs' charter due to be unveiled on the first weekend of the new season.

Three in a Row

As ever, most match-going fans were under-whelmed to say the least, since the charter did not go anywhere near far enough in dealing with the difficulties facing fans in the modern commercial world of football. There was no mention of either controlling or bringing down the price of tickets, no mention of putting into place a real dialogue with fans, no measures that would help bring back young fans into Premiership grounds and what sort of sanction is a mere fine to a club as rich as Manchester United? As always, those who have the future of the game in their hands appear to have neither the understanding, nor the inclination to do any more than pay lip service to the legions of football followers who have been becoming increasingly disenfranchised from their football clubs for at least ten years.

Thankfully, the testimonial game gave us not only an opportunity to say thank you to Denis Irwin — holder of more medals than any other player in United history and a player admired by all United fans — but also to welcome back our 'friends' from Moss Side to Old Trafford.

City are Back

Manchester United 2 Manchester City 0
Denis Irwin Testimonial
Wednesday 16 August 2000

City are like that member of the family that you take for granted. You really don't understand just how much you have been missing them until they reappear after a long absence. Let's face it, we love

The close season

to hate the Scousers and playing against the likes of Juventus and Real Madrid is special, but for a game that has everything — passion, comedy, hatred — there's nothing like a clash between the Red shirts and the Bitter Blues from down the road.

I travelled to the game from Eccles, so it was a bit of a trip down memory lane for me. Walking over Trafford Bridge with butterflies in my stomach and the odd laser blue City shirt in the mainly red crowd brought back a lot of memories. I was soon jolted back to earth of course when I arrived on Sir Matt Busby Way and gazed up at the new frontage to East Stand. I suppose I shouldn't have expected anything else — United is all about selling kits these days, so why shouldn't Old Trafford look like a giant M&S store? What upset me most, though, was the placing of Sir Matt's statue above the entrance to the giant new megastore. Instead of worshipping at the feet of the father of our club, now we worship at the entrance to shopping city. Personally, I think it shows a total lack of respect, but I doubt the men in charge at OT would even know what I'm talking about. Sir Matt's statue should be with the Munich memorial — with his boys.

After purchasing all the new fanzines and a quick visit to the ticket office letter box, I headed off for J Stand and one distinct improvement on last season immediately became evident — no Keith Fane. At one point before the match began, the songster himself — the redoubtable Mr Boyle — read out a poem for Denis. Unfortunately, the PA system is so bad in J Stand I couldn't make out a single word! There were also some faxes and telegrams from absent friends — most memorably one to 'My friend Denis' from Eric.

Three in a Row

By 7.30pm the stadium was filling up nicely, apart from in the City end that is. Despite the fact they are known to have at least 12 million fans in Manchester, they only managed to sell about half of their tickets! Mostly the excuse was that they had no intention of boosting a Red pay-packet, but there were a few thousand of them huddled together in the centre of East Stand, surrounded by almost as many coppers and stewards. To be fair, United hadn't sold out either, but there was a good crowd for a testimonial, with 45,000 paying customers at a final count. Of course it was depressing looking down at the Scoreboard, half of it now covered in concrete and our seats marooned in front of the disabled section. All my misgivings about the placement of disabled fans in that section of the ground were vindicated even before the warm-up was over. Despite nets placed in the front wall of that section, balls were still sailing over and smashing into disabled fans who were not able to move out of the way. And the new singing section? Obviously it was too early to say much, but I didn't hear a peep from up there all night.

Interrupting my musings, the players came out and formed a guard of honour as Denis (with what seem to be the essential fashion accessories these days — his kids) walked between them and onto the pitch. There were omissions from the first team, as injury and international duty had called away some, but the starting line-up was a strong one, with Raimond in goal, the two Nevs, Ronny and Denis at the back, Scholes and Butt in midfield and a front line of Becks, Fortune, Cole and Sheringham. I won't detail the City line-up because the son-and- heir and I spent most of the first few minutes of the game saying: "Who's that?" as we tried to match the players

The close season

with names that had become reasonably familiar over four seasons of GMR phone-ins. The son-and-heir ended up in hysterics when I innocently asked: "Is that Shaun Goater?" when it turned out to be George Weah!

Of course, once the game started our attention was drawn away from events on the pitch as J Stand began to rock as all the unsung chants and hoarded-up piss-takes came pouring forth and we had the most fun we™ve had at a football match in months. Very early on in the game, the chant that may possibly become the chant of the season was heard for the first time: "We f**kin' 'ate City." Very simple, more than likely very childish, but very, very satisfying and the feeling was obviously mutual as the Bitters spat, gestured and snarled in our direction. This chant went on, and on, throughout the game, reaching a crescendo in the second half when for at least 20 minutes, most of J stand was bouncing up and down, clapping and banging an accompaniment. The Bitters were a bit of a disappointment and rather subdued to be honest. There were occasions when they came back at us, but most of the time they seemed to be a little overawed by being back amongst the big boys, or was that just plain scared at the sight of the shit team they had on the pitch?

Things were dying down a bit off the pitch, when Teddy came to the rescue on it, by scoring the first goal. Of course this led us to renew our efforts as the Blues cried into their beer bellies beneath us. "One-nil, in your Cup Final" and "City are back" did the job nicely and "Stand up for the Champions" brought Old Trafford to its feet. Half-time gave the old throat muscles a rest while United and City 'legends' were rolled out for a penalty competition which was won by the Reds, but to be honest, my attention was focussed on Sparky and Choccy! More misery for the Bitters.

The second half started with City attacking our end and Raimond in the goal in front of us. The real business of the night was still the terrace banter: "Who are yer?" from them, "Champions". and "Have you ever won the treble/double/a cup" from us, while the numerous aeroplane impressions were repeated back to them as some sang "Do you know who Frank Swift is?" But the chant of the night was still "We f**kin' 'ate City" as we clapped and bounced through 20 minutes of the second half, before the sad bastards finally awoke from their slumbers, dragged themselves to their feet and actually began to give us some back. So, we sang: "We're the pride of Manchester" as they totally lost their cool leading to much amusement in J Stand. "City come from Stockport" and "Stockport, Stockport give us a wave" raised their dangerously high collective blood pressure even higher still. And when "Going down" and "24 points" were aired I thought the red-faced Jabba the Hut down at the front was going to self-destruct all over the stewards!

At some point in the second half, Cole scored the second and we were cruising. Wes Brown came on to a chorus of: "We've still got Wesley Brown" and towards the end, J Stand came over all ironic as we sang "It's just like watching City" and "Are you City in disguise" while the Bitters gazed up at us in bewilderment. And the football? Well I saw very little of that to be honest, but what I did see couldn't have given the City fans cause for optimism. As Tim said when I met up with him later, "If they play like that in the Premiership, they are going to get a stuffing every

The close season

week" — deep joy! Walking back up Sir Matt Busby Way after the game, I overheard a Bitter say to his mate: "They took the piss a bit didn't they?" Welcome back City — the Premiership awaits.

Hit the Ground Running

The following weekend brought the return of the Premiership and it was down to business with a visit from Newcastle United and, of course that man Shearer. While one of us was fighting with the public transport system in Manchester, the other was having a rather easier time watching the game on Canadian TV while eating toast:

Cheer up Alan Shearer

Manchester United 2 Newcastle United 0
Premier League Sunday 20 August 2000

It turned out to be a long, long day. Salford were playing at 12 noon, so (probably rather foolishly) I decided I could do the two games easily. Which should have been the case, had the public transport system in Manchester not decided to fall apart for 24 hours! 10am found me waiting at the station for the train to Piccadilly. 10.30am I was still waiting, when one of my fellow would-be passengers took his life in his hands and walked off down the line to the signal box to find out what was going on. He came back to report points trouble — would the train be coming? No-one seemed to know. But not to worry, our other station had a train due at 10.48am. It would be cutting

Hit the Ground Running

it a bit fine, but with the Metrolink now going to Eccles, all would be well.

As the game kicked off at Salford, I was in the back of a cab on Eccles New Road, working out whether I could now actually afford to pay to get in once I finally arrived, but I did. Salford lost to Wigan, but not by much. So I left in bright sunshine and, despite the result, with a smile on my face and waited for a tram to Old Trafford with some very disgruntled Pie Eaters who had been looking forward to a record score!

Twenty minutes later I was at Exchange Quay to meet my daughter. The son-and-heir had deserted us to flounder about in the mud at the V2000 festival so, as it had been her birthday the day before, she had been promised his Season Ticket for the day — a rare treat! Inside the new, re-vamped Scoreboard for the first time, it was certainly different! Everything looked pretty much as normal on the concourse behind the seats, except that it was very obviously quieter, but as I first walked down the tunnel, I began to panic. I couldn't see our seats at all! What if the club had cocked up? What if we didn't have seats anymore? But as I passed through the massive (in City terms) concrete structure that is the new disabled section, there they were. Huddled together at the front, five rows of red seats — covered in dust! You'd thought they could have wiped them over with a damp cloth before the game wouldn't you? Otherwise they were as we left them at the end of last season. It was very weird though. Facing the pitch, everything looked the same. But to both sides and behind us, there was this wall, cutting us off from the rest of Old Trafford — our own little enclave filled with some with familiar faces, but most were not.

Three in a Row

Eventually kick-off approached and we were on our feet applauding Keane as he was presented with the Matt Busby Player of the Season award. Or at least we were until this rather excitable jobs-worth of a steward started screaming at everyone to sit down. And the game hadn't even bloody started! For the first time in my life, I was forced to welcome the team onto the pitch from a sitting position! It didn't bode well.

The Guardian said the following morning: "United hit the ground running" and I couldn't have put it any better. This was nothing like the performance against Chelsea, or indeed against the Bitters on Wednesday night (more's the pity — the score would have been about 10-nil if it had!). This was a team in command — and Newcastle spent most of the game scratching their heads wondering what to do about it. To be honest, with all the action going on at the other end, we spent most of the first half squinting in the bright sunshine and marvelling at Barthez's distribution. This was the first time since Peter had left us that I had felt we had someone between the sticks who can fill his boots — on one occasion he nearly bloody scored when the ball had to be tipped over the bar by Given! Some players come to Old Trafford and belong from the first time they pull on the shirt.

The Geordies were making plenty of noise up in the corner. As usual, they were telling the world they were the best supporters in the universe (yawn!) and asking us whether we came from Manchester (more yawns) and there were times when K Stand actually rose from its slumbers and sang. Like that slumbering giant in Moss Side, the effects were massive! Down in the Scoreboard, instead of being at the heart of the singing, it was like we were participating through

Hit the Ground Running

glass. We could hear it all going on around us, particularly to our right where they were standing in the small section which hasn't been decimated, but when we tried to join in we couldn't seem to get it right. We couldn't keep in time, as different parts of the stadium were out of sync with each other and our voices seemed to drift away into a void, no matter how loudly we sang. I enjoyed watching the Geordies take the piss out of the stewards though. They stood throughout the majority of the game. At various times the stewards appeared to make them sit down, but this just prompted a chorus of: "Stand up if you love the Toon" and eventually the stewards gave up, since their only alternative was to throw out 3,000 people! On the pitch, we were setting up attack after attack, with Giggs twisting their defence inside out, Keane commanding midfield and Stam and Johnsen dealing with Mr Shearer without even breaking into a sweat. There were a few near misses before Ronny Johnsen headed home the first goal from a corner and United were back in business. We informed the Geordies that they would be "crying soon" and suggested "Shearer for City" as we relaxed and enjoyed the sunshine and some excellent football.

Half-time brought four legends on the pitch. First Eusebio who received a very warm welcome, then the trilogy of Charlton, Law and Best who were to receive lifetime achievement awards. The Geordies showed their lack of class by booing Bobby and singing "Drink, drink wherever you may be" throughout the proceedings — obviously aimed at Best. But then Georgie had us laughing and cheering, and the Geordies rather shamefacedly quietened as he finished with: "And I would like to wish all the Newcastle fans all the best for the coming

Three in a Row

season". Well done George!

In the second half, United were attacking towards us. At first, the break seemed to have interrupted the smooth flow of the United game and Newcastle actually had a couple of good chances down the other end, but we were soon back in command with Giggs and Andy causing havoc and eventually it was this particular dynamic duo who constructed the second. A superb one-two with Giggs and Andy (or is it Andrew?) slotted home to the great excitement of the daughter as it was the first goal she had ever seen close-up! She particularly enjoyed Cole's reaction as he posed in front of us, grinning, as his team-mates piled on top of him. "Now I know why you like it down here," she said and from then on, it was a stroll. The Geordies tried their best to wind us up with "60,000 muppets" and "We are the cockney haters" but we just sang about City instead!

The last ten minutes were spent getting up and down for the early leavers, singing "You are my Solskjaer" after Ole and Yorke had come on, and trying to make sense of what the fellah behind us was expounding to the whole of the Scoreboard: "That Giggs is lazy, he's had a crap game, and he shouldn't even be in the team!" As we walked up Sir Matt Busby Way with the miserable Geordies, it felt good to be back — not as good as it used to feel maybe, but still good enough. The journey home is perhaps best not dwelt on, but I was cheered up immensely when, upon turning to Ceefax, I found the Premiership table was being footed by Man City!

Meanwhile, out in the colonies, our other reporter was having a rather different experience:

Hit the Ground Running

Island report

Late on the Saturday night as we were about to turn in for the night, had I been at home, I would have normally been getting up and looking forward to the first real match of the season. It was a very peculiar feeling, but there is an eight-hour time difference between home and Vancouver Island.

By the time I woke up, there was just an hour to go before kick-off. No travelling up the M6, no pre-match pint, just a cup of coffee and a piece of toast as Steve and I sat patiently waiting for the start of the new season. Well, I was sitting patiently, but the Fisherman was getting nervous about the transmission — would it appear on time — would we have to wait? We had no way of finding out until the actual appointed hour arrived. It was a tense moment at satellite city as 8am approached, but we needn't have worried — the pictures arrived smack on time and Old Trafford beamed in looking sunny and very, very big. In fact it was sunnier than the weather outside the window — with the new Stretford End casting an enormous shadow over nearly a quarter of the pitch.

What a way to start the season — sitting in Fisher Towers eating breakfast! This was the early kick-off to end all early kick-offs for this particular Brit abroad! As the game got under way, it was obvious United were well up for it with Cole and Giggs running amok. This was serious football and United were turning on the style. This was a million miles from the Charity Shield display from the previous week. Despite the unfamiliar surroundings for football watching, I was all but there — sucked into the game and transfixed by

Three in a Row

some superb football. It helped that the atmosphere was coming over loud and clear and I swear I could hear Jonah leading the troops on the second tier of the new Stretford.

At the other end (my end) the new disabled section looked so out of place and I couldn't help thinking how weird it must have been for those who had remained in East Lower, but from my present vantage point (around 6,000 miles away) OT looked immensely impressive on the inside and it felt good to be back. There were three of us watching the game — our other early morning companion was one Robert Charlton — son of Fish. A little younger than the original version and definitely without the comb-over!

The lads were completely dominant and benefiting from some superb distribution from the new man between the sticks. The confidence was high and with Cole and Giggs twisting the Barcode defence till the black and white stripes turned into Bridget Riley paintings, it would surely be only a matter of time before we were celebrating.

A corner was won down at the Stretford End. Fish had just been saying that it was about time the Jaapster opened his OT account when he rose and flashed a header that Given tipped over the bar. There was a groan, but an expectant one as the next corner came over and Ronny headed into the net for the first. Fisher Towers exploded into life and if the others in the house had still been asleep, they were definitely now awake! As the TV camera panned over the front row a familiar face came into view — it was surely the daft Dane — Leeming, but on second glance, if it was, he had definitely been doing some serious eating. Barry – you've got a fat look-a-like!

Hit the Ground Running

1-0 at half-time and Canadian TV treated us to the Charlton goals against the Bitters — oh dear!

Time for another cup of coffee. The second half continued much as the first, but while there was only the single goal in it we were apprehensive. Football has a habit of sneaking up on you and just when you think a game is easy, the opposition get a lucky break, stick one in the net and anything can happen. Just to emphasise the point, Lee encouraged a good save from Barthez. It turned out to be his swansong as he was substituted shortly afterwards and the Geordies could think of nothing better to do than sing the hideous Scouse anthem. "It's a sign they know they're beaten," said Fish, "And it's a sign they have no class."

With 20 minutes to go their fate was duly sealed when Giggs and Cole combined to score the second. Cole to Giggs, Giggs — reverse to Cole, who fired past Given to wrap up the game for the Reds. Fisher Towers exploded once more and even the young Robert C joined in — waving his nappy in the air. And that was that — the game was closed down — the first 3 points in the bag — and it was only 10am!

Two days after the Newcastle game, United were playing their first away game down at Ipswich. Unfortunately, for many United fans (including both authors) getting to East Anglia, to witness the draw, on a Tuesday evening was a non-starter especially as one of us was still on another continent!

Disappointment at the 'Appy 'Ammers

Three in a Row

West Ham United 2 Manchester United 2
Premier League Saturday 26 August 2000

The trip to the metropolis was both tiresome and disappointing. It was a long day, which started at 8.30am at Old Trafford, on a grey and very wet Manchester morning. One of those days when being an armchair fan suddenly appeared very appealing.

That was what your other reporter was experiencing, but after a late night at Fisher Towers I managed to sleep through the alarm call for 6.30am and missed the first 15 minutes, but at least the sun was shining! Back home, the first (and usually most troublesome) part of the journey passed without incident as we traversed the M6 around Birmingham, and the pouring rain without delay. Despite the boredom and the general fatigue, we were cheered to find ourselves at the services, 60 miles north of London in good time. There I stood in the car park and watched, as 'respectable' travellers and football fans alike reacted to the colourful sight of an Asian wedding party with various levels of racism — from the patronising amusement of well-dressed ladies to the outright, nasty vehemence of one of my fellow coach travellers. As one of the more tolerant onlookers said, "It makes you ashamed to be English, doesn't it?"

Then it was back on to the coach and two hours of traffic jams until we hit the streets of Newham and Upton Park came into view. As we crossed the high street, walked round the corner past the Boleyn and headed for the away section, we tried to blend in with the locals. Not very successfully, of course, as we were the only ones not wearing colours! Once through the first set of gates and into the no-man's-

Hit the Ground Running

land that takes you into the away section proper, we came across one rather wet, but remarkably cheerful, Barney. As his record for the season so far was three games and three soakings, his cheerfulness was rather surprising!

We were on row AA, I was expecting our seats to be on the front row — something I would normally be delighted about, but on a wet day like that, getting soaked to the skin before (another) 5/6 hour journey was not my idea of fun. But the gods were smiling on me at last, because row AA was right at the back behind row Z! So up we trudged, to nice dry seats, with a smashing view of the game, to watch the teams warm up and the United end fill. Well, almost fill — there were lots of empty seats. Could it be that even fanatical United fans have a limit? £33 for a ticket for a game at Upton Park might just have been a step too far, but no, it became clear that many of those missing were the execs — perhaps they didn't fancy a trip to the East End? Everyone was standing, everyone was singing, there was no sign of the usual block of ilsittersl_ in the middle of the section and also no sign of stewards or trouble.

So the day seemed to have changed for the better and I began to cheer up. It was a great atmosphere and the lads were playing well. Despite what the press and media reports said later, this game was all United and for 85 minutes we were the only team on the pitch. Even the most red-tinted commentator had to admit that Di Canio and Joe Cole were playing some excellent football, but they were getting nowhere — you can™t expect two players to do the work of eleven! It was all United off the pitch too. I have never known Upton Park so quiet. We began with a 10 minute rendition of "Fabien Barthez" (to

Three in a Row

"Dirty Old Town") which he acknowledged with a grin and a wave and went on to an excursion through all the traditional United songs. At regular intervals we sang a chorus of "Can you hear West Ham sing?" but it didn't have any effect, so we soon went back to entertaining ourselves and sang about City instead. We tried to encourage their involvement with such classics as "Going down with the City" and "Nationwide, Nationwide, Nationwide", but even that didn't raise any more than a few of them out of their stupor.

On the pitch the lads were doing the business. Well, all apart from Silvestre who was bringing not only our wrath down on his shoulders, but also had Keane purple with rage on more than one occasion. We finally got our reward when Becks curled a wonderful free kick into the net down the other end and we were one up. "One-nil in your Cup Final" brought one or two 'Ammers to their feet, but most of the rest of the stadium collapsed back into apathy as we carried on our sing-song for Jaap, Keane and Andrew ("Oh Andrew Cole, Andrew, Andrew, Andrew Cole!") although I'm not sure that particular variation will catch on!

Back on Vancouver Island there was a knock on the bedroom door: "Paul, get up! The alarm didn't wake me, the game's already started and United are one up!" I roused from my slumbers, pulled on a pair of shorts and crawled into the living room where a frantic Fish was hastily pushing the video tape into the VCR. I left briefly to switch on the kettle and was shouted back in before I'd barely passed through the door! Liquid was essential and once some of the hot brown stuff had eased its way down my throat my eyes began to open and the game came into focus.

Hit the Ground Running

The imposing banner scoreline which seemed to fill the top left quarter made pleasant reading.

The 'Ammers had a few chances, with Suker in particular missing a couple of sitters, when he wasn't diving all over the pitch auditioning for a place in Ballet Rambert that is. Di Canio should have scored when Barthez decided to go walkabout outside the area and then ran rings (again) around Silvestre, placing Joe Cole in a position where he couldn't possibly miss, but did! United went in at half-time 1-0 up. Everything looked fine except for a limping Jaapster.

During the break, we were hoping to see the Beckham free kick that we'd missed, but all we saw were the previous day's goals and tons of adverts. There were even adverts during play, but at least these days they only take up three quarters of the screen leaving you to follow the game peering down at the bottom right corner. In years gone by they didn't even allow you that privilege apparently!

At the game, Linda had returned from her half-time cuppa:

Berg came on for Stam at the start of the second half and our spirits were soon lifted as Andy scored within the first few minutes. It had been looking a bit dicey, with all the action from the kick-off down the other end where we were doing some rather desperate defending. Berg had cleared from Di Canio in our penalty area and then Stimac's header shaved the post. Within seconds we were attacking — Barthez threw the ball to Becks who lifted a perfect 60-yarder which landed at Giggs' feet on the edge of their penalty area. He passed the ball through to Andy who tapped it gently to Hislop's right and it rolled slowly into the net before ex-Bitter Lomas could get to it. Celebration time again and we settled down to enjoy the rest of the game confident in the knowledge that they weren't going to make up two goals...

Nothing over the next 25/30 minutes led us to believe we were going to do anything but cruise to an easy win, possibly with another one, or even two goals in the bag. Phil Neville was getting some predictable stick from the home fans — what makes grown men spit and scream at players? We egged them on by singing "Phillip Neville is a Red — he hates England" and "We all agree, United are better than England." This roused them from their slumbers, which says it all really — they can't be bothered to react when we insult their own team but are up on their feet screaming their heads off when we insult their precious England! So with the atmosphere much improved we were enjoying ourselves, the only real irritant being Suker — still diving all over the pitch and getting away with it every time.

Then, with five minutes to go and the game won, it all fell apart. First Joe Cole, obviously having taken lessons from the Croatian, took a flying leap in the box down the other end, and earned himself a penalty. At the replay on the big screen, there were howls of protest at our end as he could clearly be seen leaping into the air and falling spectacularly, with no-one having touched him. Di Canio duly dispatched the penalty and the 'Appy 'Ammers finally burst into life with a chorus of "You're not singing anymore" — we were, but let's not be picky!

Being rather slow on the uptake, they had obviously only just realised that if they actually got behind their team, they might just pull something out of the bag. And they did — while we were still reeling

Hit the Ground Running

from the shock of their first goal, Silvestre (who else) miskicked a clearance and presented it to Suker, right in front of goal. He headed it in, and Upton Park was jumping up and down with delight. Bloody 'bubbles' everywhere.

There were two minutes left and still time for a Barca-type comeback. And the lads nearly did it. Sheringham had a shot shave the bar and Becks hit the post, but it wasn't to be, the whistle went and the 'Appy 'Ammers went 'ome more than content with their point.

From then on, my day deteriorated once more. We left Upton Park to find the police holding back a baying mob of claret and blue. We were sent in the opposite direction and eventually ended up back at the coaches by a rather circuitous route. Once back on the coach we (rather anxiously) waited for everyone to get back. And we waited, and waited. After an hour, there were still two lads missing and all the United coaches were being kept back by the police because they wanted to escort us all out of the area together. So at 6pm we finally left Upton Park, leaving behind the two lads off the back seat, not knowing whether they had simply got a lift back or had been arrested or perhaps lying in a gutter somewhere. Luckily there were no traffic jams on the return journey so we were back at Old Trafford only 45 minutes late. It had been a long and ultimately disappointing day.

6,000 miles away from the trauma, the irony of the situation was no different:

We'd seen it all before. "Typical bloody United," said the Fish.

That evening we were to be honoured guests at the Fisher party. It was our last evening on the Island.

Three in a Row

Two very special people came to that party: Marj and Bob English. Bob played for United in the fifties as reserve wing half. He would have walked into almost any other team, but at United he waited in line behind the likes of Edwards, Blanchflower, McGuinness and Colman.

Marj was Eddie Colman's fiance. She knew little about the game and when she met Eddie she didn't even know he played football, let alone that he played for the famous Busby Babes. He had told her he worked at Trafford Park! The truth? Well, sort of! When Marj finally discovered who Eddie was he invited her to the game telling her to look out for the player wearing the number 4 on his back. As the Babes took the field no4 came into view. "I thought the red shirt must have made Eddie look big," Marje told me, "until I realised it wasn't him after all! It had been the lanky, gangling, Freddie Goodwin — Eddie had been injured before the game!

Bob was one of the squad of players who was taken to the Norbreck Hotel in Blackpool to escape media attention. He would have played in the first game afterwards, in the FA Cup against Sheffield Wednesday, had United not signed Stan Crowther from Villa that morning. He never came that close to first team action again.

It had been a superb way to end our stay on the Island and the perfect answer to any post match blues, but then we had had the rest of the day to forget it anyway — the game had finished at 9am!

Hit the Ground Running

United — top of the League

Manchester United 6 Bradford City 0
Premier League Tuesday 5 September 2000

I know I should have been buzzing the morning after. After all, United had won 6-0 and had gone top of the League, but somehow, it had all been a bit low-key. It's not that I didn't enjoy the football, far from it — it was an excellent performance from a young and inexperienced side, but......... let's not get ahead of ourselves — back to the beginning:

I had arranged to meet several people in the pub before the game but unfortunately, things didn't quite go according to plan. A combination of problems with trains and buses left me without enough time despite the fact I'd originally left plenty. I decided enough was enough and got on a bus going directly to OT instead. Why do I make arrangements before games? They never work out! I was too late for the pub, but far too early for the game. So I sat on a cold stone wall, watching the world go by. With a constant queue of United fans to my right — emptying the slot in the wall of money — and a group of Bradford fans to my left — coming out with all sorts of drivel about United and us fans — it was an interesting, if somewhat depressing, experience.

I mused about how different it was from the 'good old days', when I used to arrive all excited and where the atmosphere on the forecourt could almost be cut with a knife. Admittedly, it was Bradford we were playing and thus it wasn't exactly the game of the season, but it was a very low-key crowd. The only people who seemed excited were the kids — but

Three in a Row

perhaps that's it, perhaps I'm just getting old! But the 'good old days' I'm talking about are only a few seasons ago, when it was very different. Perhaps it's simply the size the club has grown to — I know that the ground I see when I walk over the railway bridge now looks huge and impersonal and seems to have little to do with me. Luckily, before I got to the stage where I was ready to jump off the new East Stand, I spied Big Rich and a chat with him cheered me up immensely, though I was still feeling sort of 'out of it' when I entered the ground and took my place next to the son-and-heir in the new East Lower.

Just as before the Newcastle game, the same rather rotund and red-faced steward was running up and down in front of us shouting "sit down, sit down!" before the game had even started. He came through the gate congratulating himself as the teams kicked off. Someone ought to tell him that no-one was taking any notice whatsoever — and we were going to sit down anyway! Because we are now very well-behaved boys and girls in the Scoreboard, since the Club kindly removed all those nasty troublemakers and sent them packing up to the second tier of West Stand! Talking of which, as we settled in to watch the game, the chants were coming across loud and clear from the new 'fanzone', to the extent that the son-and-heir was heard grumbling to himself that perhaps we should have gone up there after all.

Looking around us for the first ten minutes, it was hard to argue with him, except that the thought of the effect of all those stairs on my poor old knees, soon clears my head of any such thoughts! Once we got past the first ten minutes all sound from the other end of the stadium more or less ceased and the son-and-heir stopped grumbling. We did hear from them

Hit the Ground Running

occasionally, particularly towards the end of the second half, but as a 'singing end', it just wasn't working. From where we were sitting, it looked like the middle section at the front was doing its best but as for the rest of the stand — forget it! That's not to say that it was much better at our end. K Stand was silent apart from a small section next to the away fans and most of the Scoreboard was little better. The usual suspects were standing and singing to our right, but sadly I have to report that the decimation of the Scoreboard has led to the expected result. Apart from a few choruses of "Gary Neville is a Red" and "United – United", there was virtually no atmosphere at all. Even the Bradford fans were half-hearted in their efforts. A few chants of "A ground full of Cockneys" and "Yorkshire, Yorkshire" were about all they could manage and they even forgot to boo Gary Neville until about halfway through the first half. So our entertainment had to come from the boys on the pitch. And what entertainment they provided!

We had been slightly concerned at the starting line-up, with Silvestre, Fortune, Greening and Wallwork starting, but I love to see the youngsters given a chance and this was a real chance for them to show what they could do. And they all took that chance, with Greening and Fortune in particular showing why Fergie has such faith in them. With United playing towards us, we didn't have long to wait for the first goal. After 11 minutes, Cole was put through and his goal-bound shot struck the back of a Bradford defender and looped over Clarke and into the net! It was difficult to know who was more surprised: Cole, Clarke or us! It wasn't long before the Bradford fans really had something more to complain about as Gary Neville brought Windass down from behind. We sighed, expecting them to get a free kick, but the referee played on, with the Bradford fans screaming abuse. Becks crossed from the right, Fortune was waiting at the far post and we were two-up, much to the disgust of the loveable Yorkshire Tykes, who now remembered they were supposed to be booing Gary Nev, as well as Becks and Phil Nev!

After a brief sojourn in the concourse behind the seats at half-time, where the meeting of minds was somewhat depleted by the removal of so many, it was back to our seats just as the second half started. And despite the lack of atmosphere off the pitch, and the rumour that City were actually beating Leeds 2-0, the second half was very enjoyable indeed. It was a little quiet for the first quarter of an hour, but then the floodgates opened and we were treated to four goals in the next 30 minutes. Fortune scored his second and then Sheringham (wearing the Captain's armband) got in on the act by scoring two of his own! The first, a volley from 20 yards and his second, a header from a cross by Greening. But the best goal of the evening had to come from Becks who scored what appeared to be one of his free kick specials, on the move!

But the entertainment wasn't confined to the goals. With Fabien Barthez in such form, who needs Olmeta? He was in his element and having a wonderful time. Kicking for goal with 60 yard free kicks to chants of "shoot, shoot", dribbling past defenders and playing up to the crowd, it was wonderful. Okay, there were some times when your heart was in your mouth (particularly when he came out to the edge of the penalty area and the resulting shot shaved the bar), but it's impossible not to marvel

Hit the Ground Running

at his confidence and his agility. He has a huge personality and he may give a few fans heart attacks over the coming months, but I couldn't help thinking that Manchester United and Monsieur Barthez are made for each other!

So it was funny night really. A bit downbeat off the pitch, but a superb exhibition of football on it. The chant "We always beat you 4-nil" will now have to be upgraded to "6-nil" of course! Coming out of the ground after the game, the Bradford fans were grumbling about how "It's easy to win when the referee gives you a two-nil start!" If it makes them feel better — they could keep right on thinking that. The City win at Leeds was a bit of a downer, I still don't like to give the Bitters too much to get excited about — but nice to get home and find Bolton had been knocked out of the Worth Nothing Cup by Macclesfield! After the severe grounding of the loveable Yorkshire Tykes, the next opponents were the Mackems from Wearside whose last league win at OT was 13 visits ago.

September Reign

It's good to be back

Manchester United 3 Sunderland 0
Premier League Saturday 9 September 2000

Down the road from this week's Premiership visitors, the manager (one Bobby Robson) had obviously swallowed a Bitter pill having stated that Newcastle were a 'massive club'. Their neighbours, from Wearside, are forever at pains to point out that they despise their 'massive' neighbours as we do ours. So you'd think we would have lots in common, would you? But it doesn't stop us from winding each other up.

This was my first 'live' game of the Premiership season. The first of many encounters with the M6 — all part and parcel of the matchday experience for those of us who actually travel to games. This was to be an easy journey though, and we arrived at Old Trafford with time to spare to enjoy the t-shirt weather that big Rich had predicted. In fact the only cloud which vaguely resembled anything like grey was hovering over the very spot occupied by a certain fanzine editor! After a brief stop to buy a can at the offie we negotiated an extended detour around the

September Reign

lengthy queue of Mackems waiting for chips and made our way back down Sir Matt Busby Way past the same fanzine editor who still had the same cloud hovering menacingly above his head. Back on the new forecourt we were tripping over the last-minute checkout chuck out from the gigantic megastore. There were red and white stripes everywhere and seemingly as many police, but the only problems were those of language — no-one could understand a word any of the Wearsiders were saying! Not that we cared.

Inside the ground I arrived just in time to hear our new announcer dedicate a song to the 'Burnage Bard' — I wonder whether said 'Bard' was in the ground to hear the dedication, or whether he was still chucking back the last pint in the Dog? The new Stretford End dominated our view, towering over the opposite end. The disabled section looked incongruous marooning the first few rows of the Scoreboard in no-man's-land behind the goal. No-one doubts the validity of an extended disabled section — but behind the goal?

The first 15 minutes of the game were superb. The football flowed from United boots and the lads were taking potshots at Macho Man in the Sunderland goal. The atmosphere was good too and even better when we went 1-0 up as Becks provided a perfect pass for Scholesy to head home. The Mackems' response was a chorus of "You'll never walk alone" to howls of derision with "One-nil in your Cup Final" and "You're just a bunch of Scousers" from us. Apart from another Scholesy effort which smacked against the foot of Macho's right-hand post, that was it, United cruised through the game and Sunderland did little else but pump long balls up to Niall Quinn who

Three in a Row

nodded them on aimlessly.

Under the stands at half-time our group had been seriously depleted by the decimation of Block 135, but several high-rankers in IMUSA were still there — glad someone stayed behind to keep us company then. I arrived back up top as the teams came out for the second half and Barthez arrived in the Scoreboard goal to a rapturous welcome.

Whatever was said in the dressing rooms during the break had obviously had no effect, as the teams continued as before. Gradually, with the score at 1-0, we became more and more anxious and the Mackems more and more hopeful. Another chorus of the Scouse dirge wound up K Stand. "You're just a bunch of Geordies" did the same for those in the away section, and everything simmered along nicely. One-nil and you still don't sing," they sang despite the fact we actually WERE singing by that time. "One-nil in your Cup Final" we offered back, followed by "Shit on the Geordies", which had them tugging their shirts and pointing to the club crest! United were gradually working their way towards gaining some semblance of control when Coley was brought down on the edge of the box by a stray elbow. Becks stepped forward to take the kick and as per usual, a posse of red and white stripes surrounded the ref. Hutchinson was booked and the ball moved forward ten yards as per the new rule. We watched incredulously as its new position was about level with the penalty spot with the whole of the Sunderland team and half of United's between the ball and what remained of the goalmouth. It was farcical. As soon as Giggs touched the ball to Becks half of Wearside was upon him and the ball was cleared. What should have happened was that the attacking team be given the choice of

September Reign

where to place the ball — in the original spot, or the new one, thus maintaining what they considered the best advantage.

Finally United assumed control and we could at last relax, but not until Quinn had sent a number of those around scurrying for the toilets as he nudged a header goalwards, only for Barthez to claw it away from the line. This produced a series of sideways glances by all around and a distinctly unpleasant odour permeated the nostrils. Less than a couple of minutes later and it was all change. The last of the flicks of another excellent move, had been from Cole's head. The ball fell to Sheringham in the penalty area and he volleyed past Macho for the second goal. As Sheringham reeled away accepting plaudits we were collectively mopping our brows. Soon after we were a great deal more relaxed as Scholesy rammed in number three from 20 yards. A piledriver of a shot which curled past the Sunderland keeper into the roof of the net. Better than his previous effort which would have parted Jonah's hair (if he had any) in the upper tier of the Stretford.

This was the start of the party proper. The butt of our attention was a certain Mr Quinn, the ex-Bitter who had whinged his way through the game contesting every decision, whether right or wrong and, having already been booked for a bad challenge, was fortunate to stay on the pitch. "Give the ball to Niall Quinn," we sang over and over. And every time he fluffed his chance, even when in clear sight of goal. Fair play to him though, he did give us a wave after we'd asked him to! The secondary butt was Phillips, who was given the vote with "Phillips for England", but why should we even bother when we have the ace piss-taker on the pitch? With Phillips

Three in a Row

advancing menacingly, Barthez flicked the ball over his head to the feet of Silvestre, leaving Phillips searching the heavens for an answer! The whole stadium rose to a chorus of "Fabien Barthez." We have a new character between the sticks at Old Trafford. It seemed like forever since Peter left us, but now we have another fit to take his place.

The end of the game came too soon. For the previous 15 minutes we had been witness to some superb entertainment. We were also nearly witness to Scholesy's hat-trick as he scooped the ball past the advancing keeper, but in the end, scooped it just wide and was clattered in the process. But 3-0 was good enough to lift us back to the top of the pile once more. And the only good news for the Mackems as we bid them "Cheerio, cheerio" was that Newcastle had been deposed at the top.

Our long journey back down the M6 was made all the more pleasant for the numerous close encounters with returning Scouse coaches (even one disguised as a National Express coach). My two travelling companions were each alerted by my frequent exclamation "Scouse alert!" but would do no more than raise a contemptuous finger at the window while continuing to read the latest fanzine editions. This produced the desired effect of course with many a Mickey baying for Manc blood.

It was good to be back. And the telling factor? A slight gruffness to the voice the morning after — the sure sign of an enjoyable afternoon the day before. And four days later we did it all over again for our first European night of what we hoped would be a repeat of '99.

September Reign

Running on empty?

Manchester United 5 Anderlecht 1
Champions' League Wednesday 13
September 2000

Anderlecht were United's first ever European opponents back in 1956 and the second leg of that tie is still United's record European score — a 10-0 win, under the floodlights at Maine Road. The first man to ever score a goal for United in European competition was the late Tommy Taylor — and that was against Anderlecht. Taylor went on to score a hat-trick that night while Dennis Viollet bagged four, Whelan two and Berry one. Last night it was Andrew Cole who scored the hat-trick. And, 44 years later, the 300th goal for the Reds in Europe. He also smashed the Lawman's European scoring record. too So, not a bad night — but we nearly didn't make it at all.

A small matter of a fuel crisis had plunged the country into chaos. Big Rich had been offered a lift straight from work — so he was sorted. Nigel and I were originally going to be picked up by the BDS, but he had had to call off the trip because of lack of petrol and remained marooned down south, clutching his ticket while driving around rather aimlessly in a sad, but belligerent and lonely protest.

So, we were forced to make other plans and it was the local Supporters' Branch who came to our rescue. At 2.30 the official coach left Leamington and headed north. The news had been filtering through all morning from our local informant — Linda, who had been warning of various protests in and around militant Manchester. It wasn't Manchester that concerned us at first though, it was what route we should take to bypass Birmingham, because all the motorways were blocked by police. They were gridlocked with ten-mile tailbacks! Anyway it gave us a chance to take an extended detour round the West Midlands through the surrounding countryside until we arrived back at the M6 and were able to continue the journey without problems other than the driver's appalling choice of radio stations! By the time we pulled up outside the Dog and Partridge it was only 5.30. The place was swamped with Belgians, swilling back the local brew.

Linda's day had taken a different route:

It had been an interesting day! Since I was working at home, I was the one put on GMR duty to keep track of the fuel crisis. I've got used to supplying regular weather reports to long-distance travellers, this time it was traffic and travel reports! As the day brought protests by taxi drivers in city centre Manchester, lorries blocking various motorways and dubious reports of filling stations with a couple of litres of unleaded to sell. So it was with some trepidation that I set foot outside the house and headed for the railway station with fingers crossed. Of course, as always seems to happen to me on these occasions, the journey went without incident and I ended up arriving at the top of Sir Matt Busby Way an hour-and-a-half before kick- off and as I stepped down from the bus, the pavement in front of Macari's was awash with mauve — yes, mauve! Hundreds of Anderlecht fans in their mauve and white shirts, singing "Who the f**k are Man United?" and trying to get over-friendly with the local coppers.

Apart from the 'Mauves' (as their flags proclaimed) Sir Matt Busby Way was quiet. Barney was in his usual spot, though he had set off at some ungodly hour in the morning to ensure that United fans would not be deprived of the latest edition of Red News. I could hear the Anderlecht fans moving down Sir Matt Busby Way towards the stadium. Then, all of a sudden, there was a surge of fans around the corner — spilling onto the forecourt. Feeling that discretion was the better part of valour, I moved onto the raised walkway that used to be the entrance to the Superstore and watched the events unfold. Following the first surge there was some chaos for a few minutes as United fans (allegedly) charged Anderlecht fans on Sir Matt Busby Way. The police, both on foot and the mounted patrols, charged towards the trouble. My small oasis of calm became crowded as people tried to get out of the way. Then it was over as the police regained control and began to shepherd what had become a very large Anderlecht presence towards L Stand. As we watched them pass, still singing "Who the f**k are Man United?", I could see United lads hanging around the edges of the group, looking for a way in, but the police were present in numbers and all but a few stragglers were eventually herded into the stadium. As they argued with police, insisting that all they wanted to do was make friends, a small group stood below us offering us beer. One of the women agreed and was instantly surrounded by drunken Belgians telling her how much they loved English women in general, and her in particular. When asked to move on by a copper, the main suitor pleaded, "But I am only being friends with this beautiful lady," and even the copper had to smile! As so many times in the past, it's a shame that fans of two great teams couldn't socialise before or after a game, because a few arseholes have still not yet

Three in a Row

managed to rise above the neanderthal level of development.

Once the forecourt had cleared a bit, I headed off into an empty East Stand. The teams weren't out yet and fans were outnumbered by stewards by about three to one! Luckily, the son-and-heir had left early too and he turned up after a few minutes, so we wandered back behind the seats for a chat. Ten minutes before kick-off, we headed back up top and much to our surprise found the place full! There might have been a fuel crisis, but over 62,000 fans managed somehow to get to Old Trafford. Even the Leamington Skinhead was there — I could see his bald head glowing under the K Stand lights.

Up in my usual spot, high up in K Stand, I was feeling confident about the result. Our friendly steward had predicted 4-1 and I was happy to go along with that. As the game got underway, it wasn't long before the Reds wiped the smiles off the Mauve faces. After 15 minutes Giggsy came bursting down the left and sent over a peach of a cross for Coley to nod in for number one. Andrew (still doesn't sound quite right does it?) had beaten the King's old record at last and didn't he know it?! He was serenaded in the usual fashion, but it didn't shut the Belgians up! They were still standing up and hating 'Man U' and telling us that "You only sing when you're winning." And we did only sing when we were winning, but as we were winning all night, we were singing all night! After half an hour Giggsy went on another extended run and while we stood transfixed, we were witness to an Arse-type semi-final replay repeat, except this time he was brought down from behind in the penalty area and collapsed in a heap of blur. Up stepped dependable Denis and dispatched the resultant

September Reign

penalty — just.

The Belgians were lost for words for once, while we lauded it and suggested it was "Just like watching City." To which they responded by chanting for Chelsea! Eh? "You're just a bunch of rent boys" was met with howls of derision plus the odd nod and wink, so we thought better of it from then on!

Becks should have made the score 3-0 soon after, but five minutes before half-time he did cross for Sheringham who scored at the second attempt, past a prostrate keeper who had palmed out his first effort. "Chelsea, Chelsea — what's the score?" echoed round K Stand as we went below for a half-time cuppa. But, first of all a trip to the gents was in order and while waiting in line I noticed (how could I miss?) that I was adjacent to one of the tallest creatures I've ever seen. He was so tall (about 8 foot) he had to bend his head to avoid eyeballing the spiders who had amassed on the top ledge to see what all the fuss was about. As the giant left, several sideways glances followed as the next in line ruminated on the size of.................wait for it................the task facing the Belgians in the second half of course — why — what did you think?

Still suffering from shock, I went back upstairs. Barthez was already down at our end as I got to my seat and within a few minutes we were 4-0 up. A long ball by Becks was sliced and laid out nicely on a plate for Coley to extend a foot and prod the ball which trickled over the line just before the keeper scrambled himself in the rigging. By this time we were back on track with the vocals: "We're gonna eat all your chocolates", "We're gonna drink all your Stella" and "We're gonna nick all your petrol" served only to confuse the Belgians, but encourage a certain copper, stationed nearby, who took exception to the nicking of petrol song and made it clear — in no uncertain terms — that he wasn't going to tolerate such anti-social behaviour. "You can stick your f**king petrol up your arse" was the immediate response. More hard stares from the agitated policeman in the riot helmet and eventually the song died a death, giving way to "Are you 'avin' a laugh?"

The only person who was having a laugh a few minutes later (apart from the Belgians, of course) was the steward who'd predicted 4-1. As Koller beat Barthez to the ball and prodded it past both Irwin and Johnsen. We thought Johnsen had prevented it from crossing the line when he back-heeled it away, but apparently not. Linda had actually missed the goal:

It was 15 minutes before I glanced up at the scoreboard and realised that the score was 4-1 and not 4-0! "Didn't you notice the teams going back to the centre circle to kick off?" asked the son-and-heir. "No," said I. "I was too busy gesturing at the away fans with a big grin on my face — I thought I was getting some funny looks!" 20 minutes later order was restored as we got our fifth and Cole got his third. Another long ball from Beckham found his head and the ball was looped over the keeper and into the net off the underside of the bar. Hat-trick for Mr Cole and the best possible way to break the King'sl record. A couple of minutes later and he was off the pitch — substituted for his buddy Dwight. The game was tied up at 5-1 and fizzled out as the ground slowly emptied with minds now on how to get back home successfully. We waited till the very end and as we sang the "Red Flag" the ref blew for time.

Moment of the match off the pitch? A bloke in the back row of the new Scoreboard, up against the front wall of the disabled section was with two youngsters. As Barthez turned to pick up the ball the guy shouted out: "Oi, Barthez!" Just at that moment the stadium went quiet and his cry echoed around Old Trafford. Barthez looked up quizzically — directly at this guy who was now standing there, his young son beside him, with everyone, including Barthez, waiting expectantly for him to do something. Looking very, very embarrassed he weakly raised his thumb. And Fabien Barthez, world superstar, had the humility to grin and give him the thumbs-up sign back. From then until the end of the game the guy stood there with the biggest grin on his face — wonderful.

Graveyard Stomp

Everton 1 Manchester United 3
Premier League
Saturday 16 September 2000

There had been a threat of a 70s compilation cassette tape hanging over us all week. And considering the fact that big Rich and I were being driven to Murkeydive by Nigel and in the same car as the doctor, the threat had to be taken very seriously indeed. Fortunately we were spared this time. But the threat still hangs over us. We arrived in sight of Anfield and about a mile from Goodison, at around 1pm, parked in a pub car park next to Asda and spent the next hour or so sampling the local brew. Big Rich decided (rather rashly we thought) to purchase food. To then choose seafood while being so close to the Mersey was taking things too far, but he did! What he'd neglected to do was to read the small print on the menu which would have informed him that the scampi in question was actually 'reformed scampi'. Whether that meant they had previously been involved in rebellious action and had since been shown the righteous way forward by the scampi religious revival school, we weren't sure. But it mattered little now the little devils were battered and about to enter the cavernous wasteland of Big Rich's stomach. Richard left shortly afterwards to make his own way to the ground leaving us to ponder on whether we would be passing evidence of his lunchtime folly on the murkey streets.

It turned out it was he who was witness to folly and not us. When a sporty jag driven at some speed by two of the young local scallywags (thieving Scouse bastards to the rest of us) careered off the road, crashed through a garden and into a living room while the inhabitants watched Football Focus. TV dinners everywhere as chaos reigned and the sirens sounded in the distance. We took the rather more peaceful route through the cemetery, where we had no trouble from the residents at all, and arrived at Goodison Park with ten minutes to spare. My seat (or where I stood) was near to the doctor, and as the teams came out on to the pitch, my next-door neighbour appeared — it was T-shirt Jon! Now, what are the chances of that happening then?!

The game started as it continued for practically the whole of the first half and most of the second — more or less one-way traffic towards the Everton goal. It was as if United were playing at home. Before the goal that started the rout went in, United could have already been two up. There should have been a penalty when a blatant handball by Dunne was waved away by the ref and Gerrard had already

September Reign

made his first good save. But there could also have been a goal at our end but for Gary Nev (who had a superb game) just got in front of the attacker, poked out a toe, and hooked away a long ball which dropped into the netting at the back of the United goal.

From then on the first half was signed sealed and delivered as a masterpiece of skill and power. Ole crossed for Nicky Butt to score the first off a part of his anatomy usually reserved for games of a more intimate nature and we went mental. As I heaved my body from beneath what seemed like a dozen people, which it turned out was only T-shirt Jon, I became aware of problems to my right. Well actually, problems is a slight exaggeration. The Scousers (for Evertonians are still Scousers) were beside themselves with admiration for the way we were celebrating our good fortune. Okay, so they were actually well pissed off and baying for blood. Spitting phlegm in our direction and making an undignified fuss!

A line of stewards and police appeared to double in strength within seconds as the soft lads growled and grimaced their way to ejection. What made matters worse, of course, was not only were we one-nil up, but we were also singing songs they weren't overly keen on. "In your Liverpool slums", "All the Scousers on the dole" and "Get to work you lazy twats" all got an airing. Meanwhile things were moving on a pace on the pitch too and before we knew it (or at least before I knew it) United had scored again. The first thing I knew was that Giggs had turned away and I had disappeared once again under T-shirt Jon and also, this time, his daft mate! Off the pitch, the atmosphere was helped in no

Three in a Row

uncertain terms by a 'lady' of the Scouse persuasion who decided to stand up and show off her obvious assets to 2,000 plus United fans. At the request to "Get you tits out for the lads", she obliged as her boyfriend stupidly grinned up at us miming "all mine". For the next few minutes all attention at our end of the stadium was focused on the lady in question, when a cry of "You Scouse slapper" went up. No-one had a clue what was going on on the pitch! "They're the ugliest tits we've ever seen" was followed by allusions to her professional status. After ten minutes or so, she finally realised that it probably wasn't the smartest idea she'd ever had, and she then proceeded to try to ignore us for the rest of the first half!

Back on the pitch, we were building up for our third (and unfortunately) final goal — the best of the bunch. And if the previous goal had made them mad, this one made it much worse. Silvestre spotted Becks running all of 60 yards away down the right wing, he passed to Ole on the right, in the penalty box, and Ole placed the ball unerringly into the net past a desperate Gerrard. "Ole, Ole, Ole, Ole" echoed around Goodison as the disgusted Evertonians either left early to get their pasties or stayed behind to mime aeroplanes crashing. Naturally it all went off again and the local bobbies moved in and ejected several Scousers. Most of them went with a fight and an arm or two around the neck, but one offered himself as a sacrifice (obviously not too bright) and was duly escorted from the stand by a rather bemused copper as we sang "Cheerio, cheerio, cheerio!" We then turned our attention to the Bitters instead. "And Joe Royle said, is that a potato for my head? Are you 'avin' a mash, are you 'avin' a mash?"

September Reign

The Scousers had, by this time started to leave in droves, preferring their half-time pies to more humiliation. They were shell-shocked, and in truth, so were we! The half had been one of the best displays I'd witnessed, and below stairs at half-time we were buzzing. Actually Jonah was humming and swaying, but that's another story!

Back up top Giggs had been replaced by Yorkie for the start of the second period and United carried on where they had left off. Ole fired well over the top when it looked easier to score, to a chorus of "What the f**kin' 'ell was that?" He returned a wry smile, promised to improve and should have been allowed to, rather than being hacked down for a blatant penalty, which the ref also decided not to give. Then something very strange happened. Everton broke away and scored. Gravesen tucked the ball between the legs of Barthez and the Scousers woke up and started to make some noise.

The game suddenly became more of a game and the showboating had to be called in. United had a fight on their hands for at least five minutes until they powered forward once again and forced the Toffee keeper into more great saves. Yorkie hit the post, Teddy had the ball in the net but was ruled offside and Ole had another kicked off the line. Eventually Dermot Gallagher blew for the end of the game and saved any more embarrassment. The second half had been a better match (not that we were interested in that as we'd have been even more content with another three or more goals!

We had arranged to meet up after the match by the Anfield Cemetery, but Nigel found me before we got there. It had been hard enough to contain a snigger as I'd left the ground on my own, but almost impossible now that the two of us were together. The Scousers were snapping and snarling their way home as we walked among them trying desperately to remain incognito whilst muffling a smirk! The doctor eventually joined us at the gates and as we walked the long walk back, we listened in to conversations. We passed two girls, one of whom was chatting on the phone and saying, "I saw dis red shairt wid Yorke on it and couldn't resist mouthin' off. De coppers trew me out!" We were then passed by two Scallies with trouser crutches dangling almost on the floor. One said to the other, "F**kin' Manc scum. Dey don't desairve to live. Dey should all be buried in 'ere." It was wonderful entertainment, as was hearing that Leeds had lost at home to Ipswich!

Rain in Ukraine

Dynamo Kiev 0 Manchester United 0
Champions' League
Tuesday 19 September 2000

This was billed as the hardest game of the group — little did we know what would happen the following week! Bearing in mind that last season Kiev took their League title with a record 18 point margin, the same as United, you could see why. Since 1992, when the Ukrainian Championship was restarted, they have won seven League titles, one more than United during this time. In addition they have achieved the League and Cup double six times! A frightening record by anyone's standards! Was it something in the local water? There was certainly enough of the stuff falling from the sky that night and

United just about managed to keep their heads above it!

Back home, United were due to entertain one of the bogey teams who had just introduced a new manager who at least spoke their language — Italian!

And the earth moved, but not a lot

Manchester United 3 Chelsea 3
Premier League
Saturday 23 September 2000

I had set my alarm clock to make sure I didn't oversleep as this was an 11.30 kick-off, but I needn't have bothered. At 5.30am we were awoken by a huge noise which literally shook the whole house. It sounded as though someone, or something, had landed on the roof. A whole posse of over-sized burglars were at that very moment preparing to force an entry – oo-er!

I was out of bed and up to the top floor in a trice, but there was no sign of anything untoward. Downstairs was the same. Very strange, but something of a relief! It turned out there had been an earthquake. 4.2 on the Richter Scale and we had been less than a mile from the epicentre. By the time we had satisfied ourselves that we were not going to be the victims of a dastardly intrusion we were completely awake so there was no problem picking up big Rich at 8am – I'd been ready at 6.30! We arrived at the Throstles just over two hours later. The mad Dane was already outside being interviewed by the BBC. Bill and his Dad arrived and ultimately a full complement of Red Eleven websters were

Three in a Row

assembled for the first time ever. The www.Red11.org team were all in town and the mad Dane was set free on the bars of Manchester. The weather matched the occasion — the sun was shining when we left the pub and as we walked together down to Old Trafford we passed Mud-slide Slim — a certain fanzine editor who was looking fragile to say the least! He muttered something about tumblers of Ukrainian vodka and a bite on the bottom! His exploits in Kiev will no doubt shock and baffle, if he can remember any of them! A quick meet with Pat, the doctor's Mum, who skipped off (literally) with her ticket for the game, and Nick, who nearly did the same with his!

Linda hadn't made it to the pub, but had gone straight to the ground:

It was quite pleasant standing on the forecourt watching the world go by, or at least it was until the Rent Boys started to turn up. I've never seen so many tattooed scalps and beer bellies in one place before! They seemed harmless (and gormless) enough, with the biggest danger coming from the assault on my eardrums from the Del Boy accents. After a while I got bored listening to the two lads standing near me wittering on about how it must be difficult to get excited about winning the League title after three or four times (no lads — it isn't, not that you're ever likely to find out of course!) and I wandered into the ground. The son-and-heir had turned up early, having set three alarm clocks and his radio to make sure he didn't repeat his Sunderland no-show, well no show until half an hour into the game anyway.

Up on the mantelpiece, the Execs had obviously won in whatever passes for an away ticket allocation system at The Chelsea Village. I think it must have been the quietest Chelsea away following in years.

September Reign

Having said that, they didn't have a lot of competition from our lot as the improved and extended Theatre of Dreams snoozed in the late morning sunshine. At times it was so quiet, I could even hear Keano blasting Gary Neville, Ryan Giggs, and anyone else in a Red shirt who wound him up, which was virtually all of them! Whatever Roy had had for breakfast hadn't suited him as he stomped and snarled around the pitch, terrifying friend and foe alike. The crowd, of course, loved it and after one particularly aggressive tackle on a Rent Boy actually woke up long enough to chant "Keano is back". Once the ref had produced the first yellow card, Keane calmed down a bit and the stadium fell back into its slumbers.

We were awakened in a disturbing manner when the Rent Boys went in front after seven minutes. A seemingly harmless cross was heading out of play when the lanky beanpole Flo wound out his leg extension and looped the ball back into play. It fell to ex-sheep, Hasselbaink, who volleyed it past Raimondo at such a pace that Rai was more inclined to dive the other way than risk it smacking against any part of his body. We weren't happy. The first goal conceded in the League at Old Trafford this season and the lads just couldn't get a grip of the game.

Old Trafford sat in sulky silence and couldn't be bothered responding until, down at the Stretford End a corner was won. Sheringham crossed from the right and the ball eventually fell at the feet of Scholes who blasted it into the net on the half volley from the edge of the box. A goal every bit as good as theirs — but this time it was ours.

Only 15 minutes gone and it was 1-1. That felt better, and it shook the visitors who started to make mistakes. The Rent Boys simmered sourly up in the

Three in a Row

corner and the usual Chelsea/United aggro broke out on the pitch as the Old Trafford crowd woke up at last.

After about 20 minutes, Becks went off covered in blood after an argument with a Chelsea elbow. He returned five minutes later, looking like he'd changed his religion, with a huge white plaster covering the wound on the very top of his head. In the meantime United had gone close to scoring again and the Chelsea boys were becoming increasingly nervous. The morning was definitely improving as Nev lobbed the ball into the Chelsea box. It eluded Scholes and Cole and several defenders when it fell to Sheringham who blasted it into the net. A couple of minutes later and we were coasting to an easy victory when Cole was put clean through on the keeper, lobbed it over him and watched it hit the post. Everyone, including the Chelsea defence, thought it was 3-1 until the ball bounced back into play. Fortunately Becks was the only player with enough nous to realise there may be a little extra to do and was on hand to tap in the rebound and it was 3-1. That really woke us up and we celebrated by informing the Rent Boys that they were "Going down, going down, going down", and that we were going to "Shit on the Cockneys".

The Rent Boys slumped into bad-tempered lethargy and the lads decided they had done their bit for the day and were already halfway to the airport and a Euro away game on Tuesday night. Sitting next to me, the Sausageman was muttering: "They're going to score in a minute," when they did just that. Raimond fumbled a header from Flo and the ball wriggled straight through his hands and into the net. Bugger! What a blunder.

We returned to our seats for the second half

September Reign

believing that Fergie would have read the riot act and that all we had to do was score another goal to sew the game up. Unusually, the lads were shooting towards us in the second half and we settled optimistically.

Unfortunately, whatever Fergie had done at half-time hadn't had the desired effect, because United never really got into their stride and were sloppy and far too generous — giving the ball away with a worrying frequency. Of course the crowd could have raised the level of play had they been bothered, but Old Trafford slumped back into bad-tempered moaning, with only a notable few realising that getting behind the lads rather than slagging them off, might have the desired effect. Of course, the atmosphere wasn't helped by SPS going in on the only area of the Scoreboard where there is still a large group of fans who actually get up and sing. The Sausageman was muttering with even more conviction now of course and when Cole's shot was impossibly cleared off the line by Le Saux it dawned on all of us that this just wasn't going to be our day. There was an awful inevitability about the game, and sure enough, within minutes Chelsea were away on the break with Le Saux beating Becks for speed (!) and Flo had his second and we had yet another draw with the Rent Boys!

For the last ten minutes, the residents of the mantelpiece found their voices and actually made some sustained noise. I thought it a bit much when they told us we were "Sixty thousand mappets" — apart from the obvious incongruity of a group of new-age Chelsea fans calling us 'mappets', the memory of vast expanses of empty seats on the telly the week before at their European game, led to K Stand chanting back at them "You couldn't sell all your tickets". There was some excitement towards the end as United woke up out of their lethargy and actually seemed to want to make a fight of it. Fergie brought Ole on and we began to think perhaps he could pull a Barcelona-type recovery out of the bag. But when Giggs ballooned the ball over the bar just before the end, we realised it wasn't about to happen. When the final whistle blew, the predominant feeling in the Scoreboard was relief — it could have been much worse!

Ryan's express leaves Old Trafford

The feedback from the first Fans' Forum, which was held after the Chelsea game, had certainly been positive, if guarded, but the feedback from certain members had not been the same regarding Alison Ryan, who had been present at that meeting. Suspicions amongst the fanzine fraternity were pointing the finger at the 31-year-old and the very next week she was removed from the post of Director of Communications before she'd had a chance to communicate. The fact that her initial form of communication had been to tell a bunch of porkies hadn't helped her cause. But the fact the fanzines had very quickly picked up on this, but the club hadn't was par for the course. Her official start date was to be 16th October and her appointment had lasted only 13 days — unlucky for her, but lucky for United that someone was on the ball!

Three weeks later and United had a new Director of Communications. Patrick Harverson, a former sports correspondent with the Financial Times, was that man. He had the Wizard's backing, but would he win over us lot? He said he would be 'listening and talking', but we would have to wait and see.

Before the game in Holland against his old club, Jaap Stam announced that he was booked in for an operation at a Manchester hospital that Saturday to sort out his Achilles problem. What a pity as there was no doubt the team missed the big Dutchman as PSV ran riot in the second half and could have come away with an even greater victory margin than 3-1. Scholesy had given us the lead from the penalty spot in the second minute after Ole had been brought down. But apart from a Yorkie miss soon after, it had been one-way traffic. United played most of the game with an inexperienced team and it showed.

Goon Island

Arsenal 1 Manchester United 0
Premier League Sunday 1 October 2000

Every time the Big Daft Sod hitches a lift with his Gooner mates to the game at Highbury, we lose. Mick — they may be good lads, but next year when they offer you a lift — just say "No!" Everything was fine until we got to within spitting distance of the ground. We were driving down the Holloway Road and were suddenly confronted with several police vans and a whole posse of their former occupants blocking the way. We turned right and headed down Liverpool Road towards the pub where we had arranged to meet the aforementioned and his Gooner mates. An hour or so later, fuelled by a couple of pints, and with Nasher now amongst us, we left the Gooners and the five of us headed for Highbury.

Back on Holloway Road the situation had become worse and the police presence had been expanded. We crossed the main drag and walked on the opposite side of the road to a huge line of United lads who were flanked by police. They were being herded slowly and unceremoniously towards the ground while we walked free on the opposite side undetected in amongst the regulars. Well, we did until we got to the next police cordon. Everyone around us was allowed through. But not us! We were singled out and encouraged across the road to join our compatriots in the Red Army. How did they know? What gave us away? We wore no colours and there wasn't a hint of Stone Island amongst us. But somehow the Redness still shone through and we were soon walking alongside our own kind before we could even consider questioning their judgement.

We were then frog-marched along at the front of the queue directly behind a shoulder-tight line of coppers who were wearing bullet-proof vests! Had we entered a time warp? We had obviously regressed at least 15 years. There were flashing blue lights, vicious alsatians baring their teeth (or was it their handlers?) and a helicopter hovering overhead. All that was missing were the sirens and search lights.

Periodic incidents broke out and the procession frequently drew to a halt as the miscreants were ejected. What we didn't find out, until later, was that when Mick's Gooner mates left the pub (shortly after us) they saw what they described as "4-500 Gooners charging down Holloway Road". They were obviously wanting to wish us luck then?

It was touch and go whether the coppers would

allow us into Highbury especially as one of our number was intent on winding them up by singing songs he'd have been better keeping to himself! Every now and then there would be a break-away from the line as lads disappeared between the houses, but because we were at the front, we could see the police tracking them and picking them off one by one. So we bided our time until we were at a complete standstill right next to the ground. While backs were turned we managed to slip quietly away and then split up, blending in with the crowd. From there we funnelled through the cordon and into Highbury. There were only a couple of minutes left before kick-off and a journey that should have taken ten minutes had taken over 30, but at least we were in.

I climbed to my spot towards the back at the Clock End. My seat was smack behind an enormous pillar which, had I been forced to sit there, would have obscured, not just some, but all of the pitch apart from the extreme right corner. It didn't of course, as everyone was standing, and accommodated those of us less fortunate in the ticket draw. I ended up next to Walshy and Nigel, with Nasher nearby and big Rich a few rows down where Nigel should have been!

The Arse were attacking our end, but United seemed in control of the game. Apart from Keano forcing an early save from Seaman, the lads were getting close to the box, but not into it where they could cause real problems. Then 30 minutes into the game Becks gave away a free kick. I'd momentarily looked away, when all of a sudden the ball came looping over Barthez and dropped into the corner of the net. There was a split second of disbelief and then mayhem to our right as the Gooners went mad.

Three in a Row

Up until this point we had hardly heard a peep from them, but now they were grimacing and gesturing in their gloatfulness.

The goal turned out to be a touch of class from Thierry (or Terry as one of our own insisted) Henry. A flick up (with his back to goal), a turn and volley from 20 yards out took everyone by surprise, and maybe even the man himself. To think he'd not scored for six games — why did the bastard have to choose that particular moment? 1-0 down, and for the next fifteen minutes the lads found it difficult to get a grip. In the stands they were singing "Who the f**k are Man United", and we were reminding them that we were "Champions". At least they were singing.

The second half brought Seaman down to our end. It also brought about a change in the crowd as BDS appeared and so did a bunch of Cockneys in the row behind us. These were some of the most nauseating so-called Reds I've ever come across. New-age fans without a single clue between them. They slagged off everyone that moved without exception and came very close to ejection on the end of a few boots.

Lucky for them, United had started the second 45 minutes with renewed vigour. They attacked with flare and invention and within seconds Giggs had caused Seaman to make a point-blank save and United were encamped in our half of the pitch. A few minutes later and we should have had a penalty when Johnsen was blatantly barged in the area just as a free kick from Becks would have been arriving at his head, with only Seaman to beat, but the ref saw nothing untoward. Scholesy was then put clean through on goal but was blocked by Seaman, and Wenger decided to reinforce the defence by taking off Kanu.

September Reign

"They're swopping a Kanu for a sub," said Nigel, who admitted he'd been waiting months for such an opportunity!

The atmosphere had started to die which prompted someone (who will remain nameless) to pipe up with a new version of a Wenger song. This particular person, who has a very loud voice and is on the tall side, was easily clocked by the police. They had started to radio others and were pointing him out. I managed to shut him up just long enough to inform him of the possibility of imminent ejection. The reaction was swift and a disguise manufactured, allowing him to disappear. It did the trick and completely baffled the local constabulary. Throughout the next half hour you could see them searching our part of the crowd. At least it took our minds off the moaning Cockneys behind us.

For most of the second half the opposite end of the pitch was empty apart from the lonely figure of Barthez. The Arse had an 11-man defence and United a 10-man attack. But whenever a mistake was made (and it happened twice in the second half) the Arse broke away at some speed. Fortunately, Barthez was equal to the task on both occasions, pulling off superb saves at the feet of each attacker. At the final whistle the Gooners to our right went berserk as we trooped out of the ground defeated and disconsolate but not downhearted. The lads had played well enough to have earned at least a draw and for long periods had dominated the game, but it wasn't to be our day.

Outside the ground the police presence was as heavy as before, but this time we weren't surprised. As Nigel, BDS and I made our way back down towards the Drayton pub we were wary. This time we

Three in a Row

were expecting problems. And we got them! Down by the pub there was trouble, with sirens blaring, dogs barking and police everywhere. Something was going off to our left but we managed to slip through unnoticed to the right, and made our way back towards the Holloway Road where it didn't quite go to plan. The rest of the United faction had arrived at the same time from the other direction and we found ourselves in the midst of it all. Stuck on the central reservation in the middle of one of the busiest roads in London, we watched and waited for the next move to take place. The United lads went one way and we the other, trying our best to blend in with the surroundings. We thought we'd escaped, and were literally seconds away from our refuge, the pub where we had arranged to meet up afterwards. As we made our way up the side street past a group with phones glued to their ears, we were suddenly surprised by the sound of the Red Army belting down the road behind us. Momentarily we stopped, but realising this was not a good idea, we continued in the same direction as the United lads — only a little slower. Behind them came a posse of police, and for a moment we found ourselves in no-man's-land between the devils and the blue line.

Fortunately we were ignored and the Red Army was ambushed — rounded up and cordoned off not more than 20 yards in front of us. There appeared a procession of police vehicles and personnel and the road was cordoned off. When the coast seemed relatively clear, we turned and wandered back from whence we had come and finally made it to the pub we had left hours earlier. The street where we had been marooned was no more than ten yards away. The blockade fully in place, there was nowhere to go.

September Reign

So we stayed there for a while and waited on the arrival of big Rich who had managed to avoid most of the problems by leaving bang on the final whistle.

It had been a throwback to times gone by. They were not pleasant times then, and should not be welcomed back. There is always an edge to meetings between certain clubs and I have never been to Highbury yet without encountering some sort of trouble — but I'd seen nothing like this since the 70s.

After an unsettling afternoon in the Capital, we had two weeks to reflect on what was, for United, a poor run of games. The 5-1 win against Anderlecht seemed a long time ago as we looked back on draws against Chelsea and Kiev, followed by two away games lost. Being United, however, there is always something going on off the pitch to keep fans' minds off a few poor results. This time it was the announcement that Man United — The Movie was about to be released, with Becks making his 'big screen debut'. To say that the hardcore fans were underwhelmed would not be an exaggeration, but at least proceeds from the film were to go to Unicef.

Have we become a bunch of spoilt brats?

I wrote this the day after United lost their second game of the season and already the panic buttons were being pressed and the doom and gloom merchants were out in force.

Listening to all the moaning and whingeing going on in the radio phone-ins, on the mailing lists and site forums and in the pubs of the North West, anyone would think we had not won since August, like the Bitters down the road. The fact that the game at Highbury was the first time we'd been beaten in the Premiership since February seemed to have little bearing on those who were already glumly forecasting we'd win nothing this season (or ever again!), or indeed on those who would like us to sell virtually every player and start again. There were even those who were questioning the abilities of the great man himself!

To someone like myself, with rather more years under my belt than I care to remember, it can certainly seem as if the modern United fan, a set of fans with less to complain about on the pitch than any other group of fans in history, seem to do nothing but moan. And it's hard not to feel some sympathy with fans of other clubs when they say that we have been spoilt by our success. But is it true? Have we really become just a bunch of spoilt brats?

Certainly, the typical United fan has changed enormously since I first fell in love with the Babes and Manchester United. In those days the crowds were predominantly male, working class and local. The game was an escape from what to us these days would seem grim lives, working on the docks and in the factories of the North West. And it was cheap. Even if you didn't have much in your pocket, you usually had enough to get into the match.

Apart from the few unforgettable years when the Busby Babes were setting Europe alight and the Holy Trinity were sending the Stretty into ecstasy, we didn't win an awful lot of silverware. Indeed, for 26 long years our cupboard was bare (of the one Cup that counted anyway).

So if we weren't winning anything, and we were

September Reign

often watching the most dire football you could imagine, what kept us going week in, week out for all those barren years? I've hinted at one important factor already — it was cheap escapism. You could stand on the Stretty and sing your heart out and be part of something bigger than yourself. Because it was the whole experience of going to the game that was the drug. The match-day routine, meeting up with your mates, standing in the same place on the terraces, singing the songs, worshipping the legends and jeering at the useless, all part of the match day experience. That was what it was all about. To me it wasn't (and still isn't) just about the result of the game.

Of course it's nice to win – I'm not a masochist, I'd rather be in the Nou Camp on a balmy evening in May than be losing away at some God-forsaken second division dump on a wet Saturday afternoon in the middle of January. But when it comes down to it, when it comes down to the fundamentals of what being a football supporter is all about, whether your team wins or loses doesn't really matter, because it's the experience and the supporting that counts — after all, what else would keep me going to watch Salford for over 45 years?

These days we get a different type of crowd in the ground. They (we) pay more and expect more. Football is no longer the escape from a harsh life it used to be. These days, those who need the escape most are those least likely to be found watching a live game. You have to have a decent job to be able to afford to go to Old Trafford in the new millennium. And, instead of the players being lads we can relate to — earning not much more than we do — they are now multi-millionaires earning more in a week than

Three in a Row

most of us do in a year (or three!). Because we pay so much and they earn so much, we feel entitled to complain if they don't give us what we want. And what we want is more and more trophies.

United's wider fan base has also changed in many important ways. Now spread way beyond the confines of Old Trafford, United fans overseas outnumber those in and around Manchester, and they certainly outnumber those of us lucky enough to still be able to attend live games. The most important part of supporting your team, if your team happens to be Manchester United, is no longer going to the games. It's now just as likely to be travelling a hundred miles to the pub or supporters' club, or contributing to a mailing list or fans' forum or buying the latest kit at the new megastore. The regular match-going experience is no longer what being a supporter is about for thousands of people, that's become a dream, a once-in-a-lifetime experience. To the modern Manchester United supporter, it is all about winning, about trophies — after all, what else can it be about? Putting money into the pockets of the PLC in the latest megastore in the Far East? And can we really blame them for feeling this way? How can we match-going fans expect those who rarely, if ever, set foot in Manchester to have the same priorities as us?

And of course, there is the pessimist in all of us. The bit of us that still can't believe we have won all these trophies. That it won't all go wrong — probably in a very spectacular fashion in the near future! When we're winning everything in sight, it's easy to convince ourselves that it will go on forever. When we lose a couple — then we can see the chasm of another 26 years opening up in front of us and we panic. "Change the forward line", "Get in a whole new bunch of defenders", "This keeper is crap" (despite being our saviour the week before). We've heard it all before. And where have we heard it all before?

Well, back on the terraces of course, in amongst the old fellas in their caps and their macs, whirling their rattles over their heads. Because the truth is that football fans have always moaned. There is nothing more likely to get a good moaning session going than a group of people at a football match. Moaning about the team selection, the manager, the result, the weather – it's all part of the enjoyment and escapism of a good afternoon out at the football. It was then — in football's golden age — just as it is today. The only difference is in the fact that these days you can't get away from it!

In the good old days, you left it behind when you left the ground (unless, of course, you were unlucky enough to live with one of them!). At the end of the game, if you'd lost, you felt miserable for a few hours and then you got on with your life until the next game came around and you could start afresh, with the highest of hopes. These days you can't get away from it. It screams out at you from the back pages of the papers, the mailing lists and internet forums. But the worst of all is the football phone-in, that most horrendous invention that gives the moaning football fan his or her five minutes of fame, over and over again! Because these phone-ins don't only happen on Saturday afternoons like they used to — these days you can find one 24 hours a day, seven days a week, if you surf the airwaves. And of course the presenters who run these so-called 'programmes' love it. Because there is nothing that they, or their listeners, love more than hearing someone slag off

Three in a Row

United. Particularly if that someone is a United 'fan'. So the answer to the question is no — I don't think we have become a bunch of spoilt brats. But what we have done is allowed those who should shut up and say nothing, the run of the airways. You know the type — they know more about tactics and team selection than the Wizard himself and don't hesitate to offer him, and the rest of us, the benefit of their advice. In the old days, it was only their immediate neighbours in Old Trafford they drove to distraction — these days, they have become the public face of the Manchester United fan and they are not doing the rest of us any favours.

I will leave you with one fine specimen I heard after the Arsenal game. Calling himself a 'fanatical United fan', he came on the air to complain about the "disgraceful performance at Highbury". His solution? We need three new strikers and a whole new back line if we are to win anything this season. In fact, in his opinion, we will never win anything again. Not unnaturally, the presenter assumed that he had been to the game. Oh no, he hadn't been able to get a ticket. Had he watched it on Sky then? No again. How had he followed the game? He had listened to the game on the radio! I rest my case!!

On the morning of the Leicester game, news broke that the 'feud' between Sir Alex and our rather plump Australian keeper had been intensified with Ferguson refusing permission for Bozzy to go on loan to Rangers. And we thought he'd wanted rid of him!

Back to the Top

Normal service is resumed

Leicester City 0 Manchester United 3
Premier League
Saturday 14 October 2000

Three games without a win and the critics were having a field day. United were on the blink.

With Peter Taylor named 'Manager of the Month', the Leicester faithful gathered expectant. Even their favourite son, Lineker, was there with his two sons — but displaying split loyalties. One a United fan, Gary? That can't be right, can it?

It's a leisurely drive over to Leicester from here. Just over 30 minutes and we were parked up in the doctor's 'lucky' parking spot and walking down to the pub. This year it was almost exclusively Leicester both inside and out. Apart from a brief chat with Andy from UWS we saw no-one else we knew, so adjourned outside carrying pints in flexible plastic 'glasses', which is not easy, or to be encouraged in a crowded bar. Half an hour later, three more familiar faces appeared from within. Buz and the Hargreaves, that well known musical trio, had been tucked away in a secluded corner — the same corner they'd stood in

Three in a Row

last time. Superstition abounded. After a brief chat, they left, preferring to get to Filbert Street early, while the doctor and I stayed for some more medicine in another flexible friend.

Down at the ground we split up. I was in 'U' Block, the doctor in 'T'. There were twenty minutes to go before the off. Plenty of time I thought, but the queue for the only two open turnstiles became longer by the minute. As the pubs disgorged their devotees a situation developed that I've encountered many times before. As Reds funnelled into the small gap made available — those of us in the centre were being crushed from both sides. The police didn't help much either. They surrounded us and penned us closer together as the late arrivals of the blue persuasion trooped past. Much snarling and posturing and the odd skirmish followed. After several more minutes I was finally extruded through the gap and almost popped into the turnstile channel where I came to a complete stop. The gatekeeper was unsure what to do about the fella in front of me who had a ticket for 'T' instead of a ticket for 'U'. He wouldn't let him through to 'U' and there was no way back! Over the top of the barrier he struggled, to be led away to his rightful place by a helpful, if slightly flustered, steward.

When I finally reached my seat, or at least a vacant spot I could call my own, the game was already five minutes old. I hadn't missed much. In fact I could have arrived 30 minutes later and said the same thing! Apart from a Leicester free kick which eluded everyone in the penalty area except Rowett, who then volleyed no more than a foot over the bar, there was nothing to report. The atmosphere off the pitch was far better. It was from the United side,

Back to the Top

anyway. The Leicester lot did nothing. We had discussed the game in the pub after we'd heard the team news and thought it probably had 'nil-nil' written all over it, and for the first 35 minutes, we'd seen little to dispel that theory.

Then Teddy took control. Denis the dependable crossed from the right and Sheringham glanced a flick of a header in off the far post. One-nil. Within a minute the score was very nearly doubled as Ole this time crossed from the right and Fortune missed by inches as the ball flashed past the gaping goalmouth. Leicester already seemed beaten. Devoid of invention, they succumbed to United's play all too easily and half-time came as a welcome relief for them. It was also a welcome relief for me as I'd forgone my visit to the gents before the game having arrived in the ground so late.

As I returned to my spot during the break there was a great deal of activity to my left in the next section. Infiltrators. Two of them spotted and set upon. The stewards were going to have to be diligent in their efforts to ensure the safety of these two. But it wasn't what it had seemed. It was Becks and Nev — thinly disguised! They'd been spotted before, but just as at the Baseball Ground a few years ago when Keano appeared in our midst, the reaction was cool and composed. Not the undignified rush for autographs from the Red Army. So it wasn't until the mid-term break that anyone descended upon them requesting signatures. The two obliged with smiles and without question.

The second half resumed. We were one goal to the good and Leicester would have had to double their season's tally so far in order to beat us. And they had shown little indication that this was anything but

Three in a Row

a remote possibility. I had moved further down the row by this time as my former spot had already been taken. It soon became all too clear I had made a poor choice. It didn't change the fortunes on the pitch, as the more superstitious may have expected, but off it things became almost unbearable. Any sign of the merest hint of excitement in the United penalty area and someone in the near vicinity would express themselves in such a way as to render the rest of us, and presumably themselves also, gasping for oxygen. The offending culprit was never identified and there wasn't a bright yellow jacket to be seen, so it wasn't the Sausageman, although it was definitely on a par with some of his best efforts. The low ceiling of the old Leicester stand didn't help either as the offending odour lingered in what was left of the air.

We were half hoping for the game to either peter out into a tedious non-event, but preferably for United to encamp in the Leicester half to dispel the tension. For a while all seemed to be progressing nicely but then Leicester had a corner which provoked more sensory depravation. The corner had resulted from Robbie Savage being up-ended in the penalty area by Wes Brown. Bearing in mind that Wes hadn't even touched the ball and had dumped Savage in a heap, it doesn't take a genius to work out that the Leicester faithful were not best pleased. Seconds later, as the worst corner ever had fallen at the feet of Fortune, he was speeding down the pitch in a moment straight out of the 93-94 scrapbook. Fortune on the left, Keano on the right and everyone else charging upfield or, in the case of those wearing blue, frantically backpeddling. The ball eventually landed at the feet of Mr Dependable who hammered a shot goalwards which Flowers could only palm away.

Back to the Top

Sheringham, in the guise of a latter-day Lawman, pounced and smashed the rebound into the top of the net. 2-0 and the game was more or less over.

That was the first time I spotted the Nevada Smiths flag a few rows down from me — obviously a couple of New Yorkers had somehow managed to acquire tickets. They were joining in with the rest of us in choruses of "Taylor for England", "It's just like watching England", "Leicester, Leicester top of the League" and even "Muzzy Izzet is a Red — he hates England". Again no response from Leicester as they sat in stony silence. We were content to let Dwight know we still cared with a rousing chorus of "Dwight Yorke, King of pornography". He turned to face us and beamed, briefly glancing back to check the ball was nowhere near, he turned again and gave his shirt a tug so that he could kiss the badge. He was then very nearly rewarded with a goal when sent clean through by that man Sheringham, but his powerful volley was well saved by Flowers.

Not long after Becks and Nev took their leave. A strategic retreat was to be the only option open to these two, and would have gone largely unnoticed had those around not given the game away. "We can see you sneaking out," they sang, as the two disappeared after a happy close encounter with the Red Army and a reminder to us that they are still supporters at heart.

When Sheringham went off for Giggs, it was time for the Ole show to take over. By the time he netted the third, in injury time, he had already forced a couple of point-blank saves out of Flowers. It was another quick-fire breakaway out of defence which produced the final goal. An interchange from Yorke to Ole — to Yorke and finally back to Ole saw the ball nestle in the far corner of the net. The ref blew for full time with Ole, Barthez and Dwight bidding us an extended farewell. A very important victory which restored the Reds at the top of the heap.

The doctor and I had arranged to meet on the corner by the main road, about a couple of hundred yards from the ground. I was there well before him and stood waiting with several others when an all-too-familiar sound rumbled in. I looked back towards Filbert Street and relived the Arsenal experience. A group of lads came pounding past and after a brief struggle at our corner, ran off to the right pursued by the local Dibble who were thrashing their white truncheons at anyone looking remotely threatening. Most of us stood stock still as the ensuing chaos entered the next phase. Fortunately this was further up the street, with the area then sealed off and the sound of ambulance and police sirens becoming more prominent as I made my way back towards the ground finally meeting up with the doctor.

As we prepared the pens in L Stand for the visit of the Sheep to Old Trafford, the mini 'crisis' of late September/early October was very much in the past as the wins against Leicester and Eindhoven cheered us up immensely. United were also probably feeling relieved as Paddy Harverson, the new Director of Communications, arrived at Old Trafford to replace Alison Ryan, who had disappeared into the sunset under a very black cloud.

Inflated ideas

Manchester United 3 Leeds United 0
Premier League Saturday 21 October 2000

Back to the Top

A certain little girl had been looking forward to this day for weeks. It was time for me to vacate my usual seat and trek around to the new second tier of the Stretford End. This particular morning Gina (our lucky charm) was with me again and was ready and waiting way before time, even though it meant an 8am start on a weekend morning, something which would normally be out of the question. Despite the hour, the M6 was still jam-packed and as we pulled in to the Birmingham services it was full to overflowing. Were United at home then?

The journey was slower than expected but we managed to get to the Bronnington carpark, down by the canal, with 30 minutes to spare before kick-off which allowed Gina and I just about enough time to find the entrance to tier two. There we were met by a question which was no surprise. "Can I have a look in your bag please?" "Yes," I said, handing it over to the steward. "Open it for me then," as it was handed back. "No, you open it, you're the one who wants to look inside." As the steward reluctantly agreed, I asked what she expected to find. Bearing in mind I was standing at the gate with a 10-year-old child who was desperate to get inside as there were less than ten minutes to kick-off. "Bottles and cans," came the reply! I wonder if they also have a directive to search megastore bags. The search unproductive, we were allowed inside. After a climb that seemed to go on forever, we took our seats and gazed down at Old Trafford from a perch so lofty, we were in danger of nosebleeds. So this was the new 'fans' section'? Not bad, but a pity it didn't replace the lower tier of the Stret, then those who make a noise (and they do) would actually be heard in the rest of the stadium rather than the sound be lost to the skies.

Three in a Row

Linda's journey was altogether different:

Coming into Manchester from Stockport at the unearthly hour of 9am, I happened to catch a Cardiff train on its way to Piccadilly. I sat down in the only available seat, which was opposite a group of six Welsh Leeds United fans. Please, dear reader, don't let anyone try and convince you that United are the only club to attract the Club Class hangers-on — this lot were awful. Loud, arrogant and ignorant, they spent the ten minutes I was on the train spouting forth about United in general and Beckham's 'poor attitude' in particular, when they weren't discussing the limo that was to bring them back to the station after the game, and the benefits of the Executive Box in which they were to watch.

Most other people on the train, who had obviously had the pleasure of their company for at least a couple of hours, were glassy-eyed from the effort required to cut out their intrusive tirade, apart from one lad in a United shirt who had steam coming out of his ears. As we neared Manchester, it was obvious they had never been near the place before. Having tried to leave the train at Stockport (unfortunately, a 'helpful' guard had pointed out their mistake), they realised they had no idea how to get to the ground. The possibility of getting a taxi being beyond their intellectual capabilities, they then made what could have been a fatal mistake.

Turning to the lad in the United shirt, one of them said belligerently, "You probably know the way to Old Trafford, how do we get there?" He stood up slowly. Leaning across the table and placing his face so close that their noses were almost touching, he paused. I cringed as the tableau held for a few seconds. Then he looked around at all the families on

Back to the Top

the train, visibly shook himself and said quietly, but distinctly, "Find your own way there, and on the way, f**k off!" With that he rose to his full height and walked away, to the silent applause of the whole carriage. With that we came into Piccadilly.

Smiling to myself, I arrived at Old Trafford 30 minutes later. Seeing as it was breakfast time, I was standing on United Road, eating a bacon barmcake, when I saw a familiar figure walking towards me. Big Norm, in the flesh. Coming over all girly, I couldn't help but grin at him as he walked by. Catching my eye he must have thought I looked a right fool — with a mouthful of bacon and a daft grin on my face, but being the star he is, he smiled and winked at me, leaving me to run around the forecourt looking for someone I knew so that I could tell them what had just happened! It seems there are ways in which I will never grow up!

As soon as I walked into the Scoreboard, it was obvious that this was a game against the Sheep. Old Trafford was full and it was buzzing with anticipation. Up to our left, the neanderthals were grunting and screaming like something out of a horror movie based in a Victorian lunatic asylum. Down at the other end, hanging from the front of the second tier we could see the new banners and they looked brilliant. "One Love — Stretford End", "Munich 1958 — Flowers of Manchester" and one that simply read "24/5 Years", with the '4' just about to turn over into the '5' and apparently with the provision to extend it to 999 years if necessary! The Bitters will love that one! The players came out onto the pitch to the announcement that it was 'World Fair Play Day' – it's funny sometimes how fate can throw up such amusingly contradictory events. United v Leeds on

Three in a Row

'Fair Play Day'? As Joe Royle might say, "Are you 'avin' a laugh?" The Wizard had changed things from Wednesday night. It wasn't a surprise, with the away game in Belgium coming up on Tuesday. Ole and Dwight started up front, with Phil Neville, Nicky Butt and Quinton Fortune coming in as well. Giggs, Becks and Cole were on the bench alongside Wes and Bosnich. It didn't seem to matter. United piled into Leeds with a vengeance and from as early as the third minute their young keeper was having to make saves.

Barthez was temporarily busy too, thanks to another very poor defensive header from Silvestre. Luckily he, and we, got away with it, as Bowyer lobbed over the bar, prompting the first of many renditions of "He's going down, he's going down, Bowyer's going down. Now that his and Woodgate's trial has been brought forward to January, it may have been the last chance to let them know. That breakaway and another half chance five minutes later were about all we had to put up with from Leeds down at the Stretford End.

Eventually those loveable Sheep couldn't contain themselves any longer and across the air of Old Trafford floated that tasteful ditty: "Who's that lying on the runway?" Some of my neighbours got very worked up at this point. Personally, I found the behaviour of both sets of fans reprehensible — how can we complain about the Munich song if we come out with "Always look out for Turks carrying knives", about their fans getting murdered in Istanbul? It all stinks and I would like to think that United fans have too much class to indulge in that sort of shite. Obviously not.

But back to the action, which, until the last ten

Back to the Top

minutes of the half, apart from a couple of efforts from Butt and Fortune, was centred around midfield. The game was a boring stalemate and up in the second tier Gina was yawning:

With the half-time break nearly upon us Gina was harbouring thoughts about drinks and crisps when Phil Neville sent Ole away down the right. The ball was dispatched at a low trajectory in the direction of the penalty area, bounced in front of the keeper and Yorke dived in to head it into the back of the Leeds net. Now we celebrated, and all thoughts of half-time treats were banished for the time being. The goal gave everyone a lift and the noise level increased. By the time the players had returned to the centre circle, an embarrassed man trudged back to his seat holding a cup of coffee with everyone chuckling and pointing out his misfortune, as if he didn't know. He'd missed the goal in favour of beating the rush for refreshments! I've never fully understood why anyone would want to do that.

As the whistle blew we went below stairs to purchase those crisps — we already had a bottle of juice in the bag, undiscovered at the steward's enquiry! We then went in search of ex-K Standers in the next section and found many familiar faces. So that's where they all live these days? The half-time award went to the person who had obviously made a superior effort to get 'off his head' and had definitely succeeded. "Gina, this is Jonah." Gina was bemused!

The second half continued where the first left off but got progressively better as the clock ticked on. Flossie, the inflatable sheep had transferred itself from K Stand and had appeared at our end, but unfortunately never reached the dizzy heights of tier two. It was batted around the lower Stretford and I'm

Three in a Row

sure I spotted Leeds keeper Robinson eyeing it up as a possible post-match companion!

Leeds were getting more and more indisciplined — fouling our lads and diving all over the place, as decision after decision went against them. And the United lads have obviously learned a vital lesson — whereas at one time they would have been losing their rags as well, that afternoon they were winding up the Leeds players, but only taking it so far, then coolly standing back and watching the results. Eventually it all became too much for Burns. With three minutes of the second half gone he and Ole tangled on the edge of the area. The overenthusiastic push on Ole resulted in a yellow card for the offender and a free kick for us. Becks placed the ball as we waited expectantly. The whistle blew. The ball was sent on its way. The Leeds wall jumped and the ball struck Bowyer which deflected it past Robinson who was left looking rather stupid as he was in the process of diving the other way at the time. We cared not a jot as father and daughter bonded! By this time we felt free to give an airing to "Shit on the Leeds scum, shit on the Leeds scum tonight." Naturally, everyone knew it was morning (possibly with the exception of Jonah) but it made no difference. Those are the words to the song so why let a simple matter of the time of day interfere?

United ran riot during the following few minutes and could easily have doubled their tally. "It's just like watching City" quickly became "It's just like watching England". They didn't like that! "Who let England down — Man-ches-ter — Man-ches-ter," they retorted. "Are you England in disguise?" we asked. They responded with a chorus of "Rule Britannia" which we followed with "Ar-gen-ti-na" and "Stand up

Back to the Top

for the Champions" as everyone stood bar the fellah behind us, who resolutely remained seated throughout. Finally, to the immense amusement of the whole stadium, they gave us a chorus of ifGod save the Queenlm. It was absolutely hilarious!

Down at the other end Barthez was getting more bored than he had been on Wednesday night. It was obvious that as soon as he was presented with an opportunity, something out of the ordinary, as far as normal goalkeeping traditions are concerned, would happen. When the ball was eventually passed back to him he decided to join in with the other outfield players by taking on Viduka. Unfortunately, Viduka had his measure and won the ball. Fortunately he fouled the Frenchman in the process. After that our wayward keeper looked sheepish, which was a huge mistake given that the opposition supporters were far too close for comfort. He behaved himself for the rest of the game — no doubt fearing the possibility of having to endure the Wizard's hairdrying treatment at full time! The fact he doesn't possess any would make no difference whatsoever!

We were just into a rousing rendition of "What a friend we have in Jesus" and getting to the "Ooh aah Can-ton-aah" bit when Becks crossed the ball from the right. It, and Ole, caused such confusion in the Leeds defence that Jones steered it into his own net. Someone bat Flossie down to the poor man — he was in need of consolation! 3-1 and we were just two in a sea of smiling faces. "We all hate Leeds and Leeds and Leeds" was sung with gusto — followed by "If you all hate Scousers clap your hands" with Gina joining in enthusiastically — but don't tell anyone!

The play was almost exclusively down at our end,

but the superiority was built on sound defence, with Gary Nev outstanding, as he had been on Wednesday. His brother was also turning on the style. Both he and Ole came very close to a goal several times more. Ole was particularly unlucky not to have scored. Another day and he'd have had a hat-trick at the very least. Becks also got in on the act but unfortunately skied his effort so high it very nearly reached us up in the gods. "What the f**king hell was that," we sang at him as he grinned and acknowledged our efforts with a raised arm! Late in the game, even Fergie got in on the act by telling Barthez he could go forward for the last corner, but he declined, deciding instead to wander back and collect his towel in time for the final whistle. The game ended with the "Red Flag" to establish credentials and put the Yorkshire rascals firmly in their place. On our way out of the ground, with Gina gripping my hand firmly she said, "I want to do that again and again." I know exactly how she felt.

Our next game was the return against Belgian champions Anderlecht, who United tonked 5-1 in the home leg. Most of us who were there that night thought the score had flattered United and were prepared for a tough ride in the return. We got it!

A Bunch of Softies

Anderlecht 2 Manchester United 1
Champions' League Tuesday
24 October 2000

Before this game United sat on top of the group on seven points, PSV Eindhoven and Anderlecht next

Back to the Top

with six points each and Dynamo Kiev trailing with four. A win would have ensured qualification to the next stage, but on Belgian territory, United knew it would not be easy.

The 22,000-seater Constant Vanden Stock Stadium was crammed to capacity. Anderlecht had never lost a European tie in 26 years against English opposition, including a notorious UEFA Cup victory over Nottingham Forest, which was proved to have been achieved with the aid of financial inducements to the match referee.

The 6 foot 25 inch Koller proved to be the threat — along with the inability of the linesman to raise his flag for offside. It had been reported that Koller had broken his leg but unfortunately for us there was no plaster cast in sight. Maybe the reports were actually true and when their coach, Aime Anthuenis, called his team a bunch of softies after the game at OT, Koller wanted to prove he could play on, even with a broken leg!

Despite recent good results, fans who had made the trip to Anderlecht came home feeling depressed as United, yet again, had made life harder for themselves with a poor performance. Bozzy had also made his life harder than it needed to be by arriving late at the airport for the flight to Brussels. Just when it looked as if he might be back in Sir Alex's good books, he pressed the self-destruct button again and it was beginning to look as if his next move would now be a permanent one, rather than a loan deal.

Back at Old Trafford, the club finally honoured James Gibson, United Chairman (1931-1951) and saviour, with a plaque on the railway bridge on Sir Matt Busby Way. Those of us arriving for the Southampton game were able to pay our respects as we passed.

Three in a Row

The Taibi Factor

Manchester United 5 Southampton 0
Premier League Saturday 28 October 2000

The Time Lords decree that British Standard time changes twice a year — so, late on the Saturday night, the clocks were dutifully put back an hour. Earlier on Saturday afternoon, however, for a brief period, the clocks were turned back thirteen months.

It was to be another early start as the whole family would be travelling with me. My mission was to drop them off in Liverpool where they would be spending the day and we would all be spending the night. I know it's not ideal being in the land of the bin-dippers, but sometimes fate takes a hand and even full-blooded Reds have to bite their lips and visit relatives! At around midday we arrived at the wrong end of the M62 and I abandoned my precious cargo leaving them to their fate. Thirty minutes later I was on my way out, leaving the 'Welcome to Liverpool' sign behind and still pondering on how anyone could find the place welcoming.

I was due to meet up with Gary in the Throstles Nest. Gary is a friend of Fish from Vancouver Island. I don't mean he likes fish, although he may well, I mean he is a friend of Steve Fisher, who incidentally doesn't like fish! Anyway, it was to be Gary's first time at Old Trafford. The Nest was hardly full of listees that afternoon. Buzz arrived, closely followed by Pete and Hal, but that was all. Maybe it was because rain had been falling incessantly all day, and still was as we left for the ground.

Walking down Warwick Road, we stopped briefly

Back to the Top

to pick up the latest Red News and exchanged greetings with a whole bunch of ex-K Standers — Barney seems to be attracting crowds these days — I wonder why? After issuing instructions to Gary on where to go, what to do, and where to meet up after the game, I made my way to K Stand. I reached my seat just before kick-off and slightly before Chris, my next-door neighbour of the last eight years, appeared. It was good to have my old sparring partner back. The teams were out and the Saints fans up to our left were quietly seated. The game got under way and all was normal. But that was when the space-time relationship got messed up. The dark, menacing storm clouds had gathered over Old Trafford and the wind howled. It was almost supernatural. Within a few minutes we were all transported to a parallel universe. There can be no other explanation. The Time Lords were having a laugh! September 25th last year became October 28th this year. Only certain aspects of the situation changed. The same two teams were involved (obviously), the venue was the same (obviously), but the circumstances varied. In this new universe, it was United who were kicking towards the K Stand goal and it was in the first half — not the second. But the funny thing was, the exact same thing happened, although this time, it happened to them. It was bizarre enough the first time — but the second time it was weird.

Around the eight-minute mark Andy shot hard and low from just outside the box. Jones, in the Southampton goal, got down to take the ball. It was a decent enough shot, but one which he would have been expected to save as the ball was heading straight for him and at a good height. He grasped the

Three in a Row

ball in his arms and had it under control. But then, as if the ghost of Massimo had entered his body, the ball wriggled free of his grasp, trickled through his legs and ever so slowly over the line. An exact carbon copy of the infamous Taibi incident from the year before. The Time Lords had decreed his fate and the ghost of Taibi was exorcised. There was a gasp of disbelief and then a mixture of guffaws and hysterical booze-laden laughter filled the K Stand air. Jones was incredulous but to his credit, refused to examine his studs as the Italian had done. "Hello, hello, Taibi is back, Taibi is back," we howled at the keeper, as K Stand collapsed in fits of giggles.

If the game had ended there and then it would have been enough. In fact for the next 30 minutes, as the two universes were re-aligned and normality restored, it was about all we got. You could just about detect the spirit of Taibi leaving Jones' body as he wrestled to reclaim his identity and everything was reverted to the present day. Apart from that, nothing else happened until Teddy Sheringham took control near the end of the first half. The ball had reached him on the left by the corner of the penalty area and, with Jones off his line, he sent a splendid Cantona-esque chip over his head and into the far corner of the net. It was the sign of things to come.

The ref blew for half-time and all manner of gubbins appeared on the pitch. The half-time draw took place while the Scoreboard net had some sort of paper or plastic sheet stretched between the posts, which Steve remarked was rather unfair on Southampton who would be kicking in our direction for the remainder of the game. It turned out to be for a competition to see if this bloke could score, Beckham-like, from the halfway line. Three shots and

Back to the Top

three misses later he trudged off — not £1,000 richer! Oh well!

The second half resumed as the first had finished, with a Sheringham goal. Scholes had stolen the ball in midfield and fed Becks, who cut it back for Sheringham, who passed it into the net. So simple yet so effective. Minutes later and Teddy Sheringham had his hat-trick. Coley ever-so-slightly miscontrolled the ball which sat kindly for Sheringham who again passed it into the net. 4-0 and three to Teddy.

Not to be outdone, Andy then scored his second after a Becks corner was headed on at the near post by Scholesy and he had the simplest of tasks to nod it into the net. 5-0 and it was time for Andy and Teddy to wave goodbye! (That was one for the old farts amongst us!) The rumour which went around at the time was that Martin had sent a 'post-it note' down to Fergie saying he couldn't cope with the possibility of Andy scoring a third as he would be expected to donate another match ball on top of the one he was having to give away to Teddy. It was a rumour which had everyone nodding in agreement!

That goal actually woke the Southampton supporters up. Or maybe it was our piss-taking. "Are you England in disguise?" didn't provoke a response but "Are you Portsmouth in disguise?" did! "Do you come from Manchester?" was their all-too predictable riposte — definitely execs then! "City come from Manchester," they added before we replied with "You even lost to City", which finally shut them up and they settled back into comatose mode. They were treated to a couple of choruses of "Hoddle for England" and "Portsmouth, Portsmouth, give us a wave!" before we shut up as well. The interesting thing was though, that the second tier of the Stretford was audible. In

Three in a Row

fact, it was very audible all the way through. We even heard them provoking us with "K Stand, K Stand, give us a song". It didn't do any good though, as K Stand slumbered.

Ole and Dwight were on by now but, with Jones fully restored to his former self, he made several excellent saves from both of them and the score remained the same. As the game ended the heavens opened once more. We had been bathed in sunshine for the whole of the second half but were only too well aware of the storm approaching. Some left early to try and avoid the deluge but didn't succeed. We stayed to applaud the players off the pitch and then waited for Gary at the corner by J Stand. He arrived trussed up in his all-weather jacket looking very pleased with himself but then he blew his cover. It was as we were passing the megastore at the front of K Stand. He was desperate to go inside and purchase a souvenir for his young son. I looked at Steve. Beads of perspiration had already appeared on his forehead. There was no other way, we were going to have to be brave! And as we made our way towards the doors with Steve crossing himself, we were granted a last-minute reprieve. The place was jam-packed. The tills were overloading and the thought of spending half an hour in a queue was even too much for our Canadian friend. An audible "Phew, that was bloody close" slipped out as we turned and walked away.

The next game came sandwiched between a home against Southampton and an away at Coventry. Two not very high profile games you might think, but all Premiership games are high profile, especially for opponents of Manchester United. It was always likely, therefore, that a team made up of youthful non-first team regulars would take the field.

The Value of Youth

When Matt Busby took over at Old Trafford after the war, he had the relative luxury of a mature team — no ground, as Old Trafford had been bombed — but a good team! He realised, though, that the team would not serve him forever. So he, along with Jimmy Murphy, set about the task of encouraging the best young footballers available to join them at United. The resultant 'Busby Babes' became the toast of Britain before they were cruelly taken from us at Munich. After Munich it was mainly the youth team, plus a few reserves and a couple of hastily-signed additions, who took United to Wembley in 1958, only to lose to Bolton.

We look back on those days with great affection and pride. Those lads were the essence of Manchester United — the phoenix vanguard that helped the club rise from the flames. It has always been a tradition at United to give youth a chance, but no more so than now. We have a special relationship with those who have progressed through the ranks as we know they are steeped in United tradition. We look upon them as our own. In recent years the talent has rolled off the conveyor belt. The press and opposition who have complained in the past about Sir Alex fielding so-called weakened teams in this competition have been made to eat humble pie. The 'Class of 92' that formed the backbone of the team that defeated Port Vale in '95, now form the basis of today's team. The Nevilles, Butt, Beckham, Scholes and not forgetting Giggs, all graduated from that

Three in a Row

class, and have all progressed to full International level. Who would be next? Wes is an obvious choice, but what about Wallwork, Greening, Chadwick, O'Shea, Stewart and Healy?

Everyone at United talks about the victory in Europe and the return of the Holy Grail, but there isn't a true Red anywhere who wouldn't want to be at a final of the Worthington Cup watching the young lads battle their way to victory. Unlikely? We would have to wait and see.

The clubs had met just once before in this competition — back in October 1978 at Old Trafford when Watford were in the third Division, but still managed to go away with a 2-1 win. Joe Jordan scored for us that night but Luther Blissett netted twice to send Graham Taylor's side through to the next round.

As the Red Army made its way down South to Watford, news was coming through from Holland that personal terms had been agreed with Ruud van Nistelrooy.

Fireworks, but only just

Roots

Watford 0 Manchester United 3
Worthington Cup
Tuesday 31 October 2000

Watford manager Graham Taylor couldn't keep it zipped up could he? Before the game he'd been berating clubs like Manchester United for fielding under-strength teams in the Worthington Cup! Wonder what your thoughts were after the game then, Graham?

To think we nearly didn't make it to this one. A Tuesday evening in Watford was becoming less likely as the day approached, but finally Nigel and I were spurred on by the fact that it wouldn't exactly take us hours to get there — so why not? Luckily for big Rich we had already decided to make the trip by the time he phoned on Tuesday morning to say that the journey he had planned to make on the train had been scuppered by some poor bastard who had decided to end it all by chucking himself in front a train at Euston station. The station was closed down for obvious reasons and the result — a delayed kick-off. Not that we found that out until we were at the

Three in a Row

ground.

Prior to that we had met up with Nasher and the Lipstick Queen in a local pub. They had originally been in the place next door until problems occurred, due to infiltration by a couple of scarf-wearing Reds who had done nothing more than walk inside. A local had taken great exception and they had been asked to leave along with any other Reds inside wearing any kind of insignia. Problem was, we couldn't get to the bar in this other boozer so we checked out the place next door anyway. What we didn't realise was that the local bruiser who had caused all the trouble was still in there and was eyeing up the pin badges Nasher and I were wearing. I'd like to think it was the hard stare I administered that prevented him from causing more problems, but I doubt it! In any case, we were in and past the self-appointed guardian so didn't care.

Half an hour later we took a leisurely walk down to the ground past another well-policed trouble spot by the Burger King which had suffered some considerable damage. It was then we were informed of the 15 minute delay to kick-off by Barney, who added the proviso that we shouldn't necessarily believe him! We did though Ron, and waited outside dithering over whether we should return to an off-licence or enter into conversation with a certain Brummie who was telling of an imminent trip to Reykjavik (try saying that with a Brummie accent!) Before we had been bothered to make a decision either way, it was getting too close to the off, so we went in and paid a visit to the pathetically inadequate toilets before finding a spot to stand. When we did, we were directly behind the IMUSA Chair and Vice-Chair. Better be on our best behaviour then!

Fireworks, but only just

Fireworks heralded the arrival of the teams, and as the two Hornets in the centre circle disentangled themselves from their lovefest, the smoke cleared and the ref blew for the start of the game. No-one on the United team had a number less than Phil Neville's no12 although we did have three (or four if you count Jonathan Greening) European Champions on the pitch! Both teams seemed fired up, but the initial thrusts came from Watford, with Nielsen going close from a Wooter cross. That was about the extent of the threat from the Watford boys in the first half as our lads soon bossed the game.

In the stands the atmosphere was one of the best I can remember for ages. The Red Army went through the full repertoire: "Hello, hello, we are the Busby boys" ran and ran and ran. It was still running past Fortune's free kick, which curled just past the corner of post and bar, and continued up to the first goal when Wallwork won the ball on the right and fed Chadwick. Chamberlain flung himself in front of his shot and it fell to Ole Gunnar who lashed it into the top of the net.

Chairman Mark was complaining that we shouldn't be winning in the Worthington, but celebrating all the same! He then noticed what could have been a familiar face next but one along. Was it or was it not Rick Parfitt from Status Quo? Nah – couldn't have been' could it? From that moment on United assumed full control and the lads who we watched get beaten last year at Villa Park in the same competition had matured. They were assured, strong, skillful and a joy to watch. This game gave me the same feeling as the one against Bolton several years ago when a certain group of young lads turned on the style and comprehensively thrashed the yonners.

Three in a Row

There were no poor performances.

Just before half-time, Nigel disappeared behind the scenes to get a couple of beers. Down at the bar, they have a strict policy not to serve alcohol before the whistle is blown. As the moment approached, the queue for alcoholic refreshment was already four deep, and some were becoming animated. When the whistle blew and the nod to begin serving was given, Nigel just happened to ask at the right moment, was served first. The moment I came down the stairs he handed me a plastic bottle of beer — nice! Meanwhile, back at the bar, things were getting silly. The latest variation on the City chant was "24 beers, 24 beers, 24 beers, 24 beers!"

If you have ever been in the away section at Vicarage Road you will be aware that the area behind the stand is cramped to say the least. In fact there is just about enough room to lift one's elbow. To illustrate this, a couple of local coppers were foraging their way through the crowds filming the chaos. "It's about restricted access to the back passage behind the stand," they explained. Oo-er, we thought, and decided we'd be better off upstairs! The second half continued where the first left off. There was an early break out of defence by Phil Nev, after being set up by a great tackle by O'Shea. Nev galloped half the length of the pitch and laid the ball off to Yorke who sent it out to the wing for Chadwick. Chadwick returned the favour by passing inside and Yorke dispatched number two. That opened the door for some Watford management piss-takes. "Taylor for England" soon became "Turnip for England" which then developed into "We'd rather have a turnip than a Swede!" We didn't expect him to respond to "Turnip, Turnip, give us a wave!" but Fergie did when he was

Fireworks, but only just

asked — which was nice.

With about ten minutes to go, Raimondo let fly with a belting kick which flew over everyone and right into the path of Ole. As the ball bounced on the slippery surface, Ole rushed towards us and the goal. The Watford keeper was rooted to his line as Ole controlled the ball on his chest after the second bounce and volleyed it into the net. A route-one goal had made it 3-0 and Ole stood before us beaming.

But there was still one last twist of fate. In the last couple of minutes, Raimond allegedly brought down a Watford player in the box. As we were way down the other end and more concerned with a chorus of "They have Curly Watts as a celebrity fan", we weren't taking much notice until the Watford player enacted his impression of Greg Luganis. BDS said afterwards that no-one had thought it a penalty on the Sky Sports Panel other than Alan Mulligatawny. The Watford fans bayed for Rai's blood. It was the first time they had done anything. The ref, having given the spot kick, then sent Raimond off. United sent Rabchubka on and took Fortune off. The Watford fans were beside themselves with glee, but not for long! Rabchubka immediately stood centre-stage to face the penalty. Mooney stepped up and ballooned it way over the bar. Was he 'avin' a laugh at us singing "City, City sign him on"? And was the 'Man of the Match' adjudicator also havin' a laugh when he awarded it to Mooney, who had spent more time on his arse than his feet and was the butt of most of our taunts? Perhaps he felt sorry for him.

As we stood on the corner of Vicarage Road after the game waiting for big Rich, young Vimto came past wearing the same daft grin as the rest of us. It had been an excellent evening's entertainment. One we hadn't expected as Watford were lording it at the top of the First Division at the time and everyone had been singing their praises. At that moment Tim was absolutely right — we all loved the Worthington Cup!

Just like watching City

Coventry City 1 Manchester United 2
Premier League Saturday 4 November 2000

Thankfully, Greater Manchester has got off relatively lightly with the storms that have battered the UK over the last weeks or so. Nevertheless, there has hardly been a day when I haven't got soaked at least once — usually a few times! I arrived in the car park to find the son-and-heir had also got there early and the first shower of the day had arrived with him!

As we arrived in Coventry, we saw something strange — what was it? Round, golden and warm — bloody hell, it was the sun! We went through the turnstiles and stood on the walkway between the two seating sections, our faces turned blissfully to the sun, and watched the lads warm up while a group of very heavily made-up young ladies cavorted about in the centre of the pitch. Eventually, we were asked, "Kindly take your seats" by a very over-bearing female steward. As she ushered us towards the upper section, we tried to move towards our seats which were in the lower section! After a brief struggle we managed to loosen her vice-like grip and were able to finally move down to the third row from the front, nice and close to the pitch, exactly where I like to be! The journey to Highfield Road was a mere 'taxi' ride away for our other reporter:

Fireworks, but only just

Down in this neck of the woods we love this fixture for obvious reasons – it's our only 'home' game. But, for some reason, for the majority of United supporters it has always been one of the most desirable 'aways' of the season.

The local trains were running an hour late so Karen drove me over to Nigel's place and then Cheryl drove us to the pub. Not bad, eh? Neither of us driving anywhere for once. We were due to meet up with the Chairs to drop off leaflets to advertise the IMUSA meeting with Peter Kenyon the following Tuesday. As soon as we entered the pub there was no doubting it was full of United. There was no singing (at first), no club colours, but no mistaking — United were in town and the Rose and Crown was packed with metaphorical red and white. After an hour or so in the pub with the Chairs and Doctor Death spent, for the most time, marvelling at Chair's two-to-one ale intake, we left and walked down to the ground. Fifteen minutes later and after a brief chat with Barney, who proclaimed himself both very optimistic and very drunk, we went inside.

From the start, the atmosphere in the upper tier was excellent, as always befits this fixture. Down to our right, the Coventry West End boys were standing but they weren't doing much else. Apathy still reigns supreme in Coventry. In truth, they had the look of those who knew the result before the game even started. Poor Cov, they probably thought we were singing about them, what with all the 'City' songs dusted down and given an airing ready for the Derby in a couple of weeks. We weren't of course, but there were a few puzzled looks from the West Enders when we were singing: "24 years — f**k all, 24 years — f**k all." You could see them deliberating on just how long

Three in a Row

it had been since they'd won their one and only major trophy. And when they'd worked it out that since 1987 it had only been 13 years, a few of them took the trouble to point it out to us — waving their calculators in the air and looking very indignant! "Are you 'avin' a laugh?" we asked. What really confused them was when we sang "It's just like watching City." A few of them actually imploded at that point — unable to comprehend the irony. What a mess!

It was as easy on the pitch as off it. Right from the first whistle it was easy. In fact it was so easy you could almost envisage something very strange happening — City breaking away from their own goal line and scoring. Almost! Surprise, surprise — it was United who scored first, in a move of stunning simplicity. A short pass out of defence from Teddy to Scholes who sent a 50 yard diagonal to Becks on the right wing. Becks took the ball to the line and crossed for Cole who met it on the volley and fired it past the enormous Cov keeper. At that moment the celebrations in the upper tier became slightly overstated due to an excess of alcohol. Within minutes Giggs went on another mazy run and was brought down on the edge of the Coventry box. Beckham stepped forward to take the kick and stroked the ball through the wall and watched as it squirmed through Kirkland's grasp. "Taibi is back, Taibi is back" greeted the second goal.

United cruised through to half-time. When the whistle blew it was time to brave the gents which had the appearance of the majority of the surrounding countryside. In other words — it was wet — very, very wet! It wasn't as though the roof had been leaking either — so exactly what was it that had been leaking? It was a mystery of Wembley proportions! It

Fireworks, but only just

becomes obvious why flip-flops are not on the United fashion accessory list.

The second half started with United still completely dominant although Coventry had brought on a Peruvian who was later to cause us some angst. We welcomed Barthez down at our end while the West End boys stood silently, apart from the odd one or two who consistently gestured in our direction. They seemed to be indicating that they had missed the opportunity to visit the gents during the break and were getting quite desperate. A funny lot — the Sky Blue army. We gestured back that we thought they'd be better off going and left it at that.

In the upper tier the complete version of "The Twelve Days of Cantona" was sung with rousing reverence and "We are the Busby boys" lasted forever and ever. The action on the pitch was becoming less of a distraction except when a City fan ran on. And no-one did anything to stop him. He ran on unhindered. The stewards looked at him, shrugged their shoulders and, in typical Coventry fashion, couldn't be bothered. Barthez waited to take the goal kick and the rest of the players stood stock still as the lad, who was so pissed he could hardly keep his feet, wandered over to our side of the pitch and pathetically gave himself up to the nearest steward who carted him off. "Who the f**kin' hell are you?" echoed through his empty skull as he was escorted out of the ground. But at least it seemed to wake the Sky Blue army.

Up until this point, this had been a game so dominated by one team, that a scoreline of anything less than half a dozen to nil was doing it no justice whatsoever. But.........after there had been several more chances down at the other end, Coventry actually won a corner. The small bunch of toilet humour devotees stationed down there became very excited. For the first time they were fixated on their team rather than us. The ball was flighted over and the resultant header tipped into the net by the Peruvian. The Sky Blue army was beside itself with glee. They went wild, and those who had been desperate to gain our permission for a visit to the gents dropped their guard and disgraced themselves.

Our attentions had been diverted by the mopping up process over to our right when they were diverted back to the pitch where there had obviously been a misunderstanding of some sorts. Keano was leaning over Eustace with that certain look on his face which was nothing to do with "Please allow me to help you up old chap." We had no idea what had happened, but there was a theory. The ref, our good friend Mr Graham Poll, reached inside his pocket. There was a huge intake of breath. A moment later the yellow card was brandished and a huge sigh of relief expelled. The same was administered to Eustace after he had been helped to his feet and the game was allowed to continue.

The home boys were only a goal behind and now fancied themselves to draw level. Fortunately they didn't possess the wherewithal to complete the comeback and after a brief, if frantic spell of about two minutes' activity, they settled down again. United regained control and we hardly saw the ball in our half again. Keano let fly with a snarling volley which the keeper did well to push behind. Cole and Ole both came close, but not as close as Yorke, who hit the inside of the post and watched the ball cannon out along the goal line. Eventually, Poll blew for full time and United's record against Coventry in the

Fireworks, but only just

Premiership now reads: won 15, drawn 1, lost 1 and the Coventry comeback of a couple of seasons ago was not to be repeated.

On our way out of the ground (massive) City's loss at home to Leicester gave us something more to cheer and even the Sheep beating the Dirties was greeted with a muted, but positive, response. We briefly met up with Linda, the son-and-heir and big Dunc, all looking very pleased with themselves. For Linda it was a trouble-free return journey back up the M6. 8pm found her back in Piccadilly Station amongst the City fans, as they waited for their trains back to the Moss Side suburbs of Milton Keynes, London and Cardiff. For Nigel and I the journey did not, for once, include the M6.

At the gate the Police were directing the United support to the right, in the opposite direction to which we intended to travel, but Nigel and I gave them the slip and mingled with the West Enders on their way out. By this time even the most fervent of locals had forgotten about the game and were chatting about what they were going to have for tea. Don't forget, this was Coventry!

Down on the main road, however, things were slightly different. There were Police vehicles everywhere. Ambulances were already wailing their way to the hospital and the world had shifted once again. Further down the road a huge police blockade had been set up. Blue lights flashed, dogs snarled and strained at the leash, as traffic ground to a reluctant halt. We had no idea whether we would be allowed through. It was chaos as some were being pulled aside and hauled into the vans. We kept our heads down and just walked. As we reached the multi-vehicle road block an argument erupted which diverted attention and we slipped past unnoticed. Once again, the familiar sight of lads with phones,. Police with truncheons drawn and snapping alsatians had all been part of the post-match experience. The frantic cry of "GET EVERYONE OUT!" was the last thing we heard as we quickened our pace and disappeared.

Kiev — chicken?

Manchester United 1 Dynamo Kiev 0 Champions' League Wednesday 8 November 2000

Well, we survived — just! Not the players — us poor buggers who were close enough to see just how near we came to going out of the Champions' League that night. It should have had a health warning — "Not suitable for those of a nervous disposition." And from Keano's reaction after the game, we fans weren't the only ones suffering from the stress! I should have known what to expect when I arrived on Sir Matt Busby Way to find a grinning Barney confidently predicting an easy win. After all, when was he last right about the outcome of a game? Walking towards the ground about 30 minutes before kick-off, I tried in vain to spot some Kiev fans. But it was all United — thousands of us all heading for the Mecca that is Old Trafford. Its Marks and Spencer-style frontage lighting up the night sky for miles around, drawing the modern United fan towards it like moths to a flame. Clutching their credit cards they queued, row upon row — their eyes glazed, repeating the MUplc mantra: "Spend, spend, spend!" Minutes later they

Fireworks, but only just

emerged, eyes blinking as they looked around them at the crowds, bright red megastore bags clutched in their hands, filled with Beckham duvet covers and alarm clocks that sing "Glory, Glory" at you at 6.30 in the morning. As I pushed my way towards the line of stewards at the entrance to East Stand, a group of men in suits passed me discussing how convenient it was that Old Trafford was so close to the Lowry, they could 'do both' in one trip! Feeling slightly nauseous, I escaped into the relative sanity of the concourse at the back of the Scoreboard. Or at least it used to be! The typical OT experience these days.

It was a strange night for our other reporter as well:

The afternoon had started all right without a motorway in sight. We decided to travel up on the A roads. Let's put it this way — the decision was not hard to make. As soon as we saw the jam (traffic) on the M6, there was no contest. Right up through the Staffordshire countryside we went, eventually stopping for a much-needed break in a country pub. However, the beer was good and we stayed a while too long — finally arriving at the car park with not too much time too spare. It seemed as though several others had also arrived in the nick of time, as there was an almighty exodus from various coaches and what resembled the London marathon snaking its way to the ground. Our bevy of passengers disappeared to the four corners of OT and I joined the lengthening queue for K Stand.

Once inside, I was glad we had arrived a little on the late side as the team announcements were being made. Memories of the Nou Camp came flooding back, but not in the way you might expect. Our new PA was announcing the United team in the same way

Three in a Row

the Bayern Munich PA had introduced theirs on that balmy night — in other words, he said "Fabien" and the crowd responded with "Barthez". Why couldn't we have left this to the Germans? That memory had been nicely confined to the category labelled 'things I like to smile about', but now, thanks to our 'friend' Mr Keegan, it's now in the category labelled 'things I don't like to smile about as much as I did before'. As soon as this new-wave madness ended, I ran up to my spot, getting a quick Euro prediction of 4-0 from our friendly steward. When I got to my seat I found that Steve had migrated to the row in front and in his place was a woman wearing far too much jewellery and dressed in a white polo neck jumper and beige camel coat. Good job there were several familiar faces around or I'd have worried I'd ended up in the exec section by mistake. I don't think she'll be bothering with our part of K Stand again though — apparently we're all far too 'uncouth'!

Down in the lower Scoreboard, the mood was tense but fairly upbeat:

Actually, worry dripped from the corrugated roof on those below. As the players lined up in front of South Stand, I leaned across to the son-and-heir and said, "Now this feels like a real European game," and it did. I was nervous and edgy, it was cold and damp, but not raining and the waterproof provided by the Mad Dane stayed in its plastic bag under my seat. The floodlights created an eerie, misty, cast to the evening and this wasn't just an almost meaningless 'league' game where a loss wouldn't be the end of the world, this was the moment of truth. In a couple of hours time, we would know whether we were to go on to the next stage, drop down into the UEFA Cup or be out of Europe altogether.

Fireworks, but only just

Even when the game kicked off it didn't help alleviate the situation. It had been a good job that Kiev showed a remarkable lack of ambition for a team supposedly within a draw of the UEFA Cup. They stacked up an eleven-man defence and United fiddled around in midfield for the first fifteen minutes. Then came the breakthrough which caused an immense wave of relief to spread its wings around OT and give us all a much-needed hug. Kiev had broken into the United half down at the Stretford End when the ball found its way to Sheringham who lobbed it forward to Cole. There was a brief exchange between Cole and Giggs before the latter back-heeled a return to the former who promptly lost control but still managed to flick the ball into space where Keano waited. Slightly surprised by the appearance of a ball he'd given up as lost, he hit a tame shot goalwards which the keeper batted away. But, there was Sheringham to add the final touch and looped the ball over the keeper and into the net. A huge collective sigh of relief accompanied an equally huge roar, as the whole of Old Trafford celebrated.

For a while the expectations inside the ground rose as we waited for United to take the game by the scruff of the neck and toss the former Russians aside. They didn't do anything of the sort. They seemed to be nervously sitting back on the single goal and consequently the atmosphere evolved from positive expectation to negative expectancy. By the end of the first half, Kiev had inched their way back into the game and had ventured forth, daring to attack the Stretford End. It was only fortunate that none of their forwards came anywhere near to the skill of their former compatriots, Shevchenko and Rebrov or the unthinkable would have been on the

Three in a Row

menu. Half-time was a welcome relief but short-lived.

The game had already re-started by the time I got back to our spot. Nothing had changed. Kiev were getting closer and closer, more and more confident. The linesman to our left was still raising his flag and waving them offside and they still couldn't shoot straight, but we were all only too well aware of the consequences of a single lapse in concentration. The atmosphere was becoming more tense by the second. We tried to get the singing going, but whenever we thought we had, Kiev broke again and the sound petered away into a nervous rendition of the "Last Post". The closer to the final whistle, the worse it became. One goal against would condemn us to the UEFA Cup, two would send us spinning out of Europe altogether.

As we drew nearer and nearer to full time, the Kiev players looked more and more dangerous. It was absolute agony, as we could see the pit yawning in front of us, its rim surrounded by jeering Leeds and Arsenal fans. With five minutes left, our worst fears were all but confirmed. There was a break on the Kiev right and this time the linesman's flag had remained firmly by his side. Oh shit! The United defence had been caught out and failed to turn in time. The ball was in crossed low and towards the near post. Everything seemed to happen in slow motion, and it all happened right in front of us — almost within touching distance. There was a huge intake of breath as we faced our fate. Images of loved ones flashed in front of our eyes as we said farewell to life in the Champions' League. The ball fell perfectly at the feet of Demetradze no more than five yards out. He'd left Nev and Wes for dead. Only Barthez stood in his way and even he seemed transfixed and leaden footed,

Fireworks, but only just

by the swiftness of the attack. The axe was about to fall. We stood unable to move a muscle as Demetradze, the executioner, brought the heavy blade down on our necks. But then a miracle happened. The ball flew a fraction of an inch past the post. We had been granted a last second reprieve. The air was thick with the stench of tension. We had been ready to accept our fate. Ready to be confined to the Euro dustbin but had got away with it.

They should have scored, we should have been out. Old Trafford finally woke up. Roaring "We love United" and "We shall not be moved", 67,000 United fans finally got behind the team. Except, of course, for those who (as usual) were leaving early. Even on a night like this one, and with the game poised on a knife-edge, some obviously thought that getting away five minutes quicker in the car was more important than what was happening in the drama unfolding on the pitch. As Barthez took the resultant goal kick the fourth official held up the electronic board — three minutes of extra time. No-one was sure where it had come from but it had to be endured anyway. A cacophony of whistles encouraged the referee to blow, but he refused. My head was buzzing with the noise, it was so loud it hurt. One minute ticked by and then the next. With literally seconds to go, Kiev forced a corner. The ball was flighted into the box and was heading straight for a foreign head when Barthez somehow managed to claw it away to safety. The end, when it came, was almost an anti-climax. I didn't hear the whistle. One minute I was biting my nails and almost crying with the tension, the next minute the referee had his hands in the air, the players were shaking each other by the hand and the tension filtered away.

Three in a Row

The following morning I awoke to GMR and Roy Keane's comments about 'prawn sandwiches'. He was right, of course. Looking back only a couple of years, the atmosphere at Euro home games has all but disappeared. But it's probably not fair to blame it entirely on the fans. Listening to Andy Walsh on GMR as I had my breakfast, he spoke for many of us when he said that it is the Club who are really to blame. They wanted to do a little social engineering in Old Trafford. They wanted to get rid of the troublesome fans who stood up and swore and sang rude chants. Well now they have, and you can hardly blame the new fans for not being what they're not, can you? Perhaps they should have thought of the effect it would have had on what was left of the atmosphere in Old Trafford when they concreted over the Scoreboard and moved the singers up to the second tier, instead of giving us back the real Stretford End. When they made Season Tickets and LMTBs in the so-called 'Fans' Zone' adult prices only. When they hiked prices to the point where even those of us in a reasonably paid job can't afford it anymore.

The game against Boro, a couple of days later, was the fans' chance to show what they thought of our captain's comments.

A divided city

Pass the canapes

Manchester United 2 Middlesbrough 1
Premier League Saturday
11 November 2000

On the Friday morning, the Mirror had been predicting a 'backlash' from the Old Trafford crowd for this game. Rubbing their hands with glee at the thought of the mileage they were going to get out of it, they dedicated their back page to winding up the prawn butty brigade. Of course, if they had any brains at all, they'd have realised that not only are the prawn butty brigade highly unlikely to be reading the Mirror, but that ordinary United fans are right behind Keane when he has a swipe at the corporate portion of Old Trafford (even if thousands of them conveniently forget that they weren't singing on Wednesday either). If that particular journo from the Mirror was in the ground at 2.58pm that afternoon, he will have been tearing up his copy for the Sunday paper and starting again as the team was greeted onto the pitch with "There's only one Keano!" Just as with all the bad publicity about his new contract, the Old Trafford crowd was right behind our captain.

Three in a Row

Of course all the jokes before the game were about prawn sandwiches. I had been on the five-mile trek to the membership office to get coach tickets for the Derby game and after swimming back through the lake (sorry car park), I got into the Scoreboard about 15 minutes before kick-off. There seemed to be a lot more fans than usual remaining behind the seats until the last minute and thankfully, the noise was such that I couldn't hear Mr Keegan's efforts to get us all to sing. Judging by the number of people saying they weren't going to their seats until "that bastard has finished farting about", I think it's all a master plan to get us to spend more on beer and pies!

Rain had been threatening all day and there was a huge black cloud overhead as we entered the surreal world that is now our section of the Scoreboard. The Boro fans were getting a little above themselves in their corner — chanting the pathetic "Let us sing a song for you". "Let us win a cup for you," we countered and turning my attention to the pitch, I noticed that dear Mr Ince had chickened out again. Injured? Funny how he has been 'injured' every time one of his new teams have come to OT, isn't it? Gary Pallister was there of course. Still a big presence at the back and when he cleared a couple of important balls early in the game, I just couldn't help but applaud.

What was clear from the off was that Keano was out to prove a point. He wanted to win and he wanted it badly! Any critics of what he said on the Wednesday could not have doubted his commitment at this game. He was everywhere and he was determined to take the rest of the team along with him. Keane was at the heart of most of the attacks

A divided city

and Yorke alone could have had three before Boro managed to score a goal which came completely against the run of play. One minute we were watching attack after attack on the goal in front of us, and the next minute the ball was down the other end and in the net! The following day the newspapers said the goal "silenced Old Trafford" — it didn't. The whole ground sang "We love United" and demonstrated how intimidating OT could be. While the Boro fans sang "It's like watching City", the lad behind me sang "You can stick you f**kin' prawns up your arse". It seemed to make him feel better anyway! Half-time saw us head off for the concourse still one down and the with the son-and- heir muttering "What have they bloody got against scoring in front of us these days?"

The lads began the second half where they ended the first, bombarding the Boro goal. Scholes put a shot the wrong side of the post, Keane had a shot saved and then Scholes again put a header wide. But finally, we got what we deserved when Keane (who else) crossed in from the right and Nicky Butt tapped it into the net. Within minutes, Yorke had another shot which was blocked by a defender. The ball came out to Teddy who blasted it into the net and we were in front. "Oh Teddy, Teddy," we sang and "It's like watching City". They didn't like having that one thrown back at them!

After that brief spell of productive activity we coasted to the end of the game. At the news of the City score (a 3-1 loss at West Ham after leading 1-0) the sound of "24 years" echoed round the stadium as we made our way out. I headed for the Megastore — no, not to purchase anything, Eric forbid! The Mad Dane was in town, and we'd arranged to meet under the statue, along with thousands of others!

Three in a Row

Eventually we found each other and the Statman, and walked down to the Nest for a very enjoyable couple of hours drinking with four Norwegians and a Dane while watching the rugby league World Cup on Sky (well, I was — no-one else seemed very interested!). To top the lot though — guess what United had had printed on the back cover of the programme: "Who ate all the canapes? Fancy watching a game at Old Trafford from a hospitality box? If you want the chance to cheer on the Reds with a posh pie in one hand and a bottle of bubbly in the other, you'd better get hold of a Man Utd mobile!" Please tell me it was a joke. But it wasn't — it was reality. Only at United, eh? So it had been a good day, a good game and a good result. United were clear at the top with a two-point lead over Arsenal and the Massive Club had lost again.

The Infiltrators

The Infiltrators are a group of urban explorers. They are not your normal, run-of-the-mill towny types though. They are people who baulk the system, who do not follow the normal guidelines laid down by the establishment. They explore where they are not supposed to. Underground storage areas, disused subway systems and rooftops are all part of their domain. They do not vandalise, or pilfer — they go where the general public are not supposed to go, out of curiosity. They are explorers in the fullest sense of the word. They are seeking a REAL experience — one which hasn't been contrived and designed by those in control — sanitised by normality and homogenised for the masses. They are individuals

A divided city

with likes and dislikes and individuals who enjoy the freedom of choice.

They do this because they want to experience in a different way — their own way. They want to experience what the vast majority of general public do not. They are of the opinion that as long as they respect wherever they go, there should be no restriction. However, the powers that be, for whatever reason, have decided that the areas the Infiltrators wish to explore, should be out of bounds. The rules are set for the majority and inconsiderate of the minority. There are occasional safety issues to contend with, but apart from that, there is often little reason why the exploration of these areas should not take place.

Maybe at first glance this doesn't sound as though it has anything to do with football. But just as the Infiltrators have an unquenchable desire to explore the unchartered urban cityscape, so do we desire to make similar choices within football. Whether we will be allowed to continue to do so is debatable.

In the sanitised world of the modern-day game, I would be considered an Infiltrator! The establishment, or those who rule football, dictate what we can and cannot do. I know there have to be rules that govern the game — even rules that govern supporters — but do they have to be so pervasive? Infiltrators appreciate the more authentic, the natural state, they do not desire the planned experience. In other words, they prefer to travel alone, or with a small group of friends, rather than on an organised trip. They would choose the personal tour over the one arranged and designed for the masses. And make their own way into Europe rather than fly with the club. Infiltrators, in this sense of the word, go

Three in a Row

where they want and do what they want.

It's ironic that football, which used to be the 'people's game', has been infiltrated by those who don't understand what it's like to support a team, but who now run it. And that people like myself, who have been involved with the game for donkey's years, have now become the Infiltrators. They have taken over 'our' game, homogenised it, packaged it, and delivered it to our doorstep. Thinking and acting for oneself has become anathema. You are not allowed to exercise personal judgement. You are supposed to conform to almost automaton excess. Sanitisation, not sanity, prevails.

The effect of all this mass control is now being felt. Visible aggression is there for all to see. There is dissent everywhere you go and it manifests itself in various forms. The most abhorrent of which is the latest wave of violence. It may be society as a whole which has provoked an excuse for such behaviour, or it may be the reaction to the destruction of freedom within football. The freedom to police oneself — to sing, to shout, to stand and to create atmosphere which influences. Gradually this freedom has been taken from us and some of us don't like it. Now we are told what to do and when to do it. Herded from place to place and conducted by the baton-wielding authorities. In the face of such violence, the freedom to move around and explore — to stand with rival supporters in a bar, before and after a game, could soon be a thing of the past.

The urban Infiltrators use the word 'respect'. They respect the areas they choose to visit. They do no damage — leave everything untouched — as it was. Those of us who are the new Infiltrators of football, should surely exercise the same judgement. It is

A divided city

through respect for the opposition environment, and not through violence, that we will retain the right to be individuals and be allowed to express our feelings with passion and dignity.

As the first Derby game for more than four years approached, the police announced their plans for one of the biggest security operations since Euro '96!

A massive match

Manchester City 0 Manchester United 1
Premier League
Saturday 18 November 2000

The build up to the Derby game in Manchester was intense. I hadn't known anything like it since the week before Barcelona. The latter, of course, lived up to the build-up and more, Saturday morning at the Theatre of Comedies turned out to be a bit of an anti-climax, more of a damp squib than the glorious festival of football predicted. But then I suppose we shouldn't have let ourselves get carried away by all the hype — this was City we were talking about after all!

Like the build-up to Barcelona, I had spent the week getting more and more nervous. Until, by the time I was sitting on the 42 bus from Stockport with all the City fans, I was actually feeling sick. I couldn't really get my head round this at all — after all, this was modern-day City and the chances of them pulling off a victory that would keep them singing for years was remote. And even if they had managed to pull off the impossible, in the long-term it would mean little to us — just as the defeats at Arsenal and Chelsea and Newcastle meant little. But despite

Three in a Row

giving myself a severe talking to, I was still as nervous as a kitten. Part of it, of course, was fear. There had been a lot of rumours flying around Manchester all week about the likelihood of violence at the game and the much publicised efforts by GMP to curb our fears had not had the desired effect. In fact, just the opposite. The views of the police regarding the best way to look after a high-profile football match (early morning kick-offs, no alcohol before the game, keeping in the visitors in order to make them an even more obvious target when they leave) are way off-beam to most of us who actually attend away games. But there was also a deep feeling in the pit of my stomach which was screaming "Derby" at me. It's been a long time, but the feeling of apprehension and excitement was still there. Getting off the bus and walking down Claremont Road was weird. Weird to feel a stranger on your own streets (I work only ten minutes' walk away) and weird to feel I was in danger amongst Mancunians. And there was definitely a feeling of menace in the air, a feeling that even though everything was calm at that moment, it wouldn't take much for it to change. I wasn't worried that anyone was going to attack me personally, even City fans aren't bitter enough to attack middle-aged women (are they?) but it's very easy to get caught up in these things when they 'go off' and I was wary. I was also mildly amused by the bitterness I was hearing. And City fans really are as bitter as we believe them to be. Walking along incognito, listening in on the various conversations, even I was amazed at the level of bile spewing out in all directions. And the glum faces! They were beaten before they got into the stadium!

Thankfully, I made it safely through the narrow,

A divided city

mean streets to the police cordon thrown up around the visitors' entrance. Going through the turnstiles, I was greeted with the 'temporary' structure on which I was to risk life and limb for the next 90 minutes! What a bloody dump! A stand that looked as if it had been cobbled together by drunken Scousers, the 'concourse' — an open yard surrounded by a razor wire-topped wall, water-filled pot holes under foot, waterproof macs on sale for 50p in the ramshackle hut that was serving disgusting tea and coffee. It was like being in a bloody shanty town! And we paid top whack for this! Okay, we only paid £16 but this was a 'C' category game, according to the programme — if we'd have been Coventry fans we'd have only had to pay £12! I cautiously stepped onto the temporary stand and made my way to my seat. Looking on the bright side, at least there was plenty of leg room and the stand bounced nicely when anyone started to stamp on the wooden slats separating us from a 20 foot drop into the scaffolding below.

On our left was the Kippax, the side of which is covered in see-through perspex. And through the perspex we could see the bitter faces twisted into expressions of hatred and rage as they screamed abuse in our direction. We couldn't hear a word they were saying and they looked like goldfish, opening and closing their mouths to no effect.

The build-up to this particular game outside Manchester had been very different. It wasn't seen as a big game, never mind a 'massive' one:

"City come from Manchester," so the song goes. Well how was it that every other car we passed on the way up to the game on the Saturday morning had a driver wearing the blue shirt then? Our initial destination had been chez Hargreaves from where

Three in a Row

five of us walked the twenty minutes to Maine Road. Walking with Hal and listening to tales of Sir Matt was a great way to arrive at the first Derby in over four years. In March '94 (the day of the last Maine Road red-blue clash) a ticketless Hal was called by Sheena, Sir Matt's daughter, and asked if he could sit in with Matt because he was too ill to make it to the game. As if that would be a problem for any United supporter to sit in with the great man watching a Manchester derby on TV.

The only good thing about our seats in the Gene Kelly stand was that we could see Old Trafford. BDS and I stood on the next to the back row, which was to be fortuitous, as you'll discover. It was bitterly cold, but soon to get warmer. Within a couple of minutes of the game starting, Haaland upended Scholes 30 yards out. His reward for the scything challenge was a superbly executed free kick from Becks which curled past Weaver and nestled nicely in the back of the net. "Let's all laugh at Haaland, ha, ha, ha, Haaland, ha, ha, ha Haaland" and Becks came charging over to the Red section to celebrate. That was where I lost BDS. At first I'd worried he'd tumbled over the back and would be lying in a pool of splodge at the base of the scaffolding, but I turned to see him leaning between two bemused lads on the row behind us. With his head stuck between the rails he was chucking up his breakfast! A full sixty feet it fell. Good job we'd been so near the back of this awesomely massive structure after all then!

The early strike served to spur on the blues, but apart from a massive amount of corners and a dipping shot from Wright-Phillips (who was not at all massive) they were as troublesome as a bunch of headless chickens.

A divided city

Yorke was lonesome up front and missed a couple of decent chances, while Haaland missed one at the other end. Towards the end of the 45, Keane broke down the right and sent a ball skimming into the penalty area which Yorke missed by a strand of Tiatto's hair. A corner resulted, taken by Becks. Over to our right there was a particularly benevolent bunch of Bitters because as Beckham stooped to place the ball by the flag, he was pelted with a variety of coins. Not one to look a gifthorse etc, he picked up the higher denomination coins and stuffed them down his shorts ready for the drinks machine at half-time. The corner came to nought, the ref blew and we climbed down the gantry to inspect the damage caused by the BDS breakfast expulsion and have a laugh about the amount of gibbers who got in with snide tickets.

The teams were coming out on to the pitch as we climbed back to our spot. Standing on the touchline was Goater. We quaked in our boots! Not the Goat — we were surely doomed! At times during that second period it looked as though United would win easily — at other times the 1-0 lead seemed very slender indeed. The Bitters were raiding down the right flank when the ball came over and Nev missed it, Barthez got a fingertip to it which nudged it into the path of Haaland. It bounced off his head and was heading for the net when somehow Wesley twisted himself almost in two and somehow hooked it away for a corner.

Standing in the freezing cold on top of a huge gantry wasn't the ideal spot, but we still managed to belt out the occasional burst of song though, with "We've got Jaap Stam bigger than your ground!" which the lad behind changed to: "We've got Paul Scholes bigger than your ground!" The City fans,

Three in a Row

however, sat in silence.

With half an hour to go my nerves were about shot but I wasn't about to show that to BDS or he'd have been pebbledashing behind the gantry again. Trouble was, City were sensing the possibility of something which would have made their season. They stepped up a gear or two, Tiatto and Dickov stepping on anyone wearing United red. With fifteen minutes to go, the atmosphere was bubbling as much as the BDS gut. The cops had gone in to the stand to our right and reinforcements appeared in front of us. That was as well as those, with fearsome truncheons (oo-er missus) who were already in our midst.

Things livened up a bit in the last ten minutes when Tiatto lunged into Neville Junior and Neville Senior tried to exact revenge. Unfortunately, the residents of both benches pulled them apart and Tiatto somehow avoided the inevitable sending off. Finally the ref blew for time and put both sets of players and supporters out of their misery and the whole United team came over and celebrated with us. We had been told we would be kept in the ground until the area outside was cleared for i.our own safetylt. Quite how it's safer being kept back, only to emerge in a big group with a sign over your head saying "United fans" 15 minutes later, than it is making a quick getaway by merging in with the City fans, I'll never know! If they were really worried about our safety, they would have kept the City fans in and let us out first, only opening the gates to the Bitters hours later when we were safely ensconced in our living rooms watching Match of the Day! But what do I know? The old bill said we had to stay in, so stay in we did.

Some were standing on the top of the stand

A divided city

exchanging pleasantries with the City fans outside, whilst the son-and-heir and I made our way down into the yard to mingle. Not long after, the police opened one of the gates and we streamed towards it only to find, once we got outside, that we were only being allowed as far as the car park. There we stood, surrounded by a cordon of police, until we heard a roar from somewhere at the front. I was barged out of the way as lads behind us charged to the front shouting, "This is it, let's go." The son-and- heir could see bricks and bottles being thrown into the crowd at the front (being height challenged, I could only see the back of the jacket of the man in front of me!) and the crowd began to surge back towards us. At that point, it didn't take much persuasion from the police to drive us back into the relative safety of the yard again, to mingle once more while waiting for things to calm down a bit.

After a while, the crowd began to move outwards again, so saying our goodbyes and wishing everyone "Good luck!" we managed to talk a copper into letting us duck through the cordon so that we could mingle with the City fans who were heading in the direction of Wilmslow Road, rather than join the large United contingent heading rather obtrusively in the opposite direction. Keeping our heads down and trying to look miserable (not too difficult in the circumstances) we walked as quickly as we could through streets that resembled a war zone. We made it onto Claremont Road but then had to detour to our left as fighting broke out on the street in front of us, and some poor sod's front garden was being wrecked. Most of the crowd obviously just wanted to get away safely, with adults trying to protect the many kids amongst us.

Thankfully, we reached Wilmslow Road in one

piece and managed to get on a bus within a couple of minutes. As we moved slowly towards Manchester on the bus, there was mayhem on either side of the main road, with fights going on down side streets, ambulances, police cars and vans driving up and down with blue lights flashing, and intimidating gangs of lads standing in front of the curry houses all down the length of the 'Curry Mile'. In the midst of all this, ordinary people were going about their business as best they could.

To some of you reading this, it will all sound very exciting I suppose, but it wasn't. It was nasty and sordid and frightening and I have to admit, I no longer have the stomach for putting up with this sort of shit, just to go to what is, after all, just a game of football. Will the violence ever stop? Probably not, as there are unfortunately too many lads out there who enjoy it too much.

Scholes scores goals

Manchester United 3 Panathinaikos 1 Champions' League Tuesday 21 November 2000

This was a proper European night and there was much more of a buzz as we walked to the ground. As per usual it was bloody freezing and pissing down with rain, but what else did we expect? The preliminaries had been dispensed with and there was a feeling that we could now get on with the real competition. We were also aware that the Greeks were definitely no mugs, having survived a group which also included Hamburg, Deportivo and

A divided city

Juventus.

Our first port of call was Macari's for a couple of cans. This has been our more traditional pre-match venue for a European evening over the last few years. Stood out in the drizzle along with a hundred or so Reds quaffing a few beers is good enough for us. Old Trafford was already besieged by Greeks and the forecourt was a sea of green. By the time we'd made the decision to leave, it was later than we thought. Warwick Road was half-empty as we walked down to the ground. The steam was rising in the floodlights, the last remaining fanzine sellers were packing up and everyone was rushing for the turnstiles. This was more like it.

As I ran up the stairs to my usual spot, our steward predicted a 2-0 scoreline. If he ever predicts a goal for the opposition I'll be worried! Over to the left, the Greek section was full to busting. The drummer was pounding out his monotonous rhythm and the whole section was bouncing up and down throwing the Old Trafford architects into a state of panic lest the whole place crash down around us. Well, that's what they say isn't it? If we bounce up and down the stands are in danger of collapse. Quick, call the structural engineers! I presume the health and safety, noise abatement society and haircutters anonymous were called and were waiting outside in readiness for any eventuality. The Greeks were out in force and not restricted to the usual away section either — they were stacked out in tier three as well. Hundreds of the buggers everywhere and not a Moussaka to be had in any restaurant in a fifty mile radius.

United had no Stam, no Cole, no Solskjaer and no Giggs and it left us slightly bereft. Twice inside the

first ten minutes, Panathinaikos missed chances —
good chances too. United were attacking our end and
we hardly saw anything of them for ages. We were
getting nervous. This Greek side were good!
Gradually United made an impression and ventured
forth. Yorkie went close, as did Sheringham and
Becks while at the other end, the Red rearguard
made a depressing habit of taking European entente
cordial far too seriously by waving the Greek
attackers through to converse at close quarters with
Barthez who was getting pissed off with the whole
affair.

The off-field activity in our section was fair to
middling, but over to our left the Greeks were
pounding out the same old song, over and over and
over and over again. Had they been taking lessons
from that lot from Sheffield Wednesday? When the
ref blew his whistle for half-time I couldn't believe it.
The half seemed to have lasted about 20 minutes
and to be honest, 15 of them were played in the
United half. At least there was no more of that
incessant monotonous song for a while.

Presumably the Wizard had made an impression
during the break with some verbal dexterity, as the
game restarted. Within two minutes United were in
front. Barthez had booted the ball upfield. Yorke
headed it into the path of Sheringham who had
obviously benefitted from a glucose boost at half-time
as he outstripped the defender and tucked it away
into the corner of the net. Much relief and many
joyous celebrations followed and the Greeks to our
left were silenced for once.

We had an all-too-brief period of dominance and
relative relaxation until Nicky Butt and Nev made an
unsavoury sandwich of Liberopoulos just outside the

A divided city

United penalty area. Up stepped Giorgios Karagounis who stroked the free kick past Barthez. The Greeks woke up again and the prolonged celebrations gave way to an alternative rendition of the same old song (this time the disco mix) and the game once again was on a knife-edge. From that moment on it became more like a game of chess than a game of football as both teams applied the thoughtful approach, but it was obvious Panathinaikos were a lot happier with the draw than we were.

There were about ten minutes left when everything changed. In a magnificent moment of supreme irony (given his detractors) it was Mikky Silvestre who made the telling move. His superb Giggs-like run down the left resulted in a powerful shot the keeper could only parry. And there was Scholes on hand to tap in number two. And just as we'd been saying how he seemed to have lost his scoring touch! Check — and K Stand woke up with a chorus of "You're not singing any more!" which was bloody rich coming from those who weren't singing in the first place. Immense relief and multi-bonding ensued.

United were now making the running and surprisingly, the Greeks seemed to have resigned themselves to a loss. On the stroke of full time came the pièce de résistance. After a move which lasted for 33 uninterrupted passes from red shirt to red shirt, the ball was finally flicked through for Scholes by Sheringham. Still travelling away from goal and at an acute angle, Scholesy turned and chipped keeper Nikopolidis. The ball nestled in the corner of the net and everyone who was still inside the ground stood to applaud a magnificent goal. Checkmate — game over and United sat on top of the group.

Into the comfort zone

Demolition Derby

Derby County 0 Manchester United 3
Premier League
Saturday 25 November 2000

We arrived in Derby with time to spare and very quickly found a heaven-sent parking spot just around the corner from the pub. £2 to leave the car outside the 'Springs of Living Water Christian Centre' was considered money well spent – especially when it would have been £3 only 50 yards up the road outside an autospares retailer — a benevolent God indeed. We checked with the attendant that we didn't necessarily have to be practising Christians and left the car in the capable hands of the Almighty. A couple of minutes later we were downing a couple of pints in the Brunswick, waiting for the old fart Hargreaves and his sidekick Mr Smith who had unfortunately not been party to divine intervention as they had left the old fartmobile miles away. We finally met up with them by the island outside Pride Park where they were loitering suspiciously while avoiding the local coppers who were out in force. These guardians of the law were all kitted out — dogs straining at the

A typical matchday experience...

The Megastore and the stall holders exemplify the mercantile nature of the modern football experience...

...but it is United's attacking play which sets pulses racing.

Preseason:
A visit to watch Eric in beach mode was followed by the last Wembley Charity Shield before getting down to business in the Champions League, in the Ukraine.

Home & Away: Trips to Athens and Valencia proved disappointing. But at home United remained almost invincible. Title celebrations followed in May

The authors and United goalkeeping legend Gary Bailey.

United go up in smoke as they celebrate their third championship in a row

The lucky charm with pre-match security

Into the comfort zone

leash, truncheons strapped neatly to one side and ready for the fray. United were back in town.

Down at the ground, as we waited for the good doctor to show up, ejections were taking place every few seconds. A line of people carted away — probably for touting, we thought, as they looked less like trouble makers than the aforementioned double act. Also hanging around was soul man Edwin Starr (yes, that one — Mr Stop her on Sight Edwin Starr). A true Red, so Nigel said.

Once the doctor had arrived we went in. There were fifteen minutes to go and those inside had already been singing up a party atmosphere. As Nigel seemed to be in possession of the ticket closest to the action the two of us piled into his spot on the second row just to the left of the goal. The doctor soon joined us having decided that his seat on the front row behind the goal was far too close to that most handsome of men, the Derby keeper Poooooooooo-m. A couple of rows behind stood Edwin (Agent Double-O Soul) and a few rows behind him, the old fart who (you may, or may not be surprised to know) was eating a pie. In fact 20 minutes in to the game he was still eating a pie and obviously has an addiction to feed!

The teams appeared alongside a ridiculous ram-like mascot thing which harassed everyone who moved and got the crowd very excited — which was a worry. When he left the pitch the locals took a while to settle but eventually calmed and sat like good boys and girls, hardly uttering a sound for the duration of the half. More than could be said for us and especially the good doctor who was living up to his reputation as the one with the pitch-side manner. "Tractor-driving tosspots" was the kindest remark he uttered while the rest of us were content with singing the usual favourites.

United should have been at least three up by half-time with young Luke Chadwick seamlessly fitting in and creating havoc down the right wing. The lad looks about six years of age and is a pale-looking young man who was christened 'Caspar' by the lads behind us, for the milkiness of his complexion. They had a nickname for all the players — my favourite being 'Shags' for Yorke! Chadwick's skinny legs stick out from shorts that look too big and too long. He kept having to pull up his socks as they could find no purchase on his skinny calves, and kept rolling down round his ankles! As the game kicked off, the lads behind us were commenting on Becks' absence, having been told by a taxi driver on their way into Manchester that morning that his brother's, friend's, cousin knew someone who lived down the road from Becks' Mum, who said he was having the day off to do his Christmas shopping in the Trafford Centre with Posh!

It wasn't the most memorable first half on the pitch, but United were in control from start to finish and it was only the efforts of Poooooooooo-m in the Derby goal that kept us from going two-up at half-time. Off it, the atmosphere was good with us virtually ignoring the Derby fans and singing about "City going down". Over to our left, in the small club class section, I spotted a family of United fans. Resplendent in their red scarves and hats and twinkling lights. Okay, the twinkling lights were an exaggeration, but they did look like bloody Christmas trees! Mr and Mrs Middle Class, with their 2.4 children, were singing and chanting and clapping and generally getting behind the team. Very

Into the comfort zone

commendable, you might say, but the trouble was they were sitting right in the middle of a couple of hundred very glum looking Derby fans! That's going to cause trouble thought I, and of course it did — later.

More disappointing than the 0-0 scoreline at half-time was the fact that the Soul Man hadn't been joining in with the singing — incognito I suppose. Behind the stands the noise was louder than during the first half, especially after the score from Maine Road was flashed on the TV screen. Oh dear, oh dear — the massive Magoos losing again! Meanwhile we were late back to the action as we had been treated to tales of the Reykjavik hotspots by the jet- setting Brummie.

Linda takes the second half:

The first had been a relaxed, enjoyable affair with the Derby fans quiet as church mice and us giving a pre-Christmas outing to the "Twelve Days of Cantona" and various other old favourites, and it was all about as threatening as a day out in the local park. The second half began as the first had ended, except that half-time had quietened things down a bit at our end — everyone had sung themselves hoarse during the break! On the hour the breakthrough came after another slick passing move. The goal was slotted home by Sheringham (his 14th of the season so far) and as we celebrated Gary Nev ran back to join in with his arms raised and almost exploding with joy. "You're going down with the City" got the Derby fans going and all hell didn't quite break loose, but things certainly livened up!

Irwin picked up the ball from Scholesy, then sent it back from whence it came. Next second it was in the net! The grumbling from the Derby fans increased

Three in a Row

as we celebrated the first goal and the beginning of the end for the Rams.

Up in the corner to our left, the celebrations of Mr and Mrs Middle Class were as loud as the rest of us and the glowers increased around them. Over to our right, there was a scuffle in amongst the Derby fans. Two lads were removed by the police but someone had obviously been hurt as the paramedics gathered round a body lying prone on the steps. Eventually she/he was carried out on a stretcher as the game continued on the pitch. Then, high comedy as a young lad burst out of the Derby crowd to our right, ran across the corner of the pitch and jumped, unaccosted by police or stewards, into the United crowd!

Being height challenged, I couldn't see what happened next to this desperately suicidal young man, but the United crowd was obviously either too surprised or too amused to do much, because he soon appeared again, to be escorted out by two coppers. Down the length of the away section they came, and then down the steps in front of us. Of course this encouraged many United fans to leave their seats and rush over to the steps to wish him bon voyage. We were trying to see what was going on and only realised that Nicky Butt had scored when the United section started celebrating and Mr and Mrs Middle Class once again joined in! Apparently it was a beauty — a 25 yard curler and unlike the normal Butty effort! We had been too busy avoiding the showers of spittle being hurled in our direction by the ejectee. A belated celebration followed along with "Are you Forest in disguise", "Are you England in disguise" and "Are you Long Eaton in disguise"!

To make things worse for the locals, Dwight Yorke

Into the comfort zone

also got into the act by scoring the third and his 100th Premiership goal. Sheringham again set it up — Yorkie flicked it over the defender and volleyed home past Pooooooooooo-m. Yorkie's face then split in two as the whole team deluged him with congratulations.

That third goal was one goal too far for the inhabitants of club class on our left. As Mr and Mrs Middle Class jumped up and down with excitement it proved the final straw for one of the blokes behind them who remonstrated with Mr Middle Class as Mrs Middle Class screamed and leapt athletically across at least four rows to get away. As the stewards hustled Mr Angry away, the police were mingling with the club class taking statements and collecting evidence (they don't bother doing that in with the lower classes, do they?). Meanwhile, similar scenes were being enacted around the ground as United fans appeared in amongst the 'loyal' Derby fans. Fergie then took the piss by taking off Barthez (who was a bit taken aback) and bringing on Rai, and the ground emptied as the Rams found that bit of last-minute shopping had suddenly become the most important thing on their minds. Trouble was, Raimond was distracted by our celebrations and nearly missed the ball as it came hurtling his way. "Raimond, Raimond van der Gouw" very quickly became "Raimond, Raimond watch the f**king ball" just in time!

The locals had mostly disappeared by the time we left the ground and we were on our way by 5.20pm, the only trouble seen being a carton of Ribena thrown at the coach window! It wasn't that different for the Leamington Skinhead:

We met up with big Rich but, as it was last year, our way was blocked by a line of police and we were

Three in a Row

encouraged to travel in the opposite direction. Encouraged, but not forced – there's a big difference. If forced we will oblige — if encouraged — no! Eventually the police line gave way and passed through to mingle with the disgruntled locals. "Oh f**k it, let them go," was the cry from the Dibble and we were away back to the 'Springs of Living Water Christian Centre' in the twinkling of an omnipotent eye.

Half an hour later we were pulling in to Leicester Forest East service area so that Nigel could ease the distress caused by his expanding bladder. There we were met by the unmistakable twang which emanates from the wrong end of the East Lancs Road. Not something you expect to hear around Leicester. "Eh, eh, come 'ed lads – 'owsabout listening 'ere a while?" – a subtle sales approach if ever there was one. And there he was, a Scouser flogging credit card services! I mean, would you sign up for a credit card offered by a Scouser? No, of course you wouldn't. And neither did we and made a hasty getaway checking that we were still in possession of our wallets.

Back on the motorway we switched over to Radio Five Live's 6-0-6 phone-in just in time to catch a 'Bert from Macclesfield' prattling on and on about City being a 'massive' club'. For a couple of minutes every other word was 'massive' as he called for Mr Potato Head to be sacked and the introduction of Mike Doyle as his replacement. It was brilliant – a wind-up of immense proportions. It turned out to be a very well-known Red, but Littlejohn (the host) hadn't twigged and was said to have been severely pissed off when he later found out!

Apparently Radio Five couldn't understand why

Into the comfort zone

there had been loads of Manchester City supporters phoning in who were all called Bert or Bertie! True blue Magoos – of course they weren't!!

It Takes Two

Sunderland 2 Manchester United 1
Worthington Cup
Tuesday 28 November 2000

A late night on the tiles at the home of the Black Cats for the lads from Manchester ultimately turned on two penalty decisions made by the referee – both went against United.

The pattern of the game was dictated early on by two other crucial decisions made by the linesman and both also went against United. Both were wrong, but had they been right, both would have resulted in United attackers in acres of space with only the keeper to beat.

On the half hour Ole slipped the ball through to Yorke whose first touch pushed it just far enough ahead to give the desperate defender a chance, but the ball popped out to Greening who gave it back to Yorke. With the Sunderland penalty area as congested as the M6 on match days, Yorke somehow managed to hammer it past the crowd and high into the net. The commentator reminded us that out of the 42 games in which Dwight Yorke has played and scored, United had never lost. Thanks a lot mate!

In less than three minutes the lead was nearly doubled when Greening flashed a shot inches past the post while at the other end Johnsen and O™Shea were in commanding form. Apart from one

Three in a Row

Phillips shot, the United 'reserves' had dominated the first half. A celebratory beer was called for.

The second began with a ten-minute version of "We are the Busby boys" but it was obvious that the Sunderland players had been treated to several minutes of Scouse expectorant from their manager. Either that, or they had suffered a severe hair gelling. In quick succession Phillips had two chances to level. One was saved by Raimondo and the other hit the side netting.

With about 20 minutes to go the game opened up and the Wearsiders made themselves heard at last and five minutes later the scores were even. Phillips crossed and Arca the Argentine glanced a header past Raimond who managed to get a hand to it but couldn't stop it. For three minutes United were held back until Greening was sent through on the keeper and for once, the linesman had kept his flag down. As he pushed the ball past Sorensen the keeper brought him down. An obvious penalty. So obvious it was taken for granted by everyone. Everyone except the referee that is, who signalled a goal kick! On the touchline, Fergie was spitting gum. In the stands the Sunderland fans had woken up and on the pitch the action became a touch warmer. For Dwight Yorke it got so hot he had to go and cool off in the tub. An un-Yorkie-like tackle on Thome resulted in the ref showing red and the 42-game run was about to come to an end.

Within a minute United also lost the experience of Johnsen who limped off and on came Stewart who almost immediately got booked as the referee had started to flash so many yellow cards it made a mockery of the previous 80 minutes. The 90 minutes ended as they had begun — in a stalemate. The

Into the comfort zone

difference now was that the referee had handed the advantage to the home team — United had been denied a blatant penalty and were down to ten men — very young men at that.

Extra time and Healy replaced Chadwick. Sorensen went off suffering from double vision (ref take note) and ten minutes in, the game took another turn in favour of the home team. Phillips got himself goal-side of O'Shea who tugged him back as he was about to shoot. A definite penalty which Phillips gratefully accepted and scored by sending Raimond the wrong way and the home crowd wild with delight. "You're not singing anymore" was their ironic response. United's was to turn up the heat and go for broke. Wallwork went off injured and on came Webber, the youngest of the bunch. An attacker for a defender and it very nearly paid off. With six minutes left and me making frequent trips to the fridge for more beer, Webber headed against the bar. With three minutes left, Fortune ran the length of the pitch, gave the ball to Healy who also smacked it against the bar. So close. The Red faithful sang "We're proud of you" and the "Red Flag", the referee blew for full time, and the game was lost. The ten men so nearly snatched an equaliser. It was plain to see on their faces that defeat hurt those young lads. It hurt us all.

In early December, United completed an eight-game unbeaten run, broken only by losing to Sunderland in the Worth Nothing Cup. Commentators were already speculating that the Premiership was over! Thus the silly season began early, with United also supposedly having already booked Cardiff's poshest hotel for the FA Cup Final, whilst every half-decent player in Europe was being linked to us. Off the pitch, fact rather than fiction reported that Manchester United were the richest club in the world.

A bird's-eye view

Manchester United 2 Tottenham Hotspur 0
Premier League
2 December 2000

This was not the usual Saturday experience — we had a couple of visitors who were accompanying Gina and I to Old Trafford. John was to take my seat for the day while Gina, Shirley and I took the tickets for the second tier in East Upper, where, after an arduous climb, we were faced with quite a view, as long as you are not scared of heights that is. We were ten rows from the back with a bird's-eye view of the pitch which looked about the size of a large tablecloth. The Spurs fans were tucked far away down to our left and the only part of East Lower we could see was the disabled section and the four rows in front where Linda sits:

Arriving at my seat I found Pat Pie Lady in residence, eyeing up the "rather handsome young man" in the goal in front of us! As usual, we had a fine time with Sullivan. Apart from his obvious attractions to the females, the crowd gave him stick from the start. The Tottenham fans' early attempts at chummy togetherness — singing a chorus of "Stand up if you hate Arsenal" and encouraging us to join them — received only jeers and hand signals in return.

The game itself was nothing special, apart from it being one of the most one-sided affairs I've ever seen. United were playing well within themselves and

Into the comfort zone

didn't have to move out of first gear at any time, against a Spurs side totally bereft of ideas. But I enjoyed it nevertheless. Partly because it was so relaxed — we were able to enjoy the skills on show without worrying too much about the result — and partly because of the antics of the guys behind us who had decided to take on the prawn butty brigade single handed!

But that was later — in the first half, the atmosphere was relatively good in our bit of the Scoreboard, at least compared to recent games. There were even a couple of times at which K Stand awoke from its slumbers with a roar that was frightening in its intensity — what a shame they couldn't keep it up and surrendered once more to the veil of apathy that reigns up there these days!

The greatest threat to their goal in the first 20 minutes was from their own keeper, Sullivan. As the ball was passed back to him he sliced his clearance so badly that it came within a couple of feet of the goal, but in the end rolled agonisingly wide of the post and the advancing Yorke. He then recovered in the nick of time from a Becks corner which was heading direct for the net. So "Beckham, from the halfway line" was changed to "Beckham, from a corner kick". There followed a barrage of extra taunts for this very English of Scottish goalkeepers that continued through to the end of the first half. "Have you ever been to Scotland, have you f**k", "Do you know where Scotland is?" and "Scotland, Scotland's Number One". Poor Sullivan, he was getting in a right state, moaning about anything and everything, and with five minutes to go before the break he had even more to complain about. Sheringham chipped the ball from one edge of the area to the other. Scholes

Three in a Row

trapped it on his chest and killed it dead. Face to face with Carr, he feigned one way, dragged the ball the other and slammed it past Sullivan.

Up in the second tier:

We totally forgot about safety and went mad — leaping up and down until we realised that the pitch of the stand up there just isn't conducive — and quickly sat back down again. It had been enough to send us into the break with huge grins on our faces. Actually the family of four sitting next to us had dispatched father to fetch the drinks and Toblerone ten minutes previous. Fortunately for him, he had returned just in time to see the goal, but unfortunately for those who were sat in front, as he had celebrated rather vigorously and had to go back and get some more drinks, a cloth and a voucher for some dry cleaning!

The break over, Barthez came down to our end waving and the second half started in virtual silence as the atmosphere, fragile enough in the first half, died a death in the bowels of the concourse. Away and home fans alike sat in contemplation as the Spurs players, who had obviously been subjected to some half-time managerial abuse, appeared as though they meant business. The fact they were still totally ineffective was a sad reflection on their overall lack of quality — not that it worried us of course. Well, we weren't at first, but after about 20 minutes of United dithering, and a deal too much activity at our end of the pitch, we were beginning to get slightly restless. Gina stated that she was bored with the lack of goal action from our attackers and who could blame her? How she could see what was going on from so far away was baffling.

The away support had sensed the faintest

Into the comfort zone

glimmer of hope while large sections of the home support reached in their bags for supplies of prawn sandwiches. Tottenham should have been well and truly buried by this time, but they were miraculously still in the game. They brought on Korsten and the Wizard took off Nicky Butt and Yorkie and brought on Giggs and Ole. It was Ole who finally finished them off with about five minutes to go. Scholesy had nicked the ball off Sherwood and sent our favourite Norwegian free on goal. Sullivan came out, Ole beat him and the ball was welcomed into the Stretford net. Several choruses of "You are my Solskjaer" followed, with Gina proudly announcing that she knew all the words. "All the words?" I enquired. "Yes," she said, "all the words." Ten years old and already familiar with the ripeness of football language — oh dear!

Spurs did have one shot on goal late on when a very surprised Barthez, who had been counting the blades of grass in the penalty area for something to do, managed to rouse himself sufficiently to pull off a fine save! Many in our section decided to make a break for it, but despite lots of hustle and bustle the family of four sitting next to us remained. At the final whistle they were still organising their multifarious megastore bags so we clambered over the seats in front to avoid wrestling with duvet covers, Fred the Reds, MUplc lampshades, several unmentionable items of undergarment and a Giggsy advent calendar. After successfully negotiating the 226 stairways to heaven we found ourselves back on street level. United had claimed their 30th victory at Old Trafford in the Premier League since their last home defeat. 96 points out of a possible 108 had been won.

Three in a Row

The Comfort Zone

Sturm Graz 0 Manchester United 2
Champions' League
Wednesday 6 December 2000

This was a game too close to Christmas for me. Too much to do and not enough time to do it in. So there was no chance of ever making it to Austria, but at least the game was live on the box. Usually, at these times the rest of the family leave me to it and this time was no different. My reputation as a bad-tempered and over vocal, neighbour-scarer, watcher of the game on TV has long since gone before me!

Karen had gone out to a College end-of-term meal and Alex was out with his mates, so only Gina and I remained — and even she deserted me for MTV! As it turned out, none of them need have bothered as it was one of United's more controlled performances which led to one of my more controlled performances. And the irony was, there was no-one to witness it. In fact nothing really happened until Scholes scored. It's debatable whether anything happened afterwards during the first half either as United dominated totally. However, the goal which separated the teams at half-time was a peach. The be-gloved Becks in defence passed to Yorke wide left. He played the ball inside to Sheringham, who reversed it to Scholes. Running wide and with the keeper advancing, he chipped it over him into the net and the house exploded. Well — maybe I wasn't quite that relaxed then!

To score the first goal away from home would normally be a relief, but United had been so far out in

Into the comfort zone

front that it had seemed inevitable. Though it roused Graz, and their newly acquired tough-boy attitudes came to the fore. There were far too many sneaky challenges, follow-throughs and snidey kicks from behind, and the ref and his linesmen did very little to protect them. Yorke in particular seemed to spend more time on his back than on his feet. Not unusual for Yorkie you might think, but this wasn't as pleasant as what you may be pondering on. So concerned was the Wizard that he dispatched Giggsy to do a spot of warming-up.

Half-time came and went. Gina had decided to put herself to bed, relaxed in the knowledge that her favourite team were in the lead and in command. And with beer at hand I sat back down to enjoy the second half — and no calls from BDS — very unusual! The second half began with Graz making a game of it. Their coach had obviously nicked Fergie's hairdrier and had given his lads a severe blasting during the break. At least they made a game of it for the next 45 minutes as Barthez had been getting lonely back there on his own with no-one to talk to. But despite the renewed vigour of the Grazianos, it was Scholes who struck first — breaking through and volleying Yorke's flick. The keeper made a good save. Ten minutes later Sheringham volleyed Yorke's flick and the keeper made a good save — again. This keeper was beginning to piss me off. He looked rank most of the time, but by this time he was making saves that would have seemed well beyond his ability earlier in the game.

With 20 minutes to go, Kocijan took the ball from the centre circle and with Butt breathing down his neck, ran to within 30 yards of the goal and let fly. The ball looped over Barthez who was recumbent on his gingham tablecloth munching on a chicken leg. Fortunately for United it rapped against the bar and went up and behind for a goal kick. The embarrassed Frenchman wiped his chin and mopped his brow. It had been a let-off which had an immediate effect. Keano powered forward catching out two defenders, cut the ball back to Sheringham whose pass to Yorke was intercepted by a defender. The ball ran free to Keane who cut it back again for Sheringham who 'scored'. Except he didn't — the linesman's flag was up, and stayed up, even though the ball, which was played through to Keane (in an offside position) had been from a defender's — not attacker's foot.

With 10 minutes to go, Giggs came on for Nicky Butt who had had another good game. By this time Alex had returned and nervously sat in and watched the final minutes alongside me. There were only a couple of them left when Giggs finally put the game beyond doubt. Becks had sent Yorke away with a 50 yard cross-field ball. Giggs went on the overlap and received the ball from Yorke. The keeper stood at his near post facing Giggs, but it made no difference. Giggs hammered the ball through the smallest of gaps and past him into the net. The game was over. The Red Army sang "We shall not be moved" and the "Red Flag" and United had won away in Europe at last. In fact Graz hadn't been beaten on their own ground in Europe since United last won there — so all they had to look forward to was a visit from Arnie the following day.

Meanwhile the Red Army were kept behind and amused themselves with a sing-song. Recreating the days when the Stretford End ruled, they took the 'right side' or the 'left side' and created a spoof verbal battle which eventually degenerated into one side

Into the comfort zone

hurling abuse at the other! I have it on good authority that the 'right side' won. After, "Do you come from Manchester?" and "Two-nil in your Cup Final!" came the ultimate putdown: "You're just a bunch of wankers!"

So United go into the mid-term Euro break sitting on top of the group with a six-point maximum and looking forward to a St Valentine's day visit to sunny Spain.

At this time Sir Alex Ferguson echoed Peter Kenyon's message by assuring fans that he wouldn't be deserting the club when he retires from management in 2002. His precise role had yet to be decided, but it appears that a 'roaming ambassadorial' role was most likely.

On our way to Old Trafford to meet the Scousers, those of us able to get a look at the Observer had a little chuckle as we read of some new research carried out at Lancaster University. The research team discovered that United fans consistently failed to come to the aid of an injured supporter when he had on a Liverpool shirt, but ran to his aid when he was wearing a United kit. What a surprise! After the game we weren't chuckling of course, as the scousers ended our two-year unbroken winning run — 3,240 minutes, 296 fouls, 28 bookings and 133 goals.

Remember this

Manchester United 0 Liverpool 1
Premier League
Sunday 17 December 2000

Three in a Row

I had thought that everything would be fine. I'd managed to survive a 70s revival party next door the previous night and the subsequent fog, both inside and outside my head, the following morning. I was beginning to wonder slightly when I saw Barney smiling and joking on Warwick Road, but confined the image to the back of my mind. I should have realised the omens weren't good, but my blind faith in everything United blotted out all the signs which, in retrospect, were there in profusion. Only the doctor's mythical bearded twins were missing from the equation.

The Scousers were up for this — naturally. They all arrived late and en masse in a coach convoy and were greeted with the usual jeers from the Red Army gathered outside Macari's chippy. By the time we took our places they were howling their anthem to a background of verbal abuse. Everything seemed fairly positive at first. We were stood up, the atmosphere was good and the sight of the new "You're not famous anymore" banner, hanging in front of the Stretford tier two, did our hearts good. But the lads were as strangely off-colour as the Scouse shirts. How could eight of them be so far off their game at once, with only Barthez, Silvestre and Wes Brown displaying anything like the qualities expected from a team wearing the shirt? It was weird. The passing was all over the place and the lack of invention, very worrying.

When Nev handled the ball just outside the penalty area when there was no-one within ten yards it added to the collective confusion. When we could see a gap as wide as the Saturday night grin on Yorkie's face appearing in the wall, we were looking around at each other as though the executioner's axe

Into the comfort zone

was about to fall. And it did, in the shape of Murphy's free kick, which sliced through the gap and decapitated our expectations. Nevertheless, at half-time I was still adamant we would win, having faith in the Wizard that he would rally the lads that they would suddenly metamorphose into their real selves. Except they didn't. The only thing that turned was the flag, which became 10 years and counting, as it's that long since the used-to-be-famous Scousers won the League.

The second half was as congested as my head — a mess in midfield, which strangled the life out of the game. And when the final whistle blew, several stalwarts had already left, disillusioned and unable to take the Scouse taunts. The rest of us blasted back defiantly with "You're gonna win f**k all" and trooped out to the sound of "You'll never walk alone" throbbing in our heads. The Scousers were pinching themselves — they couldn't believe their luck. They had beaten United for the first time in five years and we had lost at home for the first time in two years.

There was a day when a loss at home was fairly commonplace. Those of us with long attendance records remember only too vividly that losing occurred with monotonous regularity. These days however, success has lulled the Theatre of Dreams into a state of apathy. Football is not about trips to the megastore to buy the latest Giggsy duvet cover, executive hotel breaks with stadium tours, buying bricks with your name on, popcorn, ice-cream and prawn sandwiches. It's about playing the game — and sometimes (if not that often for us at the moment) your team loses. Many have taken it for granted that a trip to the Theatre will mean a guaranteed win. Maybe now, the newcomers, who

Three in a Row

hadn't previously experienced defeat, will think again. Some may not want to return. And if that is the case, we are much better off without them. But those who do return will hopefully remember that when they left the ground they had to endure the baying mob of scowling bin-dippers and will never want to witness anything like it again. And if that is the case — it will not have been in vain. If it is not the case, then it's all a tragic waste of time.

A twin set and pearls

Manchester United 2 Ipswich 0
Premier League
Wednesday 23 December 2000

When I got home after the previous week's debacle against Liverpool, I asked Gina whether she was still confident of being our lucky charm as she was due to accompany me to the Ipswich game. She assured me that she was and not to worry. So, with an hour to go before this game, as we sat in a bar with Eliza, Steve and John, she rather cleverly shifted the goalposts. She declared that to be utterly confident in her extraordinary powers of lucky charmness she would need additional help. Her levels of energy needed supplementing, despite having eaten a shed load of sandwiches in the car, after dropping the rest of the family off in the land of a thousand bin-dippers. The requirement was apparently a giant hotdog. Well, what would you have done? I thought it well worth a two quid investment and quietly applauded her ten-year-old ingenuity. With the hotdog duly administered we were all set and after a quick trip round to the

Into the comfort zone

ticket office to push yet another 'away' application through their letterbox, we made our way round to the unfamiliar territory of South Stand.

I had originally made a fundamental error when applying for both this game and the next on New Year's day. I had filled in the form, where it asks you to state part of ground preference, "NOT North or South Stand". So what do we get? Obvious isn't it? South Stand yesterday and North next week! Someone obviously doesn't have time to read the applications properly do they?! So there we were in the land of the living prawns, on the second row, in line with the players' kneecaps. Flasks, flashing devil horns, Father Christmas hats and flash-bulbs predominated. But we were among native Mancunians. They didn't necessarily have the same agenda as ourselves, but that's why they were in that area and we were the aliens!

More surprisingly, so was my next-door neighbour. If there was ever a case of not judging a book by the cover, this woman was the epitome of the saying. Getting on in years and dressed in a traditional overcoat hiding what must have been a twinset and pearls, with a fur hat, kept in place by a silver hatpin atop her coiffured head, and her hands encased in close-fitting black leather gloves. It turned out she was an exile from the Stretford second tier where she normally resides with her husband. For this game she suffered the same fate as myself – if you want to take someone else (in my case Gina and hers, her mother) you have to purchase two more tickets and relinquish your regular Season Ticket to do so. We were both in the same boat! But, she sang along to all the songs and told me she had only moved from the Stretford 'right side' when they pulled

Three in a Row

the old Stand down in '92. A kindred spirit if ever there was one.

The teams came out, the Wizard walked past and gave us a wave and the game got under way. We could hear the atmosphere up in the second tier and K Stand but our lone voices from South Stand were lost in the wilderness. Still — the action on the pitch was excellent and provided considerable optimism. Our heads were turned permanently towards the Scoreboard goal where United were attacking. They set up camp in the Ipswich half and it surely was only a matter of time before a goal came, and Scholes had more chances in the first ten minutes than for the whole of the ninety against the Scousers. A festive "Twelve days of Cantona" shifted from the Stretford to the Scoreboard. For us — a stereo treat. Ole was revelling in the freedom afforded him by Ipswich and also came close before he actually scored. A superb long ball from Becks eventually found its way to Giggs who played a nice one-two with Ole which sent him into the box with only Wright to beat. A deft shimmy later and he was round the keeper and side-footed the ball home to ecstatic celebrations all round. Gina got a huge hug of thanks and said, wearing a mile-wide grin, "It's working." And even those around us broke into spontaneous song — but only a couple of verses!

George Burley was animated on the touchline as he tried in vain to get his message across, but the fourth official kept dragging him away! With about half an hour gone and ten minutes after the first goal, there was a distinct flavour of déjà vu going around. We were all at it again as Becks sent another superb long ball from the halfway line straight into Ole's path. He controlled the ball with one touch and hammered

Into the comfort zone

it past Wright. More celebrations followed and at least three choruses of "You are my Solskjaer". Two great goals and the Premier League's third-placed team were being taught a lesson in class from the Champions. That was much better. It's funny isn't it? We've been waiting so long for a goal at the Scoreboard end and then two come along at once! Similarities with global transport systems were apparent.

A packet of crisps was scant reward for such good fortune and in any case we had no desire to be watching three 'celebrity' United fans do the half-time draw. Anyway, Gina's luck quota needed stoking up — it was a cold day, and after all, she's a growing girl!

Back in time for the second half, I find the seat next to me empty and an ageing mother concerned for her daughter! "I expect she's gone to the bar," I explain. Happy with this, she sat back to enjoy the second half. A few moments later, said daughter appears carrying two very full cups of tea. Blimey, I hope we don't score just yet, I thought, or this lot's going to be all over the place and extremely hot liquid over the nether regions would undoubtedly smart. There were a couple of anxious moments and, much to my relief, she was eventually encouraged to place the cup beneath her seat, just in case. Ipswich had re-organised though and had devised a more effective brand of football. They even tested Barthez, who made one flying save. He had already demonstrated his audacious skills early in the first half by side-stepping an attacker and flicking the ball behind himself, turning and passing clear without any of us collapsing in horror. We were getting used to his antics by that time!

The renewed action spurred United. Phil Neville

Three in a Row

went close with a piledriver which was well saved by Wright, followed by a David Healy flick header from yet another Becks cross, which smacked against the post. The result was a sound which brought back happy memories of an Old Trafford folk hero — a stroppy Cockney goalkeeper from the early years of Fergie's reign of supremacy called Les Sealey. "Heeeeealeeey, Heeeeealeeey" was the cry, and for this reason alone, it would have been good to see this lad make the grade at OT.

With ten minutes to go, Fergie took Becks and Keane off and brought on Wallwork and Greening. My heart fluttered ever so slightly and in conjunction with 64,000 others fluttering at the same time, there was a ground tremor of sufficient force to register on the Richter scale. This time though, it was a seamless weld, and the game ended with three very welcome points in the bag. We wished our twinsetted friends a good Christmas, and a happy father and daughter weaved their way through the crowds to the nearest hotdog stand! After passing a beaming Barney and equally beaming Blacky and a quick visit to Lance's swagerama for a Gina-sized Barthez shirt, we headed back down to the wrong end of the East Lancs Road to the land of the bin dippers. Still the red residents of Murkeydive were also a happy bunch after stuffing the Arse earlier in the day, if you'll excuse the rather lewd, but possibly festive reference.

On Christmas Eve, Fergie was deflecting criticism of recent performances by telling the world that this present United side is the 'best ever', claiming that they have eclipsed the Busby Babes and their achievements. Meanwhile, over at Maine Road the Christmas spirit was definitely lacking as Manchester

Into the comfort zone

United players were referred to in the official programme as 'Munichs'. Apologies were quickly forthcoming, but the damage was done, as the nasty, bitter underbelly of the world's most 'massive' club was exposed for the world to see. In the wider football world, the row was continuing over FIFA's plans to reform the transfer system. With many smaller clubs relying on transfer fees for up to 80 percent of their revenue, many were worried that the proposed system could lead to ruin.

New Year honours

Last minute bargain

Aston Villa 0 Manchester United 1
Premier League
Tuesday 26 December 2000

I have now been watching United regularly for nigh on 40 years and this was the very first Boxing Day fixture I had ever been to! It's always been a family day in the past, but as this was more or less a 'home' fixture and an early kick-off, I had decided to break with tradition. The game was also significant in that United's last Boxing Day defeat on this ground was 11 years ago.

It was an easy journey, even though we had left later than originally planned. There was some congestion on the M6 probably due to bargain hunters on their way to the Boxing Day sales, but it hardly affected us and we arrived in Aston with an hour to spare. It still took half of that time to find a parking space and with big Rich multi-tasking by reading a handy photocopied map directing us to a local school given over for match-day parking while fending off a phonecall from a certain mad Dane, we eventually completed both tasks almost

New Year honours

simultaneously. A short walk down the hill, round the new stand construction and the Villa Village and we were faced with a beaming Barney slightly taken aback by the intensity of the Villa hatred for anything United. No Christmas spirit, no entente cordial, just post-1957 Brummie bile.

No Christmas jumpers on view either — well, not amongst the Reds anyway. And a prediction of a 1-1 scoreline from Barney. What with the Arse already 1-0 up against Leicester and about to make it 6, 1-1 would be okay, but not ideal. As Villa had yet to lose at home, it appeared to be a reasonably optimistic prediction, especially for Barney! In we went, past the ticket check, past the body search, through the turnstile and into the melee.

My seat was just to the left of the goal and about crossbar height, not that I sat in it! The teams appeared, Hercules and his companion, the buxom Bella (both Villa lion mascots) left the field via the tunnel beneath us, to a crescendo of unseasonal commentary. The game got under way with United attacking our end. The sun was shining, the general mood reasonably festive, but so bloody cold even Barthez wore long sleeves.

The lads were well on top, we were singing the "Twelve Days of Cantona" but stopped short on 11 as James saved a rasper from Giggs. The Villa fans were standing up and hating 'Man U' and we were just standing up — but only just — in some cases. Apart from the occasional 'health and safety' announcement from the PA, telling us to sit down, the local stewards, and coppers, were in a benevolent (even jolly) Christmassy-type mood. Not what we've come to expect from the Brummie beat, but welcome nevertheless. On the pitch, United continued to

Three in a Row

dominate. Ole flashed a header just past the post, James saved point blank from Scholes to a chorus of "You Scouse bastard" and Villa were restricted to counter attacks. With Wes and Nev in form, these were snuffed out without intervention from Barthez who had been employed thus far as more of an attack setter-upper.

Half-time came and went, with many festive greetings exchanged, and at the start of the second Silvestre was substituted for Phil Nev. Villa had been given a rocket from 'Shotgun' Gregory and Merson in particular was pressing further forward and causing problems. Barthez was at last called into action. He had spent most of the game wandering up and down to the halfway line and back and all of a sudden was called on to make a superb one-handed save from de Bilde. It was United who were now forced to counter attack, with Villa looking as though they actually wanted to win the game rather than scared of losing it. The (alleged) 'fat bastard' Ginola was also more and more involved but still managed to spend more time falling over than on his feet. As for 'fat bastard' — if I was as 'fat' a 'bastard' as he is, I'd be well chuffed! He can keep his Vosene locks though!

United were now back on the offensive with both Scholesy, Nicky Butt and Ole all going close. It prompted the lad behind me to proffer the opinion that it wasn't going to be our day. Something that didn't impress his mate who was still optimistic and suggested that: "It most definitely was going to be our day as we were getting closer and closer and were bound to score eventually!" With Dublin, on for Villa, getting the ball in the net, but being ruled offside (just) it seemed as though this was misplaced optimism. Denis, who'd been hobbling, was replaced

New Year honours

by Wallwork who had come on to partner Wes in the centre of defence, with Nev moved out right. But the lads were not giving up and came close again when Scholes headed just past the post. The atmosphere (which had died the death of post Christmas excess) was revitalised and a final round of "Ferguson's Red and White army" sent out a defiant message to Villa Park.

With five minutes to go the pressure finally paid off. Keane passed to Becks, who was moving out right, and his cross was inch-perfect for Ole to head past James. The celebrations in our part of Villa Park were both loud and prolonged with several overexuberant members of the Red fraternity disappearing under several others. The steps were awash with bodies and several choruses of "Jingle Bells" echoed round the ground as the Villains left in their thousands. It was then that Barney's prediction of a 1-1 scoreline came back to me. But Barney's predictions are never right are they? Not that it prevented me from worrying my way through the last minutes. The final whistle was greeted with relief and more excessive celebrations. A successful afternoon — we had another three points, Villa had been beaten at home for the first time this season and Tony and I had rubbed shoulders with big Norm on the way out. What more could anyone want

"Three fresh legs"

Newcastle United 1 Manchester United 1
Premier League
Tuesday 30 December 2000

Three in a Row

"Three fresh legs" is apparently what did for United at Newcastle, or so their manager said after the game when he actually meant to say "Six fresh legs"! What he should have said was that United were sunk by three subs.

With the majority of the country under a newly-formed white blanket, it was the undersoil heating which enabled this game to be played. The snow had been cleared from the pitch and piled at the edges, as over 52,000 gathered inside St James' Park and hardly a black and white striped shirt in view. It was that cold, even the barcoded Geordies had covered up!

Yorkie was back up front alongside Ole and had an early chance to crown his return when Giggs played him through on the keeper. Sandwiched between two barcodes, the keeper advanced making it a triple-decker, and the ball pinged free, but just a bit too high for Ole's outstretched leg. It was an end-to-ender and at the United end, Barthez saved at the near post to force a corner from which the new boy, Amoebi (or the single cell) headed against the foot of a post. Normally, you might say that the barcodes were playing as if it was their Cup Final, but in their case, as they haven't shown in any of their recent appearances in the Cup Final, you'd have to say that they were playing as though it was much more important than that. Down the United left Solano was giving Silvestre a hell of a time. He cut inside and hammered a shot across the area which was missed by one barcode, but not the single cell. From no more than a yard out, Amoebi somehow managed the seemingly impossible feat of lifting a certain goal so far over the crossbar even the Geordies had to laugh — NOT!

New Year honours

Still recovering from that bizarre moment, the barcodes were faced with even more hilarity when Griffin's challenge on Giggs in the area was deemed a penalty by that terribly nice man, Mike Riley. It had been a mere tickle on Giggs, but enough to knock him off his feet and enough for Riley to point to the spot. So, with our usually dependable Den out injured, Becks took the ball, placed it on the spot and blasted it into the Geordie net as Harper dived out of the way to avoid its searing speed. 24 minutes gone and the barcodes' heads were dropping. They'd have dropped off had that (now, not so nice) Mike Riley given another penalty (as he should have done) when Nicky Butt was brought down a minute later. Obviously he didn't fancy handing the Wiz an early 59th birthday present, so waved play on.

It seemed to act as a spur to the barcodes and to Solano in particular. He was down the United left again and in a carbon copy of the first time, he crossed hard and low into the box. Barthez got the faintest touch, as did Nev. The ball eluded two desperados on the back post and ultimately fell to Dyer. But Nev had recovered and hurled himself at Dyer's feet and his shot spun clear.

The lads had been refuelled by their half-time cuppas and went out for the second half with renewed intent. Four times they could have put the game beyond the barcodes but four times they failed. First Yorke broke free and fed Giggs who fired wide. Then Butt cut the ball back for Ole and the keeper saved with his foot. Keane crossed, Ole shot and the keeper saved again, and finally Becks crossed and Harper saved Yorke's header. The United faithful paid seasonal homage and sang the "Twelve days of Cantona" and the barcodes braced themselves for

Three in a Row

the inevitable.

But..........with time running out, Bobby Robson brought on his three fresh legs and it confused the hell out of our lads. It would wouldn't it? Rolf Harris doing his "Jake the Peg" down the right wing would have been enough for anyone — for United it was fatal. With ten minutes to go, the barmy barcodes won the Worthington Cup, the FA Cup, the Premiership, European Cup, World Cup and even the World Darts Championship and definitely Sports Personalities of the Millennium all at the same time. Cordone broke free down the United left, beating the offside. He crossed into the United area. Lua Lua sliced his shot so badly it turned into the perfect pass for the third sub, Glass, who half-volleyed past Barthez for the equaliser. The barcodes went mad. The three fresh legs had done it.

At least there was some consolation for the Red Army as United grumbled off the pitch. The result from Highbury (where Sunderland had drawn 2-2 with the Arse) brought a huge groan from the barcodes, but a smile to many a Red face. But the loudest post-match cheer came as the massive result from Maine Road was announced: Manchester City 1 Charlton 4. A bitter blow indeed! And, apparently, they have another inmassivel, game (according to Mr Potato Head) coming up at Coventry on New Years day. Come on City (Coventry — that is).

New Year honours

Boo Shaka

Manchester United 3 West Ham United 1
Premier League
1 January 2001

I don't know what it is about New Year's Day at Old Trafford, but I can never seem to get the name Dennis Bailey (that QPR prankster) out of my head, especially when we're playing a London team. I know it was West Ham and not QPR, but the name had been haunting me for days, if not years.

Fortunately, the snow had disappeared and it was a good deal warmer than we had expected as we set off an hour later than usual. I had thought that this was to be Gina's first night game, but I was wrong, as she reminded me later. I'd taken her and Alex to a youth team game when she was two years old! I'd encouraged her and her brother with a huge packet of sweets. She had caused consternation in the Main Stand by running in between the rows of seats flicking Dolly Mixtures everywhere, and I was surprised to hear she'd remembered the occasion at all. Funny thing was — the team she saw play against West Ham was made up of more or less the same faces, although an awful lot has happened in the intervening years. And with George Best saying this would be the first time since he pulled on the red shirt that he wouldn't have walked into the first team it was a great testament to how those lads have grown up. As a matter of fact, I think George was wrong, as he would have walked into any team, anytime, anywhere in the world — he was that good.

By the time we arrived in Manchester (in record

time) the Arse had already been spanked at Charlton, so whatever happened, United would still be at least eight points clear at the top of the Premiership come the end of the game. We were so early we had nearly two hours to spare before kick-off. What happened to those two hours I'm not sure, but they disappeared very quickly.

We began by battling past the megastore sale crowds and found a slightly hung-over Barney (not quite) regretting the night before, but nevertheless staying alcohol-free for a day at least. I had resolved to do no such thing though, as we made a beeline for the nearest offie and a couple of cans of Boddies. As we stood outside Macari's with Tim Vimto gorging himself on half a chicken, the world passed us by, including a couple of young winos who were emptying any cans of their dregs into an old sherry bottle. They were completely oblivious to anyone else — locked in their own hazy world of shakes. Big Rich had joined us, by this time. He had the look of a concerned man about him. It wasn't concern for the sweeping winos either, but concern that he'd seen the bearded twins again. Oh shit — not the bearded twins! On New Year's Day too. It threw us all into a state of alarm. First it was Dennis Bailey and now the bearded twins — aargh!

Trying to push the whole business to the back of my mind we bump into the Undertaker and then Dr Death. Jees – what's going on, I thought. Thank god the Alien hater had stayed at home! Time to go — I grabbed Gina by the hand and whisked her away down to Old Trafford. The omens were looking decidedly dodgy all of a sudden. Good job our lucky charm was with me and oblivious to all this portent. I checked she was okay and that her powers had not been diminished by such close encounters, but she seemed fine.

Back at the ground, with a reasonable level of confidence restored, we met up with Eliza outside J Stand, wished her another Happy New Year and made our way inside. Our seats were on the very front row in front of J Stand and as soon as we took our places I felt fine. Sitting down there you begin to realise just how big (not massive, mind you) Old Trafford is. We'd only just settled down after the start of the game, when we were up on our feet again celebrating a goal. That magic worked quick enough then! Only a couple of minutes had gone by when an act of supreme New Year benevolence, by the ex-Scouser Rigabert Song, gifted Ole the chance to score the first goal. It was a poor touch by Song which allowed Ole to pick off the ball and from the edge of the area and blast it into the opposite corner. Shaka Hislop, in the Hammers goal, had no chance. All thoughts of Dennis Bailey were immediately dispelled as we celebrated.

It was the start of 45 minutes of complete dominance and fortunately for us, it all happened down at our end. And with Giggs in such form on the left, a lot happened right in front of our faces. The 'Appy 'Ammers, over in the corner, were not happy. Apart from declaring that they supported their 'local' team (not that old bloody chestnut again) they were utterly silent for the whole half, whereas we went through the repertoire. Even down at pitchside, which was essentially North Stand, we were singing. Not all of us, but father and daughter, oblivious to the rest, were making quite a racket! Within the first 15 minutes we could have been three or four up. Yorke fired just past the post as did Becks (twice), and poor

Three in a Row

Shaka, in the 'Ammers' goal, was kept very very busy.

By the 30-minute mark Song had cleared a Yorke header off the line, Hislop had made a full- length save to deny Giggs and Yorkie had sent another flying just past the post. A couple of minutes later the second goal arrived in bizarre circumstances. Phil Neville had made another snaking run down the right, crossed low into the box and everyone missed it. Everyone, including Hislop, because the ball ended up in the same corner of the net as the first goal. No-one seemed to know how the ball arrived there, but no-one really cared. United were two up and coasting. Poor Shaka! He was doing his best, but faced with the lads in this sort of form, his best was never going to be good enough. And to top it all he couldn't get his goal kicks right. Every one of them flew unerringly into touch as the piss was extracted mercilessly at every opportunity. He took it in good heart though and afforded us a smile and a despairing shrug of the shoulders.

There was to be no let up, and the next 15 minutes proved as busy as the previous 30. Hislop saved again from Yorke, again from Ole, and once again from Yorke. The dominance was so complete that it encouraged the more optimistic to sing "We won the Football League again — this time on New Year's Day!" However infectious that song was (and it was VERY infectious) I couldn't bring myself to sing it. Too many memories of too many Championships 'won' that were eventually lost. We did "Stand up for the Champions" though, and so did everyone around us, even if it was only because they couldn't see if we were stood up in front of them! And the 'Appy 'Ammers were still not 'appy! Half-time came too

New Year honours

early for us, but not for them. We went below stairs to meet up with Nigel who'd achieved some local success of his own. "You've only got two songs" was his contribution to the evening's entertainment, bearing in mind that the 'Ammers had one song and another 'playing' in defence!

We went back to our seats just as the posse of photographers were exchanging their seats from the Scoreboard End to the Stretford End in readiness for another United onslaught. At the start of the second half West Ham brought on two subs — Tihinen and Joe Cole, who actually made a difference. Barthez came down to our end and prepared himself for more inactivity. Within a minute, Pearce (who had already been booked) was challenged by Ole. The two of them had formed a less than healthy relationship in the first 45 minutes and with Ole on the floor, Pearce issued a warning nudge to the lad's nads. The linesman did nothing and neither did the ref. The crowd down at the Stretford End, where the incident had happened, would have done had Pearce been closer, but contented themselves with loud jeering every time he received the ball after that.

After ten minutes, and just as the 'Appy 'Ammers in the corner had briefly awoken up to sing "We're gonna win 3-2", we went three up. The woman behind us had just re-appeared with coffee and a steak pie as Becks, Keane and Phil Nev played triangles down the right. Nev and Keane then had a quick one-two. Keane swung a cross into the box and Yorke dived between two defenders and flashed a header past Hislop and into the net. As we indulged in more celebrations and avoided hot coffee and half-eaten pie, everyone went over to congratulate Yorkie and the smile on his face was a New Year's present to us all.

Three in a Row

With half an hour left the Wiz took off Giggs and Keane and threw on Wallwork and Greening. Almost immediately Barthez had to make his first serious save — a strike from Kanouté. Affronted by having to make an effort, after such a relaxing experience, he sought retribution as, encouraged by 60,000 to shoot from the edge of his own penalty area — he did. And the ball ended up in the opposition area and caused a deal of panic as it dropped at the feet of Yorke, but unfortunately to no avail.

With 20 minutes to go the unthinkable happened. They scored! Confusion in the box, as Kanouté headed past Barthez direct from a corner and the 'Ammers woke up again. "We're gonna win 4-3," they sang optimistically, as we reminded them they were actually "gonna to win f**k all". The Wizard brought on Nicky Butt to quell their ambitions and United played keep-ball for a while to calm things down. With five minutes left, Lampard came very close to making it 3-2, but lifted his shot just over the bar after confusing Barthez. It spurred United back into action. Ole was barged over in the box and given another friendly fondle by his new chum, Pearce, which again went 'unseen' by the officials, and in a last throw, Yorkie smacked another header against the bar.

The game finished 3-1 with United sat atop the Premiership with an 11 point cushion and astonishing odds of 20-1 on for the Title.

Our journey home was as swift as the journey North — why was it always better when Nigel was driving? Encouraged by Gina's purchase in the motorway services, we spent some time discussing the merits of what used to be called 'Sweet Cigarettes' and whether they taste any different now they are 'Candy Sticks' and don't have red tips —

careful! In case you are interested (and I'm sure you're not) we concluded they were exactly the same as they'd always been. Some things never change! Let's hope it's the same with our lucky charm — better apply for the Arse game I suppose.

Room with a view

Fulham 1 Manchester United 2
FA Cup Sunday 7 January 2001

On 12 April 1968, a very youthful Windridge and his mates went down to Fulham to watch an emphatic 4-0 win for United. Best scored two, Kidd one and the Lawman one, but little did the youthful Windridge know then, that he would have to wait nearly 33 years before he returned to Craven Cottage. At the time their midfield maestro, Johnny Haynes, was losing some of his magic and Fulham were relegated that year, not to return to the top flight until now. United went down to meet them for a season in '74, but I didn't make it with them that day, or in '79 for the fourth round of the Cup. So, this was a real trip down memory lane for me and I had been looking forward to it ever since the draw had been made.

Big Rich and I set off just after 9am on a sunny Sunday morning. A couple of hours later we were parked up and waiting for a train on Mortlake station, standing opposite a poster advertising Barcelona. The omens looked good. A couple of stops down the line, we got off at Putney and stumbled over Martin Clunes pushing his kid around. Bearing in mind this Man's on-screen personality, I'd better add that he was actually pushing his kid around in a pushchair.

Three in a Row

See how things can get misinterpreted? We were obviously in celebrity city. There were BMW convertibles everywhere and Fulham even had 'Diddy' David Hamilton on the PA. I really was back in 1968!

We sauntered over Putney bridge watching the rowing eights, when we pass one of what has to be the saddest sights known to humankind. A group of anoraked bus-spotters comparing notes and getting very excited as a number 44 came round the corner. We picked up a couple of cans from the offie and made our way down towards the Cottage. Standing in the sunshine watching the world (and Stevie Coppell) go by on the Fulham Palace Road was a pleasant way to start the day, even if his son did have a Fulham hat on.

With about half an hour to go before kick-off we wandered down to the ground past the (very relaxed) police cordon and through the turnstiles. Inside it hadn't changed that much since I was last there. Our terrace hadn't changed at all — it was still open to the elements. But the Riverside had changed. The huge open spaces had gone — replaced by a conventional (covered) stand. The pitch was in an awful state and more akin to Old Trafford circa 1968 than the present day, and definitely not conducive to United's slick passing game.

A visit to the gents was in order and there followed a brief, but close and momentous encounter. Big Rich and I had already been discussing the likelihood of a meeting with the bearded twins. It seemed inevitable that I would finally encounter this (up to now) mythical vision of duality. Forty years of United watching and never before had I seen these two, but this was to be the day everything changed. I hadn't even reached

New Year honours

the gents when it happened. There they were, side by side. Not in matching jackets, but surely it was them. The bearded twins — the bloody bearded twins. I didn't know what to do. I sought confirmation from big Rich who assured me that it was definitely them. But would the doctor's curse come true for me? Every time he had seen these two at an away game we'd lost. But, where was the doctor when we needed him most? Portent hung in the air.

Thus far the day was certainly living up to expectations. I made my way back to the gents which were inadequate to say the least. With space enough for no more than a dozen! No wonder no-one bothered with them when terraces were the norm. The backs of the legs (and sometimes, in special cases, jacket pockets) of the person in front were invariably used instead!

To walk on to a terrace again was both weird and wonderful. It was nowhere near as packed as we were used to, but to be able to freely chose one's own spot and who to stand with, is something we can mostly only reminisce about these days. Nice to be back. We stood on the right side just as it was on the Stretty and the teams were still warming up as we took our place a couple of steps back from a crush barrier. The family Walsh came along and stood with us, and later Lipstick Roberts and his mate John. Poor Lipstick looked the worse for wear having been to Barney's 30th the night before. His eyes were the same colour as the United shirts, and if this was how he looked, I'm only glad we didn't see Barney!

"Viva el Fulham" blasted out over the PA. 'Diddy' David was doing his damnedest to wind up the Cottagers but only managed to wind us up by playing the march of the Dambusters. Surely an unfortunate

Three in a Row

oversight? And Mohamed Al Fayed took a stroll around the pitch whilst the Cottagers doted. As the late-comers arrived, the teams came out. BDS and his boozing buddies were havin' a disco over to our left and the game kicked off. We had room and a view. In fact there was so much room, they could have sold twice as many tickets, but we all know why they didn't.

United started off well on top, we were singing our way through the repertoire and all was well with the world — the bearded twins, and their bloody curse, temporarily forgotten. And the game was only five minutes old when Giggs was body-checked on the left. Becks took the free kick which was headed away from the goalmouth. Becks won the ball back and slipped it to Ole who blasted it in an instant low shot past the keeper. It was so easy. We celebrated and we sang. Things were going very well.

Well, they were for the first five or ten minutes anyway! Had Yorkie not been dreaming about dipping into the river Jordan and if Becks had been his usual creative self, things might have been different. Fulham immediately fought back and Raimond's goal was under siege. And all of a sudden things were not going so well. Ole did have another chance which Brevitt blocked on the line but for the most part Saha, in particular, was running riot. If it hadn't been for Phil Neville, the game could have been turned on its head within minutes. As it was, with 20 minutes gone Fulham were awarded a free kick 30 yards out. They tried to take it quickly, but Keano prevented it by kicking the ball away. He was booked and the kick moved forward ten yards. It was now well within the range of Fernandes and as the defensive wall lined up we all knew what was about to happen. Raimondo

New Year honours

had no chance as the ball looped over the top and eluded his out-stretched left hand. The Cottage erupted. Fernandes did a double lap of honour and the curse of the bearded twins loomed large. If anyone had said to me, back in 1968 (or even '98) that a bloke called Fabrice would score against United, I'd have said, "Are you 'avin' a larf?"

When Nicky Butt went off, after a wrecklessly high challenge by Boa Morte, United lost even more control of the midfield and for the remainder of the half could hardly get hold of the ball, never mind play with it. With 30 minutes gone we were convinced they'd scored a second. Their corner had been flicked on, at the edge of his own box, by Yorke (why?) and it fell, gift-wrapped, to Kit Symons who threw himself at it. The ex-Bitter could see his name up in flashing lights high over Maine Road as the ball flew into the net. Except it didn't. From no more than three yards out, it flew just past instead, and a barely audible cry of "City reject, City reject" was heard. Half-time couldn't come quickly enough. We could cope with it being 1-1 and let the Wizard do the talking.

The break was enlivened by the appearance of BDS (full to bursting with pre-birthday booze) and Paul Parker drawing the 'Fulham Flutter' tickets. When the second half began, much as the first had ended, we feared the worst. The action spread from one end to the other with the usual culprits causing the problems. Saha and Boa Morte ran riot, but thankfully Wes and the Nevilles were on their games. Gradually — ever so gradually, United got a grip and even stung the keeper's hands once or twice and we began to see more of the action down at our end which was a relief.

With fifteen minutes to go Sheringham came on

for Yorke. Wallwork moved from midfield to right back and Phil Nev the other way. Suddenly we looked in much better shape and for the first time in the game there seemed to be more red shirts on the pitch than white. With seven minutes left, Chadwick came on for Becks as a last effort to avoid the dreaded replay. By this time United had gained the ascendancy and with three minutes left on the clock Chadwick nicked a ball to Sheringham and drew defenders away with his run. This allowed Teddy the time and space to shoot. The ball flashed past Taylor and nestled neatly in the back of the net. The celebrations on Putney Terrace were prolonged and raucous, with father Walsh and me doing jigs as all around were in utter chaos. The trauma was over. The curse of the bearded twins blown away.

The game ended and our unbeaten run in the Cup had been extended. The trophy may have been lifted by Chelsea last year but as we were not there to defend it (having been sent to Brazil by the FA) it was still ours to lose. Our terrace party was over and as we trooped away past a dapper (or at least that's what he told me to say) Brummie Bedford, we were singing "Que sera, sera — in May It's iachyd da." The Thames was glowing red in the late afternoon as we made our way back to Putney station and from there to Mortlake and the M40 to await the draw for the fourth round.

A Glorious Adventure?

"Manchester United today announced that they have appointed Eric Cantona as manager, to replace Sir Alex Ferguson when he leaves in May 2002."

New Year honours

Words that will quicken the pulse of romantics like myself and have the more pragmatic amongst us chewing their nails down to the knuckles. "What a glorious adventure," I said yesterday. And, of course, adventures are by their very nature, risky endeavours.

Let's allow our imagination to run away with us for a few minutes. Let's imagine that a miracle has happened – United's money men have taken their collective eye off the till receipts for a second and gone for the dream. In the packed news conference, Eric is flanked by Peter Kenyon and Sir Alex Ferguson. Imperiously gazing around the room at the lesser beings hanging on his every word, he talks of the beautiful game, the magical adventure to come. At his feet, the lads who learned their craft under the master, await his instructions, knowing that this is their opportunity to take their football onto another level, to become the great players that Le Roi knows they can be.

A few weeks later we turn up at Old Trafford for the first home game of the season. Our hearts aflutter, butterflies in the stomach, you can cut the electricity in the air with a knife. When was the last time we arrived at Old Trafford feeling like this? It's like being a kid again, all around us adults' eyes shine like children on Christmas morning. Weeks later, we are in heaven. Game after game watching a team moulded in Cantona's image, living the dream on a glorious roller coaster ride of sublime football.

Of course this may be all romantic nonsense and we are just as likely to be mouldering away at the bottom of the Premiership at the behest of an inexperienced manager who just wasn't up to the job. Aren't we? Even if you really believe this could

Three in a Row

happen (and I don't), wouldn't it have been worth it for the chance of the glory that could have been? For the magic that even failure would bring (for with Eric as manager, even failure would be glorious!). Because isn't that magic, the following of a dream, what Manchester United is all about — has always been about? Supporting United has never been anything but a glorious adventure. And would we have it any different? Would any of us seriously consider swapping that heart-stopping two minutes in Barcelona for a boring two-one win by the middle of the second half? Wasn't it the drama of the victory that made it so memorable, so special? Is there a United fan alive, whose heart doesn't miss a beat at the mere thought of the romance and magic of those fateful ten days in May?

I didn't actually choose to support United — I don't remember ever being offered a choice! But I'm sure that if I had, I would have been a United fan anyway because, from the Babes to Barcelona, there has always been something magical about Manchester United. There has always been something of the adventurer about the club, some indefinable something that would have appealed to my romantic and emotional nature. I can't believe that I would have chosen the journeymen in blue before the heroes in flame red. And I honestly can't believe that there is a true Red heart that isn't stirred by the thought of the team that Le Dieu would build.

It may never happen, but it's a wonderful dream .... isn't it?

Cup of woe

A Separate Reality

Bradford City 0 Manchester United 3
Premier League
Saturday 13 January 2001

The day started reasonably normally, apart from big Rich who was on his way to Australia the following morning at 6am and was consequently concerned he'd allowed himself enough time to do what he had to do. BDS was also in a state of flux as he had been forced to stay at home due to circumstances beyond his control, but in the end found out far too late he could have come too. Disappointed is a word you could have used to describe his feelings, but you'd have been closer with, absolutely gutted. Apart from all this, everything was fine until we reached Bradford. In fact nothing much out of the ordinary happened until we got to the pub and it was then we slipped into a parallel universe.

The Commercial Inn on James Street is well worth a visit if you enjoy having a laugh. The bar was bedecked with more trophies than there ever have been in City's cabinet and outside (to carry on the theme) was a van bearing the name: "L. Gallagher,

Three in a Row

Building Contractor"! We ordered three pints and stood well back. A poor excuse for a DJ was playing up a storm with the type of equipment which may have been the bees' knees in 1960, but should have been binned five years later. We then realised our fate. We were in a karaoke bar, and a queue of locals were preparing themselves for their three minutes of stardom. Vic Reeves eat your heart out.

It was the sort of place where everyone knew everyone else, apart from us and a couple more stray Reds. It was also the type of pub where you get the distinct impression they all more or less permanently live there. A place jam-packed with caricatures straight out of a Hogarth cartoon. We endured Fleetwood Mac-a-like, an Englebert Humperdink who never hit a single correct note and a Conway Twitty who was a cross between Elvis and Freddie Starr and convinced us "It was only make believe". The only regular who was apparently not up to singing was the young bar 'Queen' who seemed to be deriving far too much pleasure from her new (vibrating) phone!

We were in another world far away from normality for us, but not for them. But the most outrageous stunt of all was witnessed while minding my own business in the gents. I know you've been waiting for another of these tawdry tales of life in the world of percys and porcelain, but this was very disconcerting. It's not something you expect to be happening while standing there doing what you have to do. Making sure you're looking straight ahead until you are distracted by the person standing next to you who is counting his money (using both hands) at the same time as he is relieving himself. Why had I decided to drink that other pint? We left immediately

Cup of woe

while we still possessed some sanity.

The walk down to the ground was remarkably uneventful despite being joined on the way out by the bar Queen and her mates plus Conway Twitty, the karaoke kid. After a few moments' confusion as we headed towards last season's away section and then realised we weren't in there after all, we finally found our bit — the North West Quarter. I bade farewell to Nigel and big Rich and tried to find my seat without success. I found the right row, which wasn't difficult as it was the very front one of the upper tier, but not my seat. So I stood in the first available spot. It soon became apparent there were others also having difficulty and as the small section where I had housed myself filled up it alerted the stewards. Just like the good worker bees they are they began to move the excess and replenish stocks elsewhere. Put a yellow jacket on some of these guys and you get constant bother. The rest of our lot (including Linda) were in the Symphony Stand at the other end — hmmmmm — nice!

The lads came out, and for the first time since his achilles problem, Stam was with them but there was no Scholes and no Butt. Gary Walsh came down to our end and was welcomed warmly. It was the first time he had faced United since his transfer. But as I looked over towards the goal I realised the error of my ways. I'd been far too busy working out how to avoid the over-zealous steward invasion and hadn't noticed the enormous temporary floodlight pylon thingy blocking part of my view. This pylon was as nearly as big as those massive ones down at Maine Road. It had been a good job most others had been turfed out to pastures new as it had created plenty of room so that I could adjust my position accordingly

Three in a Row

whenever the action appeared at our end. I had considered making another effort to find my own seat, but not seriously enough to put the plan into action. Anyway the game had kicked off.

United were obviously taking things easy and so were we. "We have Jaap Stam bigger than your ground" and "City's going down for their Silver Jubilee" were the early favourites. The Bantams replied with "We're City 'til we die" whereas the person behind me preferred "You're City and a bag of shite". It didn't quite fit, but we all agreed with the sentiments.

A few locals down in the lower section were already winding people up and foolishly provoking the all-too-close Reds with the usual unsportsmanlike gestures. The fact was, the segregation was woefully inadequate and it was only a matter of time before one of these idiots was going to get (at the very least) a serious ticking off! And the action on the pitch was not much of a distraction either. Sheringham went close fairly early on, while down at the other end, Windass belted one from 40 yards which Barthez tipped over the bar. Then Giggs provided the necessary distraction and took control. He picked up the ball near halfway and slipped a posse of defenders, played a one-two with Ole and was free on goal. Walsh raced out, flung himself in his path and just managed to clip the ball and it was cleared off the line by Atherton. Becks then took over, shimmied past a couple and unleashed a drive that swerved in front of Walsh who threw himself to his right and finger-tipped it away. Was Walshy that good when he played for us we mused? And if he was why did we sell him? How the score remained 0-0 by the break no-one could fathom, but it did.

Cup of woe

By half-time Nigel and big Rich had decided They'd had enough of their lofty perch and came to stand with me. Meanwhile a rather portly chap in a Bradford shirt and a bowler hat was throwing sweets into the crowd. On the pitch the local cheerleaders were strutting their stuff and waving their pom-poms while the fellah behind me did his best to find his mouth with his pie, but wasn't terribly successful at it. It had gone decidedly colder and the warmth of the initial entente cordial, while we all stood and hated Leeds, had worn off completely as we suggested they'd be better off "F**king off back to the Nationwide".

We were hoping that the Bantams would get tired chasing Giggs and Becks and would eventually succumb to the inevitable. Down by the disabled section below us, a small group of Reds had appeared at the back of the stand carrying full pints. The police who stood in front were oblivious, but a lone club official was not. He tried his best to get the rule-breakers to leave, but without success. As they argued, they drank and it became obvious that his protests would eventually run out of time as the beer was fast disappearing and he ended up laughing and joking with them as good nature, and sense, prevailed.

The second half was much more one-sided. It would have to be wouldn't it? After all they were attacking the other lot down at the Symphony Stand end of the ground. Keane was first to show intent by flashing a shot wide after another superb move. The lads were starting to look imperious. The change came as Phil Neville was replaced by Chadwick with specific instructions from the Wiz to "Use the force, Luke." Wes replaced Stam who had played as though

Three in a Row

he had never been away but who still had to ease his way back into first-team action. Selection problems at the back now eh? Whatever next?

Ole then went close with a glancing header which drifted inches past the post and the Bantams were getting concerned. United were cranking up the gears. Whether it was concern or just plain bad luck which caused the monumental gaffe by Gary, we'll never know. The ball had been played back to him with hardly a soul around. He took a touch and steadied himself for the big boot out except it didn't quite happen like that. Poor lad! With Sheringham lurking, he took a swing at the ball and missed completely. It was more akin to the Pythonesque dance with a wet fish, as Teddy nipped round the back and rolled the ball into the gaping net. Loud and prolonged guffaws from us and groans of disbelief from the Yorkshiremen. It probably didn't help matters that we all sang "Gary Walsh is a Red, is a Red, is a Red, Gary Walsh is a Red — he hates Scousers" but you have to laugh.

Within five minutes we were two up. This was a solo effort by Giggs who received a 30-yard ball from Becks, that was so perfect it dropped right on the toe of his boot. Giggs took it past two defenders and past them again, before lashing the ball through Walsh at his near post. It was the ridiculous to the sublime — a superb goal.

"Who the f**k are Man United?" confused them, but "You're going down with the City" didn't. And it all became too much for our friends from over the Pennines. The segregation (such as it was) collapsed and a wholesale barney broke out. Stewards waded in and took their toll. The Red Army was incensed as a yellow coat was seen to throw a punch. It was a

Cup of woe

fatal mistake. The line of stewards was attacked and retreated a great deal faster than they had appeared in the first place. With the Red Army chasing them down the steps it was a sensible decision. As they re-grouped for another assault a lone Red went amongst them and literally threw one of them out. The others thought better of it and disappeared. I had seen nothing like it inside a ground for years. There were two separate warring sections which were eventually brought under control.

Meanwhile, back on the pitch, Chadwick was causing problems and had already forced Gary Walsh into a good save when Becks played him through on goal. The Bradford defence was split and five defenders stood helpless as Chadwick ran free. When Walsh threw himself at his feet he stroked the ball into the corner of the net much to his, and our, delight. It was his first United goal and he did the celebrations justice. There were only five minutes left anyway, but the ground half-emptied after that. Whether it was because they'd had enough of what was going off on the pitch, or what was going on off it, it didn't matter. The locals left in droves. We stood by the exit chatting with Boylie as the final whistle blew and then disappeared into the night without so much as a problem.

On the way back we listened to Five Live's 6-0-6, Richard Littlejohn's football phone-in. It's usually good for a laugh, but this one was priceless. A caller came on talking about City. He appeared genuine and only mentioned the word 'massive' two or three times. Whether he was actually a Magoo or a Red didn't matter because Littlejohn then introduced another into the equation. Paul from Macclesfield took a bow and it soon became blatantly obvious to

Three in a Row

everyone, except Littlejohn, that 'Paul' was one of us — a Red. "There are three reasons why City won't go down," he said. "We're a massive club. We've got Curly Watts as a celebrity fan and we've got the widest pitch in the land." And then sang a chorus of "Cos City are a massive club". It was a masterpiece of deception and Littlejohn fell for it again. He was confused and definitely not happy. He became increasingly paranoid as the show wore on and the rest of the calls were very boring and had obviously been strictly vetted. Eventually an email was read out. It came from a Bitter and said: "If anyone ever came on saying, 'City are a massive club,' they are bound to be Reds. They've got this daft song they sing about us."

In the days between our short trip over the Pennines and the visit of the Brummies to Old Trafford, speculation about various United players was rife. With Beckham reportedly about to open negotiations for a new deal, there was much speculation about his future. Players such as Figo were urging him to quit United, while the papers were claiming he was about to sign for clubs all over Europe! Whilst speculation abounded about Becks' future, Mark Bosnich was definitely on his way out of the club, with journalists maintaining that he had had his contract cancelled by mutual consent. Within hours, Bosnich had signed for Premiership rivals Chelsea, with Sir Alex Ferguson said to be furious that Bosnich had allegedly duped United into terminating his contract by claiming he wanted to move abroad.

Meanwhile, over at Maine Road, it was announced that Manchester City had signed former Manchester United winger Andrei Kanchelskis on

Cup of woe

loan from Scottish champions Glasgow Rangers until the end of the season — that was going to be interesting when they get to OT.

The Deadwood Stage

Manchester United 2 Aston Villa 0
Premier League 20 January 2001

Talk to any Villa fan, and there are plenty of them down here, you will get the same story — that there are several players who are 'deadwood' and should be cleared out. It's that 'deadwood stage' when a club is so frustrated trying to oust United from the top spot that they can think of nothing more than a clearout because none of their players were a patch on ours in the first place. This doesn't just apply to Villa of course, but almost all the Premiership. Amusing isn't it?

Ever since the FA Cup Final of 1957, Aston Villa supporters have been er, frosty towards Manchester United. Alright let's face it — they hate us with a passion! They won the Cup that year. United won the sympathy vote, but not the expected double. McParland clattered into Wood, broke his cheekbone and United were minus their goalkeeper. The Irishman then went on to score the two goals that beat us. The Villa fans have never felt they received enough praise for that victory due to the circumstances and have resented it ever since. Tough — they will never get praise or sympathy from Me, especially as this was the seventh anniversary of Sir Matt's death.

Salty joined us in the car that day, a friend of many

Three in a Row

more years than have passed since City last won a trophy. We had hoped to arrive in time to make the trip to the Dog for a beer, but a multi-vehicle shunt on the M6, which caused a massive tailback, put paid to that idea. So we arrived with only 30 minutes to spare and Warwick Road was packed. A few Villa fans were being gathered together in the coach park opposite the ground ready for the short walk through the Red throngs and the touts were doing business. Scouse touts at that. I wonder if those Brummie coaches were resting on bricks by the end of the game?

As I entered the ground I couldn't believe my ears — Keegan was playing the Buzzcocks. Blimey — whatever next? It was a very pleasant change from the usual dross we've been used to. He may have also been listening in to the on-going 6-0-6 controversy as he was chatting about this 'massive' flag from Carrickfergus which was being given an airing in the centre circle. I climbed up the steps to my usual spot and was greeted by our steward who told me the score would be 2-0 and that Sheringham would bag them both. I suggested that as he'd been way off the mark last time (with the Scouse score) he should keep his predictions to himself, but it didn't stop me from hoping he was right!

We already had news, from BDS, that there would be no Becks. Apparently he had been given special leave to attend a music awards ceremony in Cannes with Posh. From Spain to the south of France in less than a week — not a bad life for a pro footballer these days eh?

Calamity James came down to the Scoreboard End and with the new England boss watching, we were expecting him to be giving the performance of his life. And he almost did. It wasn,t quite like West

Cup of woe

Ham in '95, but if the news had leaked out that he had been confirmed as a Czech national, I wouldn't have been surprised. The Villains seemed in reasonable voice as the game got under way, and so did our lot. Apparently we'd "only come to see the Villa", which was more than most of them had done the previous Wednesday night when they played Newcastle to a half-empty stadium!

Calamity had already saved well from Ole when Greening won the ball in midfield and played him through again. Only James stood between Ole and the goal when Gareth Barry appeared and just as Ole drew back his foot to shoot, he nudged the ball away. Not another prospective England recruit turning it on for Eriksson. It was difficult enough against an eleven-man defence without the Swede turning up.

Sheringham had also gone close in that first half but again Calamity was there to somehow scramble the ball clear. With honours just about even and the Villa fans singing "It's time for a sandwich" (which was pretty inventive for them) we went off for a break below stairs. So, no goals in front of us again. Our steward was repentant and vowed to zip it next time!

Confidence was still fairly high as the second half started, but we were soon having second thoughts. Villa were men possessed and suddenly there seemed more likelihood of a goal down at our end in that first ten minutes than in the previous forty five. 'Shotgun' had obviously been mouthing off (if you'll excuse the expression) in the dressing room and Dion (he of the longer than normal shorts) was causing problems. The Scoreboard goal was under pressure, not that Barthez seemed to be that bothered. He was his usual Mr Cool — returning a

Three in a Row

pass back from whence it came by flicking the ball over the head of Hendrie to Phil Neville. "For God's sake, don't encourage him!" said the fella next to me as we all sang "Fabien Barthez". "He gives me the willies!," he continued. Enough said about that I thought.

Minutes later Hendrie stole past the offside trap courtesy of the unfortunate nutmeg through Nev's legs. With only Barthez to beat he thought he had rounded him successfully and was just about to prod the ball home when the Frenchman stuck out his arm and pushed it behind for a corner. From the second of the two corners, Greening kicked off the line with Barthez beaten for once. Whether this woke United from their half-time reverie, or whether it was the sight of the Soul Brothers warming up, we don't know, but it seemed to spur them on. Yorkie (in his sparkling white woolly hat) smiled and waved at the Villains as he ran the touchline. They smiled and waved back, but only using two fingers. "You can't get in the team," they sang to him. They sang some other stuff too but no-one could work out what it was they were on about.

United stepped up their game and were being encouraged forward by Keane and Butt. And prompted by Sheringham, who had another decent volley saved by Calam, though we still had to wait an hour before we could celebrate. In the first half, we'd been up and down like yo-yos — it had been more like a Catholic Mass than a football game. When the goal finally came from a Keane free kick, we only knew it had gone in because the Stretty went up. We had been convinced the ball was saved from crossing the line, but no. Calamity had finally been beaten by another England hopeful — Gary Nev. It was such a

Cup of woe

rare occurrence for the elder Neville that the whole team surrounded him as we reminded him how "...he hates Scousers". The Villa fans, who had been declaring their love for their home town, immediately switched allegiance and sang "You'll never walk alone". Instead of the usual howls of derision from the Red Army there was an ironic and contemptuous round of applause followed by "Who the f**k do you support?" and "Shit on the Villa".

Meantime, young Chadwick had come on looking more like a coathanger on sticks than a footballer. His shirt was too big, his socks fell around his ankles because he has no calf muscles and his shorts needed a tuck in the elastic to stop them falling down, but this lad can play. He caused major panic down the right wing every time he ran at the Villa defence. The goal had opened the game up and Villa were forced from their defensive roles and attacked with a vengeance. Fortunately, not very effectively. Merson ballooned over to cries of "Merson for England" and so did Dublin to "Dion for England". Down at the Stretford End, Calamity was called on to make another save from Butt who had another superb game.

As a final effort to snatch a draw, 'Shotgun' threw Ginola into the fray. "Ooh aah Cantona" rang round OT along with "You fat bastard," which was started by one of the Euro coke drinkers who sit in front of me. The one with a neck so huge it spills out over his jacket collar and even his finger wobbles when it points! Ginola did nothing. He didn't even want to be bothered, whereas United were looking to wrap things up and did so with three minutes left. Cole had come on for Ole and was also looking to impress Eriksson. He stole the ball from the ex-Scouser

Three in a Row

Staunton, and fed Sheringham who split the defence wide open. Coley took the ball to the byeline and crossed. Calamity palmed it out to Teddy (nice of him) who volleyed home. 2-0 — Calam stood disconsolate and smiled sheepishly at the Swede and we could finally relax.

The game ended with Nev's song and him lauding it in front of us while the Villa fans Brummied their way back to the coaches and cars ready for the big moan to the talk shows. On my way out I forgave the steward who was mightily relieved that at least one of his predictions had been reasonably accurate. He'd been reprieved and ready for the next time. Back in the car we eagerly awaited Littlejohn's 6-0-6 as we'd been tipped off that a certain person had a cunning plan. It was going to be another of those 'massive' calls, but with Littlejohn on the lookout, it wasn't going to be easy. There aren't many highlights on journeys up and down the M6, but this, like the other 'massive' calls before it, was worth waiting for. The caller (let's call him Jon) got on saying he had been the one who had run on to the Highfield Road pitch and pulled down his pants as a protest at Coventry's inept display. It was obvious to us who it was and Littlejohn was suspicious. Maybe it was the accent which gave him away. Maybe it was when the word 'massive' was mentioned, or the talk of '25 years', or even 'the under-soil heating on Economy Seven,' but thousands of Reds had another massive laugh. Littlejohn laughed (well, spluttered) too — nice one mate!

Cup of woe

The bubble bursts

Manchester United 0 West Ham United 1
FA Cup Sunday 28 January 2001

I don't know what it was about this game, but something wasn't quite right. It was as though it had been pre-ordained that United would lose. There was a sense of a fulfilled prophesy in the making even days before the game. Perhaps it was the thought of the 'Ammers buying up barrow loads of tickets through United and the tour packages — hamming their way through the pathetic excuse for a screening process that the club offered as an answer to infiltration. They obviously sensed an upset — or were they just being over-optimistic chirpy Cockney types? Whatever it was, it caused unease. I was even in two minds whether I should go until the doctor and the Sausageman offered me lifts. So I put all pessimism to the back of my mind and travelled up in Dobson's fartmobile.

The day got off to a reasonable start. We drove through the fog, past the longest convoy of away fans I have ever seen on the M6 and the Sausageman hadn't let one rip all journey. However, as soon as we were in sight of Old Trafford the familiar sound of the Dobson rear end erupting caused us to reach for the window buttons. "I don't fart for the fun of it," he said, presumably in jest, and seemed surprised that neither of us believed him. We were on our way to the Throstles for a pint with the regular Nest goers. Funny that as we arrived, everyone scattered at the mere sight of his arrival. With about half an hour to go before kick-off, and with a pint or two inside us, we

Three in a Row

walked down to the ground through streets which were abnormally quiet. It wasn't until we reached White City that we encountered anything like the crowds we had been expecting. Past the stretch limos with their champagne on ice and down on to Chester Road where we could hear the noise from the stadium. Bloody hell — everyone was already inside!

The 'Appy 'Ammers were in the top tier of K Stand and police were there en masse, almost surrounding our end of the ground. By the time I had weaved my way through the web and into the ground it was nearly time for the off. The teams were already on the pitch, everyone in K Stand was stood up and the atmosphere was buzzing. The FA Cup was back at Old Trafford after its year-long sabbatical.

The first thing that struck me was the pitch. It Hadn't improved since the week before and, if anything, it had got even worse. It was no better than a cabbage patch in parts and definitely not conducive to United's slick passing game. However, the game started well enough with Barthez showing all the skill of an outfield player as he ran to the edge of his area as Kanouté approached and backheeled the ball to Stam. Cole looked sharp, Giggs looked even sharper but lynchpin Teddy Sheringham seemed fatally off his game. Down at our end there was a brief moment of déjà vu as Shaka Hislop sliced a clearance so badly the ball spun back towards the goal and had to be cleared off the line by a vigilant defender. Maybe things weren't going to be so bad after all.

The 'Ammers were blowing their bubbles and we were taking the piss. How anyone who sings "I'm forever blowing bubbles, pretty bubbles in the air" expects to be taken seriously I'll never know. It's not

Cup of woe

exactly macho stuff is it? But at least the atmosphere was more like a cup tie should be, and no wonder — the 'Ammers were there in force — thousands of them with their chimney sweep outfits and soot smeared all over their cheeky Cockney faces. They were singing songs for us (which was nice).

Down below, Giggs was turning it on with such style that even when faced with three defenders he would trick his way clear. Some of the United football was swift, breath-taking and incisive, but the midfield was choked with bodies and only Giggs seemed intent on using the spaces out wide. When the ball found its way into the West Ham penalty area it was either hoofed away, batted away, or our forwards were unusually profligate, although Hislop made one superb save from Giggs. The Hammers had been resolute and resistant and by half-time I was beginning to wonder whether my more recent optimism was well founded, or the initial pessimism would prove correct. Even our steward wouldn't offer a final score prediction and that was a worry.

All thoughts of imminent Cup exit were put behind me as the second half started. Cole shimmied past Lampard (or Lamp post as the Brummie behind me called him) and fired at goal. Hislop could only parry the ball to Sheringham, but it came at him so fast he had no chance of controlling it and it ended in the upper tier. No more than a minute later Keane put Giggs clear, but wide of goal. Giggs opted to shoot rather than return the favour and Hislop saved. Had he looked up, Keane was completely free on the far side of the goal waiting for an easy tap in. The advice Keane gave to the Welsh wonder was heard even down at the Scoreboard end. It was not pleasant and definitely not printable!

Three in a Row

That same old feeling returned. United just don't miss chances like that. But — they had missed them. and it served only to offer encouragement to West Ham who ventured forth in numbers and to some effect. With 15 minutes to go Kanouté sprang the United offside trap and set Di Canio free. Everyone bar Di Canio stopped. In fact even he hesitated, fearing a flag. Up in K Stand, we didn't even give it a second thought as we assumed he was at least a mile offside. Play almost came to a standstill. Barthez stood on the edge of his six yard box with his arm raised and reacted far too late to Di Canio's shot, which was already under his body on its way into the net. It was almost surreal. Suddenly out of the silence and disbelief, the tier above us erupted and it dawned on us that the linesman's flag had not been raised. The goal stood. "Paulo Di Canio," sang the exceedingly 'Appy 'Ammers. Paulo Di-bloody- saster more like.

In retrospect it had been incredibly naive and unprofessional of the United line. You play to the whistle and take no chances, especially when the likes of the Italian have the ball at their feet and the goal at their mercy. The Wizard showed immediate intent by taking off Butt and Irwin and throwing Ole and Yorke into the fray — and United piled forward in great numbers. West Ham had no choice but to withdraw and their penalty area became a battleground. It was all or nothing — a Dobson fart or the sweet smell of success. Even Barthez played the last five minutes as an out-and-out attacker exclusively in the opposition half.

With the clock already showing 90 minutes were up and the frantic 'Ammers' fans whistling for all they were worth, their left back, Winterburn, dived in the

Cup of woe

penalty area and saved the ball with both hands. It was the most blatant penalty, but for some reason only known to himself, the referee chose to ignore it. It had been almost a carbon copy of an incident in the first half which was also strangely ignored. They say these things even out during a season, but I am not so sure. Barthez was the last to touch the ball as Durkin blew for full time. He booted it high into the crowd out of anger and frustration and all our dreams of the first Millennium Stadium FA Cup final blew away with the East End bubbles. We were left with the Dobson fart.

There were many angry faces snarling abuse at the 'Ammers in the tier above as we left the ground. Their team had played well and deserved their moment of glory — I just turned and walked away. After our surprise defeat in the FA Cup, Alex Ferguson got into a strop over the state of the pitch: "The biggest club in the world and they have to play rugby every bloody November and the pitch is a mess after it," he stormed. "You think they would learn a bloody lesson and it's an absolute disgrace." Another member of the playing staff who lost his temper was Gary Neville who was charged with misconduct by the FA, following an incident after the West Ham game, when Gazza had allegedly upset the referee's assistant by using "foul and abusive language".

Three in a Row

Character

Sunderland 0 Manchester United 1
Premier League
Wednesday 31 January 2001

Allow a strong-willed man to build a team and he will build one in his own image. There has been no doubt about that at United over the last few years, but now there can be no doubt at Sunderland either. In Sir Alex and Peter Reid you have two of the strongest characters in the game today and their teams display the same qualities. I will never forget Peter Reid's interview after the '85 Cup Final when he gave credit to the victors — us. It took guts.

Some have said recently that the reason United seem to be running away with the Premier League is because of a lack of quality in the top flight. The Wizard has disputed this, claiming that the real reason for United's dominance is due to a settled side, while rivals have been chopping and changing, buying and selling in order to try and keep pace. In the last three years, Leeds have spent £74m, Liverpool £69m, Chelsea £66m, Arsenal £64m, Newcastle £61m and Aston Villa £60m. But I think there is another major factor and that is character. It's the character that comes from the example set by the manager and United have this in abundance. And each manager needs a strong leader to ensure that character is transmitted throughout the team. Manchester United have Roy Keane.

It would be interesting to know whether the teams that were chasing Manchester United at the top would have preferred us to win or lose this game. It's

Cup of woe

irrelevant now of course, but there was an argument to suggest they may have actually favoured this result as it gave more of them the chance of realising a place in the Champions' League next season by coming second or third. As far as I was concerned, United may have been streets ahead but the League wasn't won until it was mathematically impossible for anyone else to overtake us.

Prior to this game Sunderland were unbeaten at home and in second spot and United hadn't won on Wearside since 1983 — how times change! It was impossible for me to get to the Stadium of Light in time for this game. I had an important business meeting in London to attend which had to take priority over a football match — even this one. So it was the dreaded Radio Five Live commentary for me. The trouble with radio commentaries is that you never get a true picture of what's going on! But with Alan Green commentating on a United game you are going to get opinion. Apparently he had received an email suggesting he was a United supporter (no sniggering at the back). He replied by saying he was "hated at Old Trafford and is definitely NOT a Manchester United supporter." True!

The atmosphere inside the stadium was befitting that of a Cup Final, which for the Wearsiders, it was. Perhaps they even harboured the hope that if they had won this game they could have overtaken us at the top. Nah — they wouldn't have thought that, would they?

The game started with United in control. They had obviously put the West Ham defeat behind them. Not that anything much happened in the first half, but United took the sting out of the homesters and went in 0-0. But all was about to change dramatically.

Three in a Row

Only 24 seconds from the re-start United broke the deadlock. It was a goal which changed everything in more ways than one. During the build up to the goal the ball had struck Andy Cole's hand but was cleared. Keane headed it back into the danger area and Craddock made a real bollocks of his attempted kick. Actually he missed the ball completely, allowing Cole to collect and chip it over the advancing Sorensen. As Coley ran over to celebrate with the Red Army, Michael Gray ran over to have a brief chat with Graham Poll. Unfortunately for Gray, the ref didn't seem too enamoured with what he had to say and decided to offer him the chance of an early bath. One-nil down and one man down. The radio commentator said he thought it was a shame Gray had been sent off for what appeared to be foul and abusive language but I'm not sure I agreed, for obvious and biased reasons.

United then took complete control and could have gone much further ahead had Sheringham not headed over and Sorensen not saved at the feet of Keane. The Mackems were beside themselves with righteous indignation and amidst a crescendo of boos Giggs got free down the left and crossed into the box. Cole went up for the ball with Sorensen and lost out. There followed a bizarre and farcical situation when Rae and Cole squared up to each other and amused themselves by doing the old Glasgow kiss routine. By this time Poll had caught a nasty case of red fever and sent them both off. Andy Cole was furious. The game was now 9-10 to United and from then on you felt anything could, and probably would, happen.

Peter Reid sent on Thome who played for less than ten minutes until he had to come off again

Cup of woe

limping. A Sunderland fan ran on the pitch and started shoving and pointing at anyone wearing the United shirt and was belatedly removed. The Reds were raucous — well out in front and singing "Forever and Ever" when another fan ran on the pitch who was well out in front. Now this was different — the fan was female and dressed only in her red and white striped knickers. She made a beeline for Becks who turned away and eventually settled on (no — not in that way) Varga, the Sunderland defender. But where were the stewards? Where were the police? They were standing around enjoying the show, in the front row, as the female wondered why no-one was taking hold of her charms. She was eventually encouraged off to a chorus of "Who let the dogs out?" from the United faithful!

There were five minutes left when Green said, "Tthe game's over. It's inconceivable that Sunderland could equalise." Don't you just hate it when a commentator says anything like that? You know what happened next don't you? They threw everything at United in a last ditch attempt. Only Sorensen stayed back as the United penalty area was besieged. The defence held firm and Barthez held them at bay — but only just. The four minutes of added time for the boob break seemed like an eternity.

When the final whistle went to a crescendo of boos and a chorus of the Scouse anthem from the Mackems, the relief was paramount. Graham Poll was escorted off the pitch by the police, sheltering from a hail of spit. United were 15 points clear at the top and even Ladbrokes started paying out on all bets.

By the time we moved into February, the prospect of losing Fergie in less than 18 months time began to

Three in a Row

worry both players and fans, with Gary Neville being the first to voice his unease. "It will be frightening for a lot of us who have been here for fifteen years, all under one manager," the defender said. "Some of the lads have been at the club since they were thirteen or fourteen and don't know any different."

Return to Europe

A close call

Manchester United 1 Everton 0
Premier League Saturday 3 February 2001

On the match day closest to the anniversary of Munich, Manchester United seemed more concerned with the resumption of the Champions' League than the Premier League. Complacency was in the air, but you can't be complacent when there are Scousers about — they'll pick your pockets, and Everton nearly did.

With GMR on my bedside radio, I was awakened with the announcement that Andy Cole had signed a new contract. It's not often I get out of bed smiling (I'm not even vaguely human until at least lunchtime), but this time I did. Still grinning, I listened to the Talk Radio phone-in as I travelled into Manchester. The anti-United taunts, for once, just sounded ludicrous, and I laughed out loud at an Everton fan's disgusted description of how the red side of Merseydive is celebrating getting into the Worthless Cup Final — "anyone would think they'd got into the European Cup Final," he spluttered! I also listened to an Aston Villa fan say almost the same thing about

Three in a Row

Birmingham fans — it was priceless entertainment.

It was also a cold, murky, damp (ie. typical Manchester) day when I arrived at Old Trafford just before 2pm, for the tribute to the Babes that Gez had arranged — thanks Gez, if you're reading this. Walking across the forecourt, towards the North East corner and the memorial, I looked up at Sir Matt and thought (yet again) how sad it is that his statue is over the megastore, and not where it should be — with the memorial to his lads. I arrived on the corner to find Tim Vimto already there. The son-and-heir soon arrived, followed by the Baldy One and the Sausageman. Soon there was a reasonable crowd of fans gathered in front of the Munich plaque.

If there's anyone reading this who has the ear of our new Mr Big at Old Trafford, please whisper in that ear about moving the memorial to a more respectful position, befitting its importance. It's disgraceful that the memory of those lads should be given so little prominence in a stadium the size and importance of Old Trafford. Those who want to remember them and pay their respects should not have to huddle in such a forlorn and windswept corner of the ground, presumably out of sight and out of mind of those who are more interested in getting their 30 pieces of silver through the tills of the megastore as quickly as possible.

While all around us was the noise of a matchday, this group of a hundred or so raised our eyes to the list of names, singing "Forever and Ever" and then "The Flowers of Manchester". The singing came from the heart, and as we sang "In the cold snow of Munich, they laid down their lives, but they live on forever, in our hearts and our minds", there was many a tear blurring the words on the plaque. But I'm sure that no-one there needed to read the names — young and old, their names are emblazoned on our hearts and will be remembered forever.

So we moved on into the ground and found the Everton fans already up on the mantelpiece, enjoying the rare sight of a rapidly filling stadium. I have to say that it was pissing me off the way smalltime fans, who can't fill their own stadium, turned up at Old Trafford in large numbers and singing "Can we sing a song for you?" This lot were no exception and from the start were doing their impression of the greatest fans in the universe. Those of us who have been to Goodison know that even with their ground full for our visit (it happens twice a season — when we go there and when their chums from the other side of Stanley Park turn up) they still don't sing for more than the first five minutes! To the disappointment of many, the young lady who entertained the away section at Goodison didn't appear to have had the guts to bring her assets to Old Trafford. Either that, or she had thought better of it and was keeping her assets firmly under her jumper this time!

By 2.20, the Baldy one was also in the ground:

I had given over the token for match 14 from my Season Ticket book, even though it was actually match 13. We never use that token — it always remains in the book. I hadn't been inside a football ground with so much time to spare before kick-off since 26th May 1999 and it was a great deal warmer then. The teams were out on the pitch going through their warm-up routine as I chatted with Mr Wheeler. And that was about as entertaining as it got, or as my next-door neighbour said, "I had more fun walking from the car park." So much for Steve's prediction of the start of a new era — or was that it? If it was, then

Three in a Row

I'm not so sure I was ready for it. A premonition of another Ipswich indeed! The closest this game came to that 9-0 rout was the colour of the Everton shirts! Our steward couldn't resist another prediction either — raising three fingers on one hand and describing a nought with the other. He suffered a severe ear bashing at full time and swore never to do it again — til next time no doubt!

As the teams came out, the Soul Brothers were there, with Coley's new four-year contract tucked into his back pocket. There was no Keane, no Butt (suspended), no Gary Neville and no Giggs, although he appeared for the second half after Scholes had been injured. For all we knew, the others were pushing shopping trolleys round Sainsburys and apart from the odd one or two, the rest of the team might just as well been with them. The Wizard had ordered a rest, so they rested! At least the pitch looked slightly better, but only slightly.

For the first fifteen minutes or so, United dominated as Everton were pinned back expecting an onslaught. Steve's prediction looked more possible at this time than any other, but gradually the Toffeemen realised United were not that bothered and by the end of the half had assumed control. It has become normal of late for United not to score when playing towards the Scoreboard, so we were half-expecting a goalless 45 minutes and so it was.

The second half wasn't much better, apart from the goal. Coley had taken the ball wide right and fired a shot hard and low across the keeper. It was about all we could see down at our end as the penalty area was as congested as my nasal passages normally are at this time of year. As it sped on its way the ball suddenly took a massive deflection and looped high over the keeper and eventually plopped into the empty net. It hung in the air for so long there was an almost eerie silence as the stadium held its breath. We were dependent on the Stretford transmitting the news and as soon as their arms were raised we joined in. It may have been hard on Everton, but at that moment we cared very little as we sang "Shit on the Scousers", "In your Liverpool slums" and "You'll never get a job". The Scousers were naturally not best pleased and some of them committed the ultimate indiscretion by demonstrating how to fly an aeroplane, or rather how to crash one. So close to Munich too, and so close to the line of stewards and SPS who had, unbeknownst to them, just appeared behind. The hapless Scousers were duly ejected to a round of ironic applause, to contemplate the error of their ways in police custody. However normal that might be for those from the wrong end of the East Lancs Road it was worth the entrance fee. Well, we were clutching at straws by this time. "Get to work you lazy twats!" reverberated around K Stand as we waved them a fond farewell. In response they were singing "Stand up if you hate....." but whatever it was they were standing up and hating had been lost in a sea of phlegm. Perhaps it was: "Stand up if you've ever eaten a rat", or "Stand up if you're nicking a hubcap later", or perhaps "Stand up if you've got a job" — well, maybe not!

On the pitch the game had taken a turn for the worse as Everton looked likely to take revenge rather than United adding to their lead. They could have scored a few times and when a near mirror image of the goal at the Stretford was re-enacted at the Scoreboard, we thought they had. Fortunately the ball, which cannoned off Jaap's ample thigh, looped

Three in a Row

over Barthez, but also over the bar. Towards the end of the game Chadwick, who had been tormenting both fullbacks, was taken off to a standing ovation. "He's run his socks off today," said Chris. The truth was, he couldn't keep his socks up even if he wanted to, his calves are that thin! He had looked the most likely to create chances. Phil Neville also played well in a more central role, Wes too had another superb game alongside the big man, but Silvestre was arguably the best in red.

The game was hard work for United. It could have been made easier by a referee who seemed more concerned with prancing around like a bloody circus pony, posing at every opportunity, than controlling a game of football. And in the end he played so much extra time, the three added minutes turned to six. Finally, he called it a day and United retained their fifteen-point lead at the top while at the other end of the table it was looking like a tale of three Cities, as Manchester, Coventry and Bradford all looked doomed. Pity — Coventry's such a good awayday.

It had been a sunny day when we left the Midlands and for big Rich, it had felt more like his 'home' of the previous three weeks. He hadn't quite adjusted to his regular time zone having just returned from three weeks in the summer warmth of Oz. He had been underdressed to say the least. The rest of us, the Sausageman and my old mate Salty had been well wrapped up in jumpers, thick coats and hats., but by the time we got back to the car his tan had turned from a golden glow to a rather unsavoury purple.

Our journey home was swift. It had to be, before the packet of peanuts that he had devoured earlier, took effect on the Sausageman's deadly derriere,

Return to Europe

Thankfully we had Littlejohn and his 6-0-6 radio show to take our minds off the possibility of imminent asphyxiation from one of the bubble buster's belters. This poor chat show host was now utterly paranoid. He even cut short a perfectly serious caller because he happened to say the word 'massive' twice!

So it was with some relief that I pulled up outside my house and discharged the Sausageman and his gurgling stomach. The journey had taken place without incident, unless you consider the close encounter with someone wearing a massive afro, dressed in a skin tight devil costume, with a large tail swinging between his legs, an incident. As the Sausageman walked to his car his parting salvo was enough to leave me wiping the perspiration from my brow "As soon as I get to my car, I'm going to put one leg up on the bonnet, let rip and fly off to the moon." That was close!

Why does Munich still matter

The other day, I was asked a question by a fan of another team. Quite seriously he asked me, "Why does Munich still matter so much to United fans? After all, it was a long time ago and many United fans weren't even born then."It Yes, it was indeed a long time ago, 43 years ago to be exact, and my son is one of those who wasn't even a twinkle in his mother's eye at the time. 1958 is ancient history to him — a time before computers, mobile phones, CDs — the list is endless and makes me feel very old, so I'll stop. But you get the picture. To his generation, it might as well have been the stone age. Yet yesterday he was singing his heart out with the rest of us, in memory of a team he has only ever seen in grainy black and white pictures that make him cry. And as I looked around me, I saw that most of the crowd gathered there were also too young to have been around on that sad day in 1958, and it got me thinking.

First and foremost, of course, for many of us the Munich disaster is still a vivid memory and a defining event in our lives. Never mind what they were doing the day Kennedy got shot, or the day Lennon died, ask a United fan of my generation or older what they were doing the day of the Munich disaster and their eyes will mist over as the memories flood back. Indeed, ask anyone who lived in Manchester or Salford at that time, and they will remember — because despite the chants and the aeroplane impressions that issue forth from Maine Road these days, this was a Manchester tragedy. There was no Red or Blue in Manchester in those cold February days of 1958.

For me personally, the moment I overheard a tearful conversation on a Salford street was the beginning of the end of my childhood. It was the day that not only music, but the magic died.

So the first answer is, of course, that for anyone over the age of 45, it still matters because it's part of our life's history. We loved those lads and we miss them and always will. But there's more to it than that, much more.

When they criticise Manchester United and its appeal to football fans all over the world, many fans of other teams bitterly point to Munich as in some way being 'unfair', almost as if we did it on purpose! They say that Munich, and the death of most of our young players gave us a romantic appeal that drew

Return to Europe

fans to us like moths to a flame, and with which no other team could compete. They accuse United of having used the legend of the Babes to build the modern Manchester United and to make pots of money. And of course, to some extent, they are right. It was Munich and its aftermath that defined the modern Manchester United and attracted thousands of fans from all over the world. Many football fans, who probably hadn't taken much notice of us before, started by wanting us to win out of sympathy and then stayed loyal United fans for the rest of their lives. There is no doubt that we were carried to the FA Cup Final that year on a tidal wave of sympathy that must have helped the team on the pitch to pull out that little bit extra. And the rise of the phoenix from the flames to win the European Cup in '68 completed one of the most amazing and yes, romantic, stories in football.

But of course the Manchester United we know today had its roots in what was happening in Old Trafford before Munich. In the 50s, Matt Busby believed in playing the game the 'right' way, in entertaining football, in giving youth its chance, in a work ethic that put the team first and that discouraged the development of ego-driven stars. His lads looked up to him in much the same way that Gary Neville now talks of Sir Alex, almost as a father. When so many of his lads were killed, Matt Busby could have walked away — indeed there have been interviews with him where he admits that is what he wanted to do for a long time — but he didn't. He stayed and he re-built and he went on to lift the European Cup at last. The winning of the European Cup showed that it's possible to come back from the depths of despair and not just survive, but win. There are many parallels today and I'm sure that it is no

Three in a Row

coincidence that the lads who form the backbone of the present team, and who refuse to be beaten until the final whistle is blown, are United fans — lads who were raised on the history and legends of the Munich air disaster.

And in that last sentence lies an important truth about why the importance of Munich lives on. Because with the passing on of the stories about Munich, we are passing on to our children and their children all that is important about supporting Manchester United. The importance of youth, of playing entertaining football, of playing for the team, of supporting the team through thick and thin — the importance of history. My son is moved when he sees a crackly video of Duncan Edwards or Eddie Colman because he knows that this is the living history of a team he loves. This telling and re-telling of what is truth and what has become legend, binds generations of United supporters together across the years and across borders. Only other United fans know how we feel about Munich, only other United fans can, a form of 'them and us' that binds us into 'family'.

Today, it's hard to associate the modern Manchester United plc with the club that we knew in the 50s and 60s. To those of us old enough to remember, with our admittedly rose-coloured spectacles, those days seem like something out of another world — an innocent world, unsullied by football violence, millionaire players and rampaging commercialism. It's hard to imagine that the hard-headed businessmen, who sit on the board of United today, will pause for a moment just after 3pm on Tuesday and remember, as I will. Perhaps this is the most important thing that Munich has to teach us. It reminds us all — whether we are ordinary fans in the Scoreboard, players on the pitch, executives in a fancy box or board members sitting in the Directors' bar, that there is more to supporting Manchester United, to being a part of the dream, than just making a lot of money, buying bags full of goodies from the megastore and winning trophy after trophy.

So yes, it does still matter. Indeed, as the years pass and Manchester United grows into something inconceivable in the 1950s, it matters more and more. And this is the main reason why we must never let the memories die.

Rumours began to circulate that Manchester United and the New York Yankees were set to announce the biggest joint marketing deal in the history of sport. Sir Bobby Charlton and Peter Kenyon flew out to the States to clinch the deal which, it was claimed, would strengthen United's position as the richest football club world. Many of United's army of fans in the USA were less than pleased as they contemplated their heroes on the English football pitch being linked with their most hated rivals.

The driving force

Chelsea 1 Manchester United 1
Premier League Saturday 10 February 2001

The memories of last season's hammering at the Bridge live long. The fact that I was in the Michael Collins bar in Barcelona at the time made it slightly easier to bear, but it still hurt as that fifth goal went in. The omens were not good this time either, with Chelsea's home record since the arrival of Ranieri

Three in a Row

reading ten wins and one draw from eleven starts. Mind you, it would have been very rare indeed for them to have won two consecutive home games against the Reds since that had happened only once since 1946 and even I wasn't born then!

Far be it from me to suggest that paying £32 for a ticket to Stamford Bridge could be stretching things a bit far but, coupled with this outrageously inflated admission charge and some urgent business to attend to, I was forced to take a half-term break from live football.

Another forced on to the sidelines was Barthez, who was suffering from a slight hamstring problem and was rested in the hope that he would be fit for the trip to Valencia the following Wednesday. Raimondo deputised for the second time this season against Ranieri's rent boys and it was to be a day of mixed fortunes for him. Also starting his 250th appearance for United was Andy Cole, who would be playing his last league match until March, due to his three-match suspension.

I actually came to the game at half-time as 45 minutes of radio commentary is more than enough for me. By this time Chelsea were a goal up. I wasn't surprised at the scoreline, but was at how the goal had come about. The Dane, Gronkjaer, had caused problems all afternoon, and it was he who tricked Gary Nev and found himself in so much space he could have phoned a friend before crossing the ball. Not that it was a particularly good cross, which was headed away by Stam, but only as far as Scholes on the edge of the area. Maybe Scholesy couldn't see Hasselbaink as he headed back across a crowded area towards a surprised Raimond. It was an unfortunate and uncharacteristic error from Scholesy

Return to Europe

which cost United dear as the ball ended up with Hasselbaink rather than Raimond and all he had to do was deflect the ball into the corner of the net. It signalled the Dutchman's hat-trick of goals against United — Charity Shield, Old Trafford and now Stamford Bridge.

What more would any team want under these circumstances than captain Keane who, for the last 15 minutes of the half (and all through the next) drove United forward relentlessly. His immediate intent was signalled by a powerful run from deep in United territory to 25 yards away from the Chelsea goal when he let fly with a daisy-cutting drive which sped inches wide of the post. United were down, but not out and neither were the Red Army.

The first half had been even and open, so inevitably chances would come, but an incident early on in the second half convinced me United would not come away from this game as losers. Zola was sent strolling down the left hand side, the ball played through by Gronkjaer (again). Raimondo came out of his goal to the edge of the penalty area to cover and as the ball sped on its way towards the dead-ball line, Raimondo left his penalty area to shield and shepherd the ball to safety. While Raimond was doing the dance of death with Zola down by the corner flag, the others just stood and watched in disbelief. Was this Barthez in disguise? It certainly looked that way as the ball hit the corner flag and bounced out to Zola's feet. Mr Diminutive was away again, made enough of an angle for himself and chipped the ball into the empty net. The Chelsea fans naturally went wild. What a terrible shame it was all in vain! The linesman had already raised his flag except no-one had noticed. The ball had drifted out of play as the macabre dance was enacted down near the corner. The 'goal' was disallowed and the relief was immense.

Even listening to the radio commentary you could glean enough to know that things were going to take a turn for the better and from then on United took control. Cole went close and Giggs closer still. The rain was pissing down as Keane drove the lads forward, but it was Giggs who provided the killer ball for Cole. It split the Chelsea defence wide open and Andy was on it in a flash. When he fired low past the keeper at the near post it was the Red Army's turn to erupt.

There were still 20 minutes to go and the team more likely to were definitely those wearing red. Chelsea took off the troublesome Gronkjaer as if they were happy to settle for the point. United were not. And Scholes should have won it for us. How he didn't connect properly with a free header inside the six-yard box, after a superb Gary Neville cross, only he will know (or not). It was so typical of him that he had ghosted into that position in the first place, but for once he couldn't find the killer touch. The game ended amongst a cacophony of frantic whistles from the Chelsea Villagers and with honours even. Whilst the first team were down in the Capital, drawing with Chelsea, it was announced that the dreams of ten young United hopefuls had been smashed, as they were released by the club: George Clegg, Mark Studley, Stephen Cosgrove, Welsh schoolboys' star Wayne Evans, Gareth Strange, Michael Rose, Rhodri Jones, Ashley Dodd, Marek Szmid and Josh Walker were all been told that they had no future at United.

As the thoughts of both Red and blue sides of Manchester turned to the coming Derby at Old

Return to Europe

Trafford, City fans caused hilarity amongst their Red neighbours as the news leaked that they had booked the air space above Old Trafford on Derby day. The Blues had reportedly raised £3,000 to pay for a plane to 'buzz' United's ground on the 21st April, trailing a banner reading: "You're the pride of Singapore". They apparently had enough money left over to buy 3,000 inflatable prawns with Roy Keane's face on!

Valencia

Manchester United 1 Valencia CF 1
Champions' League
Tuesday 20 February 2001

What can I say, except that it was a most unsatisfactory evening from many points of view. The result (obviously), the atmosphere (what little there was of it in the land of the living dead in front of the disabled section), the refereeing and the ability of the Spaniards to fall down when breathed upon. In the end, it was a fair result but a highly frustrating one. I had spent the afternoon with my six-year-old granddaughter and perhaps should have stayed in McDonalds. As it was, I set off for Old Trafford through the drizzle, feeling not a little nervous. Travelling from Piccadilly to Old Trafford, the bus was full of Valencia fans. Once we got in the stadium, and saw how few of them there were, I think they must have all been travelling on my bus! They didn't look like football fans at all, not a scarf or beer can in sight!

After a coffee and a natter, we braved the elements as the teams arrived on the pitch. Looking up at the mantelpiece, I was confused. The away fans

Three in a Row

were all sitting quietly on their bums, with only the small section in South Stand making any sort of noise. "They don't look like the usual away fans, do they?" I muttered to the son-and-heir. "That's because they're not!" he replied in disgust, his more youthful eyes having spotted that L Stand was full of United fans! I, of course, should have known by their genteel behaviour!

Kick-off put paid to my reveries, as I realised that we must have lost the toss, with Valencia opting to shoot towards the Stretty in the second half. This cheered me up immensely, as I realised that perhaps we had a chance of seeing United score in front of us for a change — I really should have known better!

The first 15 minutes was pretty good. Despite the attentions of the steward who ensured that we all sat down by screeching at a level of decibels which would be illegal were it not a human voice. We managed a few choruses of "The Busby Boys" and I was cheering up. On the pitch, the lads were controlling the game. Early on, we had a chance at the other end when Silvestre and Giggs combined and Teddy rose with the keeper. Their keeper managed to get to the ball, but to the surprise of everyone in the stadium the referee's whistle was heard as he gave a completely unwarranted free kick against him. This was not his worst decision of the night, and we were soon to become heartily sick of hearing that bloody whistle!

Valencia counter-attacked and, to our relief, Gonzales hit the ball over the bar at our end. Twelve minutes in, the breakthrough came. Giggs picked the ball off the feet of an opponent and passed to Cole. It came back to Giggs and with the Valencia defence expecting him to shoot, he pulled the ball back to

Return to Europe

Cole and we were one up. A great goal, United in charge, and all was going well. "We shall not be moved," sang some brave souls up in the singing section, but I preferred to keep that one until we were in a rather stronger position. Just as well as things worked out!

As I said, the first 15 minutes were good, then it all started to go downhill. First, Giggs limped off, an enforced change that altered the whole game. Then, proving that his early effort was no fluke, the referee began to get his whistle into gear, to the point where the guy behind us began to share with the rest of the Scoreboard just what he could do with it (and very inventive he was too!). First he (the referee, not the guy behind us) penalised Nicky Butt, who had replaced Giggs, when all he had done wrong was to stand up under pressure. Then he gave a free kick against Scholes on the edge of our box, when he had quite legally got to the ball. Thankfully, the resulting free kick from Mendieta went wildly over the bar, to the relief of your reporter who was watching from behind her hands! For a while, the Valencia players were camped out in the box in front of us, with Gary Neville eventually saving our skin with a well-placed foot and we could breathe again as play shifted down the other end.

Those of you who are paying attention will have noticed I haven't mentioned the atmosphere. A simple reason for that — what there was had completely disappeared. We could hear some singing from the 'singing end' and occasionally it started something off at our end, but mostly all that could be heard in the Scoreboard was moaning and complaining and the munching of prawn butties and popcorn. What a contrast to a couple of seasons ago,

Three in a Row

when standing in the Scoreboard on a Euro night was the ultimate, hair-on-the-back-of-the- neck-rising experience. The Club should be ashamed of the wanton destruction they have wreaked upon us.

Anyway, back to the game. Butt had a chance down the other end and then the guy behind us was thrown into further paroxysms of bile when Mendieta fell over after a dirty look from Butt and they got yet another free kick. Thankfully, again nothing came of it and then a nice move involving Scholes and Becks was in vain. By this time, the booing of the referee's decisions was the only noise being made in most of the ground, with only the singing end living up to its name. Becks took out Carbonne rather crudely, but we booed the resulting free kick anyway! Just before half-time, Angula had a shot down in front of the Stretty, but it was blocked by Silvestre and the whistle blew straight away. So we went down for our half-time Jaffa Cakes in reasonable spirits, pleased at least with our one-nil lead, if not with the rest of the experience.

Of course we should have known better than to expect to see some goals in front of us. In the second half, United seemed to spend as much time heading the wrong way as they did coming towards us, when they weren't giving the ball away that is! The only question mark was not if, but when the equalising goal would come. Early on, Butt finally got the yellow card the referee had been anxious to give him all night, when Mendieta (yet again) fell over at the slightest provocation.

Then Old Trafford awoke as Carbonne cut in front of Becks, fell over and got Becks booked! Whistles and boos filled the damp night air. Ole came on and things began to look up as he had a fine run down the

Return to Europe

left, fired the ball across the face of the goal, but Cole missed it by inches and it went out by the far post. Minutes later, Carbonne cynically took Becks out from behind and should have been sent off. But despite the howls of protest from all corners of Old Trafford, he was only shown a yellow card.

With only a few minutes left, Baraja had a header kicked off the line by Scholes. Stam headed the ball clear, but only to Mendieta. The ball came back to Rodriguez on the left. He shot towards goal and Wes lunged to clear it. Unfortunately, he only managed to turn it into the goal and Old Trafford was stunned into silence as their players celebrated and we heard their fans singing for the first time. Unbelievably, with minutes left and the game balanced at 1-1, the stands began to empty as usual, as hundreds of United fans left early. It's beyond me — why do they bother? We spent the last minutes of the game getting up and down to let people out (funny how the steward doesn't shout at them to sit down, isn't it?) and resisting the urge to take out our frustrations on the part-time ********! Eventually the referee blew his damned whistle for the last time and the teams went off to a chorus of boos and whistles aimed at the officials. I then wandered up Sir Matt Busby Way, trying to avoid the horse muck, feeling frustrated, sad and angry, all at the same time.

Watching the highlights on TV the next morning, it was actually a better game than it appeared from the Scoreboard, with a result which I have to admit was probably a fair one. So my immediate feelings about the football itself faded to the point where I can be philosophical. But I was left with the knowledge that I couldn't bear the thought of being in (what was) my favourite part of the ground for much longer. If I don't

Three in a Row

get a move next season, I might as well stay home and watch it on the telly — the atmosphere would be better!

The following morning, Mick Meade posted one line which puts all of this into perspective: "21st February 1958 — Duncan Edwards R.I.P" Our thoughts were with the lads that day, as always. Sir Bobby had this to say about Duncan: "If I had to play for my life and could take one man with me — it would be Duncan Edwards."

Prized assets

The Arse spanked

Manchester United 6 Arsenal 1
Premier League 25 February 2001

On Sunday morning I woke up to bright sunshine, made even brighter by the snow which covered most of the ground. Very Winter wonderland, but with a lot of the local roads covered in a layer of ice, I drove very carefully on my way to pick up big Rich. Once we were out on to the main roads, the conditions got slightly better. By the time we reached the M6 the outside lane was still half-covered with slush. Most drivers were being sensible about the conditions, but it only takes one and when we reached Staffordshire we came to an abrupt halt around junction 11. The four-wheel drive in front of us took a turn for the worse and did a Giggs-like shimmy before skidding its way to a stop inches from the car in front while we slipped into the vacant outside lane and slushed our way to a standstill.

There had been a multi-car pile up a couple of hundred yards down the road and as we made our way past the scattered debris and on up the motorway the conditions remained treacherous until

Three in a Row

we got as far as Cheshire. The problems were not restricted just to the northbound carriageway either as on the opposite side there were several cars on the hard shoulder, halfway over the crash barrier and even one halfway up a tree. We were beginning to wonder why we'd bothered (as if). We were about to find out!

It was with some relief that we pulled into Knutsford Services for a quick break. Big Rich made straight for Burger King for a top up and was most amused at being served by a girl wearing a name-tag which read: "Maximilian Wainthrop". We finally made it to Bronnington with an hour to spare before kick-off and were surprised to find that the weather in Manchester was cold, but sunny with hardly any snow to speak of.

It's peculiar what concerns you before a big game, but definitely the most worrying sight of all before this particular game was that of a certain fanzine editor with a broad smile on his face. I thought he must have been on the 25 year Bitter bash on the Friday night, but apparently not. He was just confident. Barney, confident — that was a problem. The fact that Tony Smith was also smiling made things even worse! The Arse were bound to be up for this one and these two harbingers were involved in pre-match joking — something was definitely up.

Once inside the ground the place was buzzing with anticipation, the teams were out, Seaman came down to our end and with a nonchalant fan of his moustache and flick of his ponytail, the game kicked off. Little did he know what was to follow — not that he could have done much about it even if he had! Wonder what Sven made of it all sitting up in the Directors' Box?

Prized assets

Right from the first whistle, United tore into them — and I had been worried about our lack of width — I needn't have bothered! Before we had got used to the fact that we were still standing, Yorke had bagged number one. Scholes played a major part in the build-up by stepping over the ball as it came in from the United right. He turned, ghosted past his marker, and made the decoy run, Yorke slipped the ball through, Scholes returned the favour and Yorkie netted off his thigh. We presumed it was his thigh, but with Jordan in the stands it may well have been another prominent part of his anatomy. Whichever part it was it excited him no end.

We were still celebrating that goal when the Arse retaliated, and a close-range Thierry Henry goal levelled the scores. Two goals in a matter of minutes — this was shaping up to be the archetypal Arse game — NOT! The Arse fans woke up and we were momentarily stunned, but not as stunned as we were about to become. They were beside themselves with the deepest joy, observing that we were "Not singing anymore", when it happened again. Yorke beat the Arse offside trap and slipped another under Seaman's body. Number two for the King of pornography and Seaman nowhere. It was too much for a few of the Arse followers who were escorted out of the ground by SPS — and they were the lucky ones as it turned out!

"Seaman for England", "England, England's Number One" were the jibes aimed at the ponytail. And you can always tell when he's angry as his hairpiece seems to take on a life of its own as it flicks around, swiping belligerently at the side of his face. He was angry alright! But things were about to get even worse.

Three in a Row

Becks had already chipped the ball to Keane who crossed for Yorke whose header was saved by the ponytail itself which by this time had detached itself and taken control of its own actions. Not that it could do anything a couple of minutes later as Nev won the ball, gave it to Becks who slipped his marker and sent a 40-yard pass which fell perfect for Yorke who fired number three past Seaman. 3-1 after 20 minutes — we were in shock! And a hat-trick for the Trinidadian who was swamped by his team-mates at the corner flag. He had a grin on him as big as Jordan's assets. And we were bouncing up and down in celebration (of the goal — not the assets). Or was it the assets which were bouncing up and down in celebration?

But the entertainment was far from over. Five minutes later, Yorkie appeared on the left, turned Stepanovs (who was left in a heap) on the touchline and hared off down the wing. Ole provided the decoy this time, drawing two defenders away from Keane who was screaming for the ball on the edge of the box. Yorke spotted the captain and looped the ball across. The defenders saw it too late and Keane slotted in number four. Seaman was all over the place and this time it wasn't Yorke who was to blame. It was the captain's turn to be swamped.

There was nothing the disembodied ponytail could do. The Gunners were shell-shocked and so were we. "Shit on the Cockneys" rang around Old Trafford as the Arse tried to re-group and close the gaping holes which had appeared in its defence — oooh dear! United were running riot.

The whole ground was buzzing, except for the Arse fans of course. They sat with heads in hands. So much for their "60,000 mappets" which was rammed back down their throats with a vengeance. The Arse,

Prized assets

and especially Seaman, couldn't wait for half-time — what a pity United were about to spoil their day even more. After a period of relative inactivity in the ponytail's goalmouth, United stepped up the action once more with ten minutes left of a pulsating first period and scored another. Nev fed Butt on the right, Butt slipped past Cole and passed inside to Ole who had run near post. Ole flicked the ball past the ponytail which was left flapping. The disembodied hairpiece was distraught and lay on the ground writhing and thrashing around and only put out of its misery by the posse of red shirted heroes trampling over it to get to the Norwegian.

The Arse fans had seen enough and hundreds left their seats to find solace in a cup of Bovril. We bade them a temporary farewell with "Cheerio, cheerio, cheerio". Those who had already taken themselves downstairs were lucky enough to have missed number six. Becks took a free kick after a stray Grimandi arm had felled Ole. The ball came to Scholes in the six-yard box. He twisted and stuck out his chest to help it on its way goalwards only for Seaman to save it at at the foot of the post and the ball was cleared. The ponytail had been ground into the dirt and lay there bereft of life.

The half ended with a standing ovation. The Arse had been ripped apart (oo-er) and below stairs the mood was upbeat, if still a little shocked. For a start, not only had United scored five goals against the Arse, but they'd scored them in front of us. This was unprecedented. Could it have been the presence of a certain Mr Boyle slumming it with the rest of the Scoreboard or could it have been the fact that my mate the steward had kept his mouth shut and for once not made any prediction? Or that's what he said

Three in a Row

and swore never to make another.

Arsenal made one change for the second half, taking off Cole and bringing on Ljungberg — it made all the difference! The ponytail had been picked up and delivered back to its owner but it had lost the will to continue. The Arse fans, buoyed by their half-time Bovril, got behind their team for a while. Granted this is never an easy thing to do when you have been so comprehensively outplayed, but they made a reasonable effort. Maybe it was the sight of Teddy Sheringham warming up along the touchline in front of them that spurred (pun intended) them on. And didn't he love it? Taunted by the Arse fans as per usual he danced in front of them as we asked him "Teddy, Teddy, what's the score?" He turned to us, beaming all over his face and scratched his chin, then held up five fingers on one hand and one on the other. The Arse fans went mad! And to rub their noses in it even more, he lifted the three imaginary cups again just for them. Their attempt at an atmosphere to gee up their team was short-lived.

The second half didn't exactly drag, but it was nowhere near as exciting as the first — not that we expected it to be of course. United appeared content to make sure the Arse didn't run too much, and when time was getting short, hit them again. Meantime, poodle Parlour was subbed and endured a deal of barracking from the Stretford about there only being "One Charlie Dimmock" (his look-a-like from Groundforce). Keane and Yorke were also subbed which brought Sheringham and Chadwick into the fray. They immediately made an impact. Chadders was running at the already bewildered Arse defence and scaring them half to death and Teddy taunted his erstwhile tormentors.

Prized assets

With ten minutes remaining, Sheringham gave ample warning of what was to come when he flashed a header just wide of the post. Five minutes later, Arsenal actually threatened to score. It was Vieira who got the ball through to Ljungberg who beat the offside trap while the United defence were pre-occupied by yet another unruly attack on Wes. Barthez raced out of his goal to the edge of the penalty area and Ljungberg lobbed the ball just past his right hand and, fortunately, the far post. It was a glaring miss. He stood with his head in his hands (or rather his gloves — the big softy).

The sheer effrontery fired United once more and within a couple of minutes, Ole had smacked a shot against the inside of the Stretford post. The ball escaped to freedom until Nev retrieved it and gave it to Sheringham who passed to Ole. Ole was setting himself up for a shot when Teddy thought he'd have a go and fired past Seaman for number six. It had to be Teddy. It was only right and fitting that the butt of so much hatred which has spewed out of the Gooners over the years should wrap up the afternoon's proceedings. And all the Arse fans could do was sing "Paulo di Canio" — utterly pathetic. Most of them had disappeared by this time anyway as we sang back "You're going home in a taxi". I was already on the steps next to the steward by this time and celebrated with him as the last goal hit the back of the net. "Don't think they'll come back from this," said my next-door neighbour. And he was right! The game was brought to a close with massive celebrations and the remaining Arse fans were released from their torture as we reminded them it was "1-6 to the Ar-sen-al".

Outside the ground the atmosphere was unadulterated joy. Barney was beside himself with the stuff as I passed by on my way back to the carpark. It's always an ideal result for a Cockney Red when the Arse get tonked. And didn't they get tonked? Best result against them since 1952 and a rather abrupt end to their ten-game unbeaten run. Not the Arsenal's biggest ever defeat though — that was against Loughborough Town in 1896 — 8-0! So, with United 16 points ahead of the rest, the Championship already looked a done deal. Not that this person ever takes anything for granted until it's mathematically impossible for any other team to catch us.

After thrashing Arsenal 6-1 and stretching our lead to 16 points, Alex Ferguson wrote off Arsenal's challenge "It's impossible for Arsenal to get us now," said a beaming Fergie, at an elated Old Trafford. Speculation as to who would replace the Wizard continued, as Fabio Capello confessed his admiration for Old Trafford and admitted he is interested in the job.

In-between the two Valencia games, Jaap Stam signed a new contract that ties him to United for another five years. Good news indeed. In the business pages, 'Manchester United' was quoted as the most valuable sports brand in Europe by the Financial Times. The club beat Ferrari, McLaren, Mercedes and Real Madrid to the top European place.

The day before the Leeds game brought the sad news that Manchester United former player Colin Webster had died, aged 68. The Welsh striker played 80 games for United, scoring 31 goals and winning the League in 1956. He had missed being with the team at Munich because he was suffering from flu.

Prized assets

Yorkshire bitters

Leeds United 1 Manchester United 1
Premier League Saturday 3 March 2001

It was very, very cold at 6.30am when I dragged myself out of bed cursing morning kick-offs! I arrived at OT very early, via bus, train and tram and found more coaches than I had seen all season. For some reason, no-one seemed interested in driving to this one!

Off we went, leaving God's own County of Lancashire behind and heading over a very snowy M62 to the dark lands. It took less than an hour and we were soon leaving the coach and looking dubiously at the 'welcoming committee' on both sides of the road that leads to the away section. The usual sights and sounds greeted us. The constant whirl of the rotor blades and a cordon of police in riot gear. And this year they were wearing a very fetching outfit in black, with a hint of yellow. It had changed dramatically from last season's ensemble as our friends from the local constabulary now enjoy the benefits of plastic legwear which made them look more like Robocop than ever before. There were some who seemed to find it an exhilarating experience, but most of us just wanted to get our heads down and get in as quickly as possible.

Thankfully, apart from the jeers of the sheep safely ensconced behind a line of Yorkshire's 'Boys in Blue', and me slipping off the pavement and almost sprawling full length in front of David Beckham's mum, it was an uneventful walk and we soon found ourselves in the safety of the away section. We were

Three in a Row

in an hour before kick-off — unheard of! After 30 minutes queuing for one of the two ladies' toilets (a good place to stand — just about everyone I know, apart from the Leamington Skinhead, came past!), I arrived at my seat — on the third row, right behind the goal, and within chatting distance of Barthez, who was winking and pulling faces at the United fans while warming-up. The lads were attacking our end for the first half. I use the word 'attacking' very loosely, as the majority of the action was directed away from us. I can't remember one meaningful event in the Leeds penalty area all 45 minutes. For the first twenty, all the play was down at the other end with Barthez having to earn his money for once. Leeds were completely dominant, but for the final fifteen United came back into it and at least made an effort to come down to pay us a visit.

We were inviting enough, and were well on top of the atmosphere chart. Flossie, the inflatable sheep, made another guest appearance and seemed more than happy to be batted around. I expect she received gentler treatment from us than she would have done in the Revie Stand at the other end of the ground though. And despite the lack of action in front of us we entertained ourselves and our friends from Yorkshire with most of the usual ditties. The young lad directly in front of me, who was no more than seven years old, particularly enjoyed the lengthy rendition of "We all hate Leeds" by dancing on his seat and pointing, in perfect time with the rhythm, to all corners of the ground. His father looked on with some considerable pride. It didn't do too much for the sheep fans in the stand to our left though, as several became over excited and had to be calmed down by stewards who were becoming more anxious by the

Prized assets

second. This led to much hilarity and even more goading. "If you follow Leeds United you must have foot and mouth" was the topical favourite. With United entrenched in their own half, we had to do something to entertain ourselves.

As the 45 minutes drew to a close there was suddenly a massive shout from the other end and a melee of players in red surrounding the ref. From where we stood, we couldn't see what was going on but with the whole of the Revie Stand baying for Barthez's blood, and Harte writhing around as though he'd been poleaxed, we assumed the worst. Barthez was eventually yellow carded, when we had assumed red and a penalty awarded. When we saw the replay on the big screen it was evident that Harte had been auditioning for the dying swan role and Barthez had obviously been chatting to Eric as he'd given him a sly clip — after some provocation, it has to be said.

After a considerable wait, while referee Barber booked Ole for his continuous protests, Harte stepped up to take the penalty which he smacked low and hard to the left of the goal. Fortunately, despite being told to go one way by Nev and the other by Teddy, Barthez chose the correct way and tipped the ball out for a corner. The sheep bleated their disapproval while we were deep in celebration. As the whistle blew for the end of the first half, and with a crescendo of boos echoing around the ground, I went below still singing "Fabien Barthez" along with several hundred others. There I met up with big Rich who warned me that the bearded twins were about. See, I told you — 30-odd years having never once seen them before and now I see them at nearly every away game. How come? And was this portentous?

Three in a Row

Neither of us could work out if it was or not, so we assumed it wasn't — it seemed best.

I arrived back in front of my seat just in time for the second half to kick off and the atmosphere was even better than for the first, as we now had Bowyer and Viduka at our end. With the trial well underway at this time we sang: "Four to five years" to the former and "You fat bastard" to the latter. At their first corner Bowyer was only feet away. "Bowyer's going down," we sang, and "Bowyer for Strangeways," while he studiously ignored us for about 30 seconds! Eventually, he couldn't resist it any longer and glanced across — just as the lad in the front row held up his 'Go to Jail' card. We watched as his eyes moved across the lines — brilliant!

By the time our first (and only?) real attack came along, both Smith and Viduka had had chances. We were eighteen minutes into the second half when it happened. Whether it was against the run of play or not, we didn't care — we naturally celebrated with the enthusiasm reserved for such occasions. Scholes and Sheringham played the one-two which resulted in a defence-splitting pass for Ole to run on to. Ole shot across the keeper who spilt it like a bag of greasy chips. The ball squirmed free and Chadders was first there to tap it home. Pandemonium broke out in the visitors' section as it hit the back of the net. Barthez came running towards us, fists clenched and a massive grin on his face, but he didn't run as far as Gary Nev, who sprinted the length of the pitch to stand in front of the United section, screaming.

"We shall not be moved," we sang, as the Leeds lambs sat in silence. Actually, apart from a couple of minor bleats here and there, they had sat in silence all through, so the goal had changed nothing. Fergie

Prized assets

was encouraged to give us a wave, but Kiddo wouldn't. "Kiddo, Kiddo, what's the score?" must have struck a nerve though — it did with the sheep over to our left as the stewards were again called into action! Eventually they roused themselves as Barthez saved at the foot of his post after a corner. Flat on the ground, facing us, he tipped us the wink and mopped his brow before getting back to his feet.

All this time Yorkie was warming up along the touchline while a new verse to his "Dwight Yorke, King of pornography" song was being aired. Something to do with sticking two fingers up (Jordan?) and assets as 'massive' as Man City! It brought a knowing smile to his face anyway! Not that he made any sort of telling contribution when he came on for Teddy. With little more than seven minutes remaining we were hopeful of stealing a victory, but the sheep had other ideas. Mills broke free down their right and with Denis missing somewhere upfield, Stam went on a mission. A frightening sight for any marauding attacker — I felt Mills got rid of the ball more in panic than anything else. Unfortunately, Stam was inches too late and when Mills crossed into the box, the United defence, apart from Wes, had obviously gone searching for Denis. Bowyer got to the ball before Wes and nicked it on to Viduka who headed past the stranded Barthez.

Cue sheep delirium. From that moment on anything could have happened. The game became more frantic than ever before and the sheep woke from their slumbers and commented on the fact that (momentarily) we were "not singing anymore". Rich coming from that lot, who hardly uttered a bloody word for 80 minutes but by this time had contrived a wall of noise. "Are you 'avin' a laugh?" we asked.

Three in a Row

Things had definitely livened up. Down at the other end, Scholesy had a ball kicked off the line which we were convinced had gone in. Minutes later, the roles were reversed as Bowyer crossed into the box and Wes slid in to clear the ball, but only succeeded in directing it past Barthez and into his own net. As Wes lay prostrate, eyes clenched firmly shut and brow furrowed, it suddenly became clear that the linesman to our left had his flag raised. The own goal was disallowed for offside and a mightily relieved Wesley Brown was saved from the dreadful moment of déjà vu. And all he got was a slap on the head from the slaphead.

The final whistle blew with the sheep distraught and disturbed by what they mistook as a grave injustice. They may have had by far the better of the play, but the score remained one apiece. Of course it gave rise to the inevitable aeroplanes and the odd finger drawn slowly across the throat but it didn't alter the fact that at that time we were still 23 points better off than them. Not a great game from the Red perspective, the lads missed Keano's leadership, but we'd have settled for a point before the game, and were content with it afterwards.

I don't remember how long we were kept in but it must have been at least 20 minutes. The usual line of security stood between ourselves and the pitch while we watched the highlights on the big screen. After a while some of the Leeds players came out again for a warm down and after them strode Kiddo. Pity some chose to boo an ex-Red who had served the club well, but we all joined in with "There's only one United".

Outside the ground the Leamington Skinhead walked back to the car with the others:

Prized assets

Once back in Derbyshire to drop off Pat while the sheep bleated pathetically on the post-match phone-in we decided to take a short break at Pat's local in Clay Cross. This is where his nephew, eleven-year-old Daniel, resides. This lad is a one-off and often to be seen in the Throstles before a game with his uncle who has, by all accounts, led him astray to the dark side. He told me he was watching the game when the last-minute Wes own goal had been disallowed and his father had cheered when he thought it had been the winner. Daniel had spotted the linesman's flag and ended up leaping around shouting "Wankers!" at the top of his voice! Or so he told me.

Who do you hate the most?

As is becoming a habit these days, I've been doing some thinking following a question someone put to me the other night. I was asked who I 'hated' most: City, Liverpool or Leeds.

At the time, I answered the question readily Enough: City, no problem. But equally despised, and always will be, is Bolton and Nat 'cheating bastard' Lofthouse. And as to Liverpool and Leeds, well neither of them even come close! My friend may have been surprised (although we have discussed this before, so he probably wasn't) and as I explained some of my reasoning, I began to think about my background and why I have ended up 'hating' those I do.

When I was growing up in Salford in the 50s, Manchester City had very little impact on my life. I actually knew very little of the town of Manchester itself — I knew the City centre, Cheetham Hill and

Three in a Row

Old Trafford, and we often used to go shopping in King Street in Stretford, before it was buried under the Arndale centre. Sale and Altrincham I also knew well and sometimes we used to take ourselves as far abroad as Warrington or Wigan. But the other side of Manchester — Fallowfield, Moss Side, Hulme — they were places I'd never been and I doubt if I'd even heard of them before I was almost into my teens. As to City fans in Salford — well, there must have been a few I suppose, but I never met one! Salford wasn't a divided city like Manchester in those days, Salford was pure Red.

Liverpool, on the other hand, was somewhere I did know. We regularly went to New Brighton for days out and often sailed down the Mersey on one of the pleasure boats, and then would get the 'Ferry Cross the Mersey' into Liverpool itself. We had friends in Liverpool and I remember feeling at home there, it felt very much like Salford, with its docks and the river, and its people seemed to have the same concerns as Salford people. Back in those days, Salford and Liverpool were both Lancashire towns who had much in common. And, of course, the music of my early teens — Billy Fury, Gerry and the Pacemakers, The Hollies — it was as much a Liverpool scene for us, as it was a Manchester one. Leeds, on the other hand, seemed a strange place to me as a little girl. Far away in a dark place called Yorkshire, where people were mean and in-bred, so my Grandad told me — an avid Lancashire cricket fan by the way — nothing much changes!

The team that we Salford kids hated was Bolton Wanderers. Despite being further away in actual distance than City, on our side of town they were the local rivals — just up the road and in their prime.

Prized assets

When the council began the slum clearance programmes in Salford, pulling down the terrace streets around Ellor Street, they moved the people out to Little Hulton, then a village in the countryside only a couple of miles from Burnden Park. This, of course, increased the rivalry as thousands of Salfordians were moved into the vast estates that were beginning to cover the fields, coming into close contact for the first time with the locals in Farnworth and surrounding areas — massive (i.e. City-esque) Bolton fans. I didn't know anyone who didn't have a relative (or two) who had been forcibly moved up to Little Hulton, so with the natural hatred of a team that is as good as, or better than yours, was mixed a new ingredient — local rivalry.

So at the turn of the year in 1958, the only team I could honestly say I 'hated' was Bolton Wanderers. Then came Munich, when I was ten years old. The whole of Manchester and Salford mourned and yes, even the Scousers. As I've said before, there was no Red or Blue in Manchester in those sad days. Of course, going to school in Salford I didn't come across many young City fans, but I did come across a few Bolton fans, and to my amazement and shock they actually made jokes about Munich. The only time I met anything but sadness and sympathy in the days immediately following Munich was from a couple of young Bolton fans in my own school playground. A feeling I had never felt before began to foster and to simmer. Then, on a wave of emotion we made it to the Cup Final to win what should have been 'our' Cup, dedicated to the lads who died. But we didn't win it, not because we weren't good enough, but because Nat Lofthouse, of Bolton Wanderers, 'cheated'. From that day to this, I have hated Bolton (and Nat

Three in a Row

Lofthouse in particular) with a passion unreserved for any other team, to the point where, when Lofthouse walked out on the pitch on Feb 6th a couple of seasons ago, I was almost physically sick. Needless to say, I have enjoyed their demise immensely and have always believed that their fall from the big time was payback time for cheating us out of the trophy that was rightfully ours.

As to City, well it took rather longer to begin to feel anything very much for the club across town. I remember disliking them in the 60s, simply because they were better than us (as you do!) but it was the development of the Munich chants and jokes and particularly their increasing use of the term 'Munichs' to describe us that flipped that dislike over into hatred. To watch Liverpool or Leeds or Bolton fans doing aeroplane impressions is one thing, to see Manchester people doing it is another thing entirely. It twists a knife in my guts every time I hear Munich chants in a Manchester accent — even sometimes in a Salford accent these days — although they tend to make sure there are no Salford lads about before being brave enough to do it! For me, it's much much worse to have these sick chants coming from those who shared in the tragedy, from those who should know better. And over the last few years it has just got worse and worse. Whereas I was prepared to accept that it was a minority (if a large one) a few years ago — this is no longer true. This sickness infects the whole of Manchester City FC from top to bottom. The recent use of the word 'Munichs' in their programme illustrated that. I don't believe for a second that it was an oversight, what I do believe is that the term is now so much part of the Bitter psyche that it was seen but not 'noticed'. As I have said many times before, until

Prized assets

Manchester City stop mocking a Manchester tragedy I will continue to hope fervently for their demise, along with Bolton Wanderers.

I suppose I should now don my fireproof suit! After all, my credentials as a 'real' United fan have probably been dealt a severe blow now I've admitted to not putting the Scousers at the top of hate list! I'll join in with the abuse of course, and thoroughly enjoy it, but I don't really feel it down in my guts the way I do for Bolton or City. Since I was (am) both a woman and a coward, I never became involved in the fighting that was going on off the pitch in the 70s and 80s, so that intense and very personal rivalry was never part of my life. What I do remember about that time is hating them all — not just the 'lads' of Liverpool, but the 'lads' of Manchester too. They were all much the same to me — violent and nasty and responsible for spoiling football for me. They'd taken somewhere I felt safe and accepted — I don't remember ever feeling unsafe in the packed crowds of the 60s — into somewhere I could no longer go, without risking being hurt. And I still feel that same distaste today, for those who are trying to drag football back into the dark ages. I've little time for those who take their footballing rivalries into their real lives, and drag the rest of us into the shit with them.

March madness

Reds are here, Reds are there...

Panathinaikos 1 Manchester United 1
European Champions' Cup
Wednesday 7 March 2001

My first Euro away — away. I mean really away — as
in New York!

When we booked this trip to New York a few
months previously I had been pretty sure it would
coincide with one game or another so it was always
in my mind that I would take a trip down to Greenwich
Village and Nevada Smiths to check out the
atmosphere. And I wasn't disappointed.

Before we left home on the Tuesday morning it
was even doubtful that we would be allowed to fly into
New Jersey as a snowstorm of monstrous
proportions had hit that part of the Eastern seaboard.
It had prevented all flights on the Monday, but as far
as air traffic control were concerned there was no
way ours would be stopped! As we sat in the plane
ready for take-off, it was with a great deal of
apprehension that I looked out of the window at the
wing which was having a thick layer of ice cleared
from it. This brought back vivid memories from 1957

March madness

when members of the United party cleared ice from the wings of their plane before take-off from Bilbao. These memories were not good, bearing in mind what happened only a year later in the snow at Munich.

In actual fact, despite my unnerving recollections, the flight was fine and so too was our landing at Newark, even if we did arrive in a blinding snowstorm. Once down on the ground I didn't see one other plane land and none were leaving — all grounded! Nonetheless we had arrived and were safe.

A mere 24 hours later, after adjusting to the time difference by fending off any thoughts of sleep until late the previous night, I was negotiating the subway system and making my way down to Nevada Smiths on 11th Street and 3rd Ave. to meet up with Paul Gallen. We'd briefly met at Barcelona in the haze of the Hard Rock Café, so there was at least a modicum of recognition as I paid my ten dollar admission fee and wandered into the darkened bar. I had pre-warned him that when he saw a tall bald-headed person walk in at around 2.30 that afternoon, it was more than likely me, unless there was a preponderance of tall, bald-headed Reds in the City that is! Seamus was also over at the time, but unfortunately had been pre-booked into a meeting somewhere else, which was a great pity.

You may think Nevada Smiths is a typical American bar, and to some extent perhaps it is, but this is also home to the New York Reds and behind the bar is festooned with United flags and memorabilia. The bar itself is littered with TV screens of all sizes so that no matter how full, you would always be able to see uninterrupted coverage of the

Three in a Row

game. The place is packed out with devoted followers of the United cause and for every game featuring the lads Nevada Smiths is full to bursting with the faithful. And a more disparate bunch you couldn't wish to meet. We were amongst the Irish of course, but nearby was a Mets fan in full regalia, a local with one of the biggest beards ever seen and wearing an old 1970s bar scarf, and a giant, Giants fan sitting by the bar!

I took delivery of my first pint as the game kicked off. After ten minutes Paul's mate Aaron wandered in late because he'd presumed the match was starting at 3pm not 2.45! Throughout the game, people were arriving depending on what time they could steal themselves away from work. Odd people put their heads through the door, took one look, heard the clamour of far-flung Reds and beat a hasty retreat, but not many — most came in.

The game was far from being a classic and if Barthez hadn't been in such fine form we would have been far worse off than the 1-0 half-time scoreline. Nevertheless optimism abounded as we found solace in a pint of Guinness and awaited the second half.

More of the same followed — not Guinness — well, maybe some! The Greeks piled on the pressure and United couldn't get a grip. As the game wore on, the mood in the bar became more and more tense. No-one left. No-one moved, not even to the bar. Everyone was transfixed by the TV screens. Sporadic singing broke out, but as United started to get more involved, chances came and went at both ends as the bar became more animated and expectant. There may have been doubters, but I wasn't aware of any. Even when the game went into injury time no-one

March madness

wavered.

Another Guinness had appeared, courtesy of Aaron, and as I stood (we weren't at OT remember) nervously clutching the glass I found myself nearly drinking it, putting it down, nearly drinking again, but then having to put it down again as another attack formed. Luckily for me, and those in close proximity, I wasn't clutching that pint when it happened! As Scholesy's shot hit the back of the Panathinaikos net all hell broke loose. There was bedlam. The noise was deafening and the resultant celebrations a little more than enthusiastic! The whole place erupted in an instant. If there had been another goal, and it was a distinct possibility, I can't imagine what the scenes would have been like or whether any of us would have survived them!

As the game ended and the tension lifted the camaraderie in that bar was as evident as it is on the streets of Salford. It makes no difference where you are, or who you are — a Red is a Red is a Red. As the inhabitants spilled out into the sunlight of another Greenwich Village afternoon, the locals must have taken a second glance or three, or maybe they are used to seeing United gear on the streets. The post-match mood was upbeat! The pints were downed in record time and I was introduced to Happy Jack (star of the silver screen) and was given my honourary Nevada Smiths shirt.

This place is a must visit for any travelling Red in New York City. There is one proviso however — if you drink too much Guinness you may have difficulty working out exactly which subway train goes where. It's difficult enough when you haven't had a drink but nigh on impossible when you have consumed the odd one or two. Still, I eventually reached our hotel (more by luck than judgement it has to be said) and found a very patient Karen and Gina waiting for me!

In the days between the two European matches, a row blew up which was to rumble away for the rest of the season. United fans were warned by Trafford Borough Council that they must remain seated during matches or else risk parts of Old Trafford being closed. After observing fans standing at the Valencia game in February, the Council had informed the club that if persistent standing continued at the coming Champions League game against Sturm Graz, some areas of the stadium would be closed for at least one game. Sir Alex Ferguson supported the fans' wish for a return to safe terraces but told United fans to sit down for the time being, rather than risk stand closure.

To stand or not to stand?

Manchester United 3 Sturm Graz 0
Champions' League
Tuesday 13 March 2001

To stand or not to stand? That is the question. Whether stands should be for standing, or sitting is another. Whether you should allow a bunch of thugs to manhandle supporters is another. And I thought that the PLC were turning the corner and that they were interested in fostering good relations with those of us who actually want to support the team in the time-honoured way. After the events of last night, it seems I may have been sadly mistaken.

We were told to sit down — a plea by the manager, a threat by Trafford Borough Council and a

March madness

schoolmasterish instruction by Ken Merrett. A 'prohibition order' would be issued if we failed to comply and this would take effect in 21 days and cause the closure of certain parts of the ground. The identified areas were: West Stand second tier, West Stand lower, East Stand lower and the East Stand first tier, which used to be known as the K Stand. Still is known as K Stand as far as I'm concerned! As uncle Ken said, "That's where the vociferous support traditionally comes from." Of course it has to be remembered that there used to be a great deal more of this 'vociferous support' in the lower section of the Scoreboard End before the club extended the disabled section into it, but that's another matter, or is it? So, with all this in mind, the Sausageman and I set off for Manchester.

How I managed to survive the journey back and forth with him in the car I'll never know. But despite a couple of fairly severe braking incidents, the air inside the car remained relatively pure and we arrived in Manchester with enough time to pay a visit to Walsh towers and even the offie by Macari's, where we were greeted by a very businesslike Mr Brisco. The last time I'd seen black leather gloves like that, they were being worn by the air hostesses on our flight to Barcelona. Draw your own conclusions!

As we were about to leave for the ground, a very happy Austrian fell all over us. So tanked up on Boddies, he was more concerned that we beat Bayern Munich, who he professed to hate, than his own team beat us. In fact he predicted we'd win 4-0 in the coming game, which was nearer the mark than anyone else. His mate, who was wearing more United gear than the collective throngs hanging around the chippy, was less forthcoming, offering

Three in a Row

nothing more than one of those burbling smiles which tells you he is incapable of any sort of speech due to an extreme excess of alcohol consumption. They staggered their way down to the ground as I veered off to check on whether Barney was confident or not. He was, which is always slightly worrying. Fortunately a distraction arrived — an encounter very reminiscent to the Austrian. It was Jonah, who was incapable (of predicting anything)!

Down at the ground I met up with Eliza and enquired as to why she hadn't responded to my earlier phone message, but apparently it might have helped if I'd sent it to the correct number — whoops! We filter past the bunch of stewards checking tickets, and enter through our usual turnstile. I pass by our steward, who was keeping his mouth tightly shut as per our non-prediction agreement and we climb to our seats where we find notices stuck on the back of every one imploring us to remain seated during the game. And so at the start it was a strange sight seeing the whole of K stand and beyond, all sitting. It lasted all of two minutes, as United were straight on the attack with the Graz keeper somehow managing to claw back a Solskjaer header as he was falling backwards over the line.

United had signalled intent and attacked en masse and within a couple of minutes were one up. The build-up was messy, but the goal was not. The ball had seemed to be on elastic pinging around between Solskjaer, Chadwick and Keane on the edge of the area. Suddenly it was released and found its way out to Nicky Butt. With the whole of the disabled section ready to duck, he fooled the lot of them by bending his shot low and hard past Sidorczuk. The celebrations were protracted and some over in J

March madness

Stand forgot to sit back down.

Problems erupted soon after as a number of SPS muscled their way in. It seemed as though the objections had emanated from one of the exec boxes and the offenders were found and wrestled from their places. The whole of J Stand were on their feet quickly, followed by K Stand and the Scoreboard. The game was secondary to the action over to our left. The actions of SPS were typical. Over-zealous would be a more than sympathetic way of putting it. Pig ignorant may be nearer the truth. They were fortunate that the reaction of the crowd (and it was extremely aggressive) did not escalate and become out of control. "You're just a bunch of wankers" was spat out with venomous hatred. Reminiscent of the Arsenal game a few seasons ago, when this problem erupted for the first time. A chorus of "Stand up for the Champions" echoed around the ground and was repeated over and over. SPS eventually retreated. A strategic withdrawal perhaps? We weren't sure how such outrageous reaction could suddenly have been turned to discretionary behaviour, but concluded that the aggression directed towards them had swayed those in command, and an air of relative calm descended — but not for long.

Fortunately this happened in the nick of time, as we turned back to face the pitch. We were about to celebrate the second goal. Butt was again involved, winning the ball from a defender who was only too willing to give it up as soon as he realised Nicky was snarling over his shoulder and snapping at his heels. He slipped it through to Ole, who cut it back to Sheringham, who then beat the keeper with a low shot to his right. Two up in less than 20 minutes and both had been scored at our end. The game was all

Three in a Row

but over. There was no way Graz were going to recover. It was only a surprise United didn't go further ahead. In fact if it wasn't for Sidorczuk in the Graz goal, they would have done. He pulled off a couple of superb saves from Ole and Scholes to keep the score down to a more flattering level.

Meanwhile, events were taking a turn for the worse up in J Stand where the problems erupted once more, but this time in a far more serious manner. A line of SPS trooped up the aisle, followed by a line of coppers. They stretched from top to bottom — an overreaction of immense proportions. An SPS official appeared in one of the exec boxes and directed his men toward their targets. Everyone stood again and the same cry of "You're just a bunch of wankers" was spat out with even more rebelliousness than before. It made no difference. The gorillas moved in and dragged their prey from their positions. I saw at least three ejected, but apparently there may have been two more. They were pushed and shoved down the stairs and below. You got the impression that it was a disaster waiting to happen and one way or another SPS were going to single someone out (and the more the merrier as far as they were concerned) and make an example out of them. If the whole situation had been managed differently (in other words sensibly) there would have been no problem.

The behaviour of SPS could have caused mayhem. Ken Merrett had said, "We could try and take action against those who persistently stand but from past experience, that's self-defeating. We rule by consent of the majority and if they see fellow supporters being ejected at the behest of the local authority, it may escalate the problem into other

March madness

areas." So who took the decision to send these gorillas in then? And if it was solely the decision of SPS, then surely their contract should be withdrawn with immediate effect. Now Trafford Metropolitan Borough Council have lifted their threat to close parts of the ground as they say we showed a responsible attitude. More's the pity SPS didn't. The whole thing is a mockery.

The half ended with the whole of J, K and the Scoreboard, in an attempt to restore the evening to a more affable occasion, chanting "Fergie sit down, Fergie sit down." When he did, he got a round of applause. We didn't go below stairs straight away, we waited a few minutes while I was distracted by the chocolate fudge cake Eliza gave me and by one of our oldest supporters who was doing the half-time draw. Alice is 97 years old and a lovely lady who I have had the pleasure of standing next to at Coventry a couple of years ago. When we finally went downstairs we were astonished at what we saw. A long line of police were marching through the back of the East section. This line was so long, you couldn't see the beginning or the end. The reaction of everyone was antagonistic. The reaction of one Red was extreme. He walked in amongst them Goose-stepping and doing the Hitler salute. The copper directly behind him was least amused as he possessed a moustache not too dissimilar to the aforementioned dictator, but the Red was somehow allowed to get away with it.

The second half was more or less a non-event apart the last few minutes. The two in front of us, who usually bring bottles of Coke to Euro games, had broken with tradition and brought orange juice instead, but it had the same effect. They had also

Three in a Row

brought horns and blew them at every available opportunity until they became incapable of any co-ordinative action! On the pitch the second half started as the first had finished, with their keeper making an excellent save, this time from Stam. In front of us the only thing to keep us entertained, apart from our friends becoming less and less capable, was Barthez. If anyone was born to be Red, he was. His skill on the ball is just incredible for a goalkeeper.

Down at the Stretford, after that initial flourish, the action didn't pick up until near the end, when Scholesy smashed a 25 yarder goalwards which Sidorczuk acrobatically tipped away for a corner. The third goal came shortly afterwards. The move stretched from one end of the pitch to the other and was started when Silvestre brilliantly intercepted the ball on the edge of his own area. He passed up the line to Chadwick who slipped the ball one side of an embarrassed and static defender, ran round the other and took the ball forward to the edge of the Graz box where he gave it to Ole. This was flicked on to Keane who passed it between the keeper's legs and into the net. A superb move, celebrated accordingly. I made my way down to the stairs where I stood for the last minute chatting to a delighted steward, who swore his predicting days were definitely over.

Feelings after the game were mixed. We were through to the next round in second place in the group on goal difference, but that was not the issue — the action of SPS was. Sad to say, it dominated all discussion and overshadowed the evening — when will they ever learn?

After the joy of the win against Sturm Graz, fears were mounting for the health of one of United's favourite sons, as George Best pulled out of a charity dinner due to liver problems. A couple of days later, feelings amongst United fans were mixed when the draw for the quarter-finals of the Champions' League pitted United against Bayern Munich again.

The lucky charm leaves it late

Manchester United 2 Leicester City 0
Premier League 17 March 2001

Whichever way you look at it, sometimes fate takes a hand, and however it came about, the fact that this was Denis Irwin's 500th appearance for United and it was also St Patrick's Day, no-one could have planned it any better. Denis was rewarded with the captaincy for the day, and no one would have begrudged him that honour. A superb player for Manchester United he's hardly put a foot wrong in the nine years he has been with us. He has to be one of the bargain buys of all time — and perhaps somewhat of a lucky charm considering the honours he has won.

Another lucky charm was also with us for this game. Fortunately the ticket office had looked kindly on our application as it is Gina's birthday weekend. But there was one point late on in the second half when she tugged at my sleeve and said she thought her luck may have run out. "I may have lost it," she said. I told her never to believe she has lost it and that we should never believe we have no chance of winning a game until the final whistle blows. "As long as there are a couple of seconds left, there is time to score." By the end of the game, it was a totally different story of course!

It was 6am and I couldn't fathom out why I should

Three in a Row

be awake. I looked out of the window and was doubly disappointed. Not only was I up and about at this unearthly hour for no reason, but there was also a driving snowstorm raging outside and a fair amount of the stuff had already settled on the ground. I closed the blinds and decided not to look again until a reasonable hour had dawned. By the time I opened them for the second time the storm had past and all traces of the snow had disappeared. The weather was still crap but it was at least an improvement on what had been happening earlier.

I instructed Gina to make sure she had several layers of clothing handy and we set off earlier than usual in order to meet up with Eliza, Steve and John for a pre-match pint in Arbuckles. On the way we picked up big Rich and later on, the doctor, who was christened 'Doctor Doom' by Rich as he was in one of his harbinger moods — although I was disregarding his pessimism as Gina had already informed me that we would win, and that was good enough for me.

After a brief stop at Knutsford services to check out a certain Ms Wainthrop (who wasn't there) we were ensconced in Arbuckles just after 1.30 with plenty of time to spare. Where that time went I don't know. Where the others went I don't know, because as Gina, Eliza and I arrived at the ground there was only a minute to spare. And as Gina and I took our seats down at the front of South stand by the old Stretford Paddock and the corner flag, the teams were out, Denis had already been presented with his 500th appearance memento, and they were about to kick off.

We were glad of the extra clothing too, as it was as bitter down there as it is on the Kippax. The action on the pitch did nothing much to change our attack of

March madness

the Arctics either. All down the other end, we were continually straining to see what was going on and Leicester were playing twenty-four in defence. They did nothing to contribute to the game as a spectacle, and neither did their fans. If this is how they play away from home, then I have no idea why so many of them bothered to turn up. They were dire, and so were the fans — "Paulo di Canio" — make an effort next time will ya?

Down at our end, the Tier Two Commandos were in fine voice. If only the club would see their way to giving us back the whole of the Stretford End, the atmosphere would be superb. Credit to Tier Two though, for an excellent performance which just went on and on. The only noise that emanated from our section, apart from the usual bellowing from yours truly, was the sound of horns. Two kids in front of us were making the most of their new toys and their mother had rather inventively found a method of changing both the intensity of volume and the pitch of each so they sounded reasonably harmonious when blown together. Clever that!

So, down in the over-exposed wasteland by the corner flag we shivered our way through the first half. Good job we'd had a hearty breakfast, and probably a good job Gina had also devoured a huge bag of crisps and a giant hotdog too — or that's what she had me believe. The action was all down at the Scoreboard. Keano went very close, Ole did too (twice). Even Nev shot powerfully only to see the ball nestle in an unfortunate defender's exposed crisp packet to collective male gasps of "oooh, nasty". Tier Two stood up for the Champions, the lower part of the Stretford followed (not the execs of course) and even some of our section, which was full of St Patrick's day celebrators who'd already partaken of a few more pints of the black stuff than perhaps was good for them.

The first half finished with Ole again going close, but we had to be content with 0-0 and look forward to the change of direction when we returned from the break. It struck me, as we went below stairs, how different this part of the ground is. The SPS presence is so low-key as to be practically non-existent. These guardians of Old Trafford security (eh?) down there are naught but youngsters in massive jackets who would have difficulty recognising any trouble, let alone reacting to it. We were in the sedate part of the ground alright, but both of us prefer a little more attitude rather than this form of soporific civilisation.

We were back up top for the start of the second half just as Yorkie came ball juggling his way down the touchline. It was a sight to warm our hearts. And as the game recommenced, the atmosphere became more intense. At least we could see what was going on and felt more a part of it too. In the first minute Ole had a decent shot saved and in the next, one just over the bar. The noise level was cranked up a few more decibels and we felt as though there was a game on at last.

With 25 minutes to go Nicky Butt was pulled off, Sorry, taken off, and Chadders came on which gave us some width on the right. But it was Denis who put over a peach of a cross from that wing which Yorkie should have buried, but headed just over instead. United had stepped up a gear and things were beginning to look a great deal better from where we sat. Or at least that's what I thought. Gina thought different. She takes her assumed position as lucky charm very seriously and was professing doubt, but

March madness

as has been said before, the doubt was dismissed and the lucky charmness returned. It was just a little later arriving than we had anticipated!

With ten minutes left, Silvestre came on for Phil Neville and the mood changed again. With a mere three minutes left and the Leicester fans getting far too chirpy for their own good while singing "Cheerio, cheerio, cheerio", as a few of the less hardy OT-ites left before time, Ole found space 25 yards out and let fly towards the Stretford goal. The ball glanced off Yorke and slipped past the keeper's grasp. We were on our feet in a microsecond and a little girl, beaming all over her face, flung herself in my direction.

Just like waiting for a bus, you spend hours in the biting cold and then two of the buggers come along at once as a minute later there was another breakthrough. This time Mikael Silvestre went on one of his runs down the left flank, cut inside his man and fired from the edge of the penalty area. The keeper was covering the near post — the ball nestled inside the far post. The look on Silvestre's face, as he turned towards us, was one of disbelief and delight at one and the same time. I couldn't think of anyone (apart from our acting captain) who deserved it more.

Seconds later the referee blew for time. It only took a couple of minutes to grab all three points, but when the opposition come with the boring intention of settling for just the one, their negativity deserved nothing less and it was fitting that United should wait until the very last minute to seal their fate. The ground rose to its feet and an emotional chorus echoed around Old Trafford: "We'll never die, we'll never die, we'll never die, we'll never die — we'll keep the Red Flag flying high, 'cos Man United will never die."

During the run-up to our annual visit to

Three in a Row

Merseydive, Fergie made what must be one of his most controversial signings by bringing in Andy Goram on loan, to cover a short-term goalkeeper crisis. According to rumour, we had also been busy signing up just about every decent player in Europe. On the international scene, Becks won over the Scousers to inspire England to a 2-1 victory over Finland at Anfield. Those of us watching were treated to the surreal sound of Anfield echoing to "There's only one David Beckham" coming from the Kop!

A rather more pleasant experience was hearing the news that the player the scousers had christened the 'evil pixie', Ole Gunnar Solskjaer, had stated his intention to remain at United for the remainder of his career. "My dream is to finish my career with Manchester United, I don't want to play for other clubs. Money is not important, my love for United is greater than my need for more money," he said.

It's definitely NOT Christmas

Liverpool 2 Manchester United 0
Premier League Saturday 31 March 2001

The news of David Rocastle's death brought everything into perspective. But for me, things were already in perspective after the recent departure of someone who had been a special part of my life. I hadn't been sure whether to go to Anfield at all, but in the end I decided to. And I am still not sure why. I suppose I was searching for a link with normality. Not that I would necessarily associate a trip to that place with normality. It was, however, a chance to be amongst friends and away from stark reality — a chance to push recent events to the back of my mind for a few hours. And to some extent it worked, but for the majority of the time I was really only half there. Had the game been more positive from the United point of view it would have been a more fulfilling experience, but I'm afraid it wasn't.

After a late night, Linda was making ready for another early start:

I was later to bed than I had planned on Friday night, due to a late-night phonecall from a drunken Mad Dane who proceeded to introduce me to all his new Norwegian friends, including (he claimed!) Henning Berg's brother! So I was pretty knackered when I dragged myself out of bed at the unearthly hour of 6.30am. This was becoming a habit! No-one would believe that I only live 15 miles from OT where I was due to catch the coach at 10am, but due to Railtrack sabotaging the Stockport line at weekends, and North West Trains' inability to provide a reliable service via our other station, I decided that to be on the safe side I had to travel into Manchester by bus — a journey that normally takes well over an hour. So I set off from home just after 7am. I don't know what it's called, but there is a law that says that if you're in a hurry, the buses will be full of little old ladies with shopping trollies, taking forever to get on and off the bus making you even later. On the other hand, if you are early and wanting to waste a bit of time the opposite happens.

At 8.10am I was getting off the 192 in Piccadilly, with an hour-and-a-half to spare before I had to be at OT! So there was nothing else to do but sacrifice myself to breakfast in McDonalds. I eventually arrived at OT about 9.30am and by 10am we were on our way to Merseydive. Nothing much happened on the

Three in a Row

journey — our passage through the crumbling tower blocks of Croxteth being enlivened only by the site of spanking new purple wheelie bins outside all the houses — no doubt to match with all the old shell suits!

Arriving in Liverpool is such a non-event these days that even the local scallies don't bother to come out and welcome us anymore. As the son-and-heir said, wandering across Stanley Park just before 11am, "I wouldn't have done this ten years ago!" There are some who look back with nostalgia on this particular aspect of the 'good old days', but personally I prefer a leisurely stroll across the park in safety. So we arrived by the Shankly Gates amidst the Scousers as they met up with their tour guides to get their tickets and compare the contents of their bright red superstore bags.

At the away turnstiles, security was strict (not!). After perusing our tickets so closely that he practically wiped his nose on them, the son-and-heir had every bit of his person touched up by a fat Scouse copper who then just waved me through without so much as a glance. Gradually, the usual suspects gathered on the concourse (if you can call that dark, dismal cave a concourse!), before we went to find our 'restricted view' seats up at the back in the Anfield Road stand. Not quite right at the back though, in the rows behind us were the Leamington Skinhead and the two leading lights in IMUSA, now known as 'rug and flask' due to their suspected sympathies for the prawn butty brigade!

Before the game we listened to the PA announcer wishing happy birthday to Tor from Norway on his first visit to Anfield, Tommo from South Wales and Peregrine from Surrey. "Spot the Scouser on the

March madness

Kop?" we sang later. Once we had managed to survive the onslaught to our ears that was Gerry and the Pacemakers, we were then treated to the ludicrous sight of the Liverpool team standing in a circle in the centre of the pitch doing their Americanised huddle. That was the last time we laughed at the Liverpool team for the next couple of hours — even the obligatory chant of "Fowler takes it up the nose" was half-hearted as we watched them dominate the game. Pity we hadn't arrived late and missed the first half. I know there were two excellent goals, but when they ended up in the back of the United net it took the shine off them somewhat. United had hardly threatened and spirits were low.

We arrived at half-time relieved to have kept the score down to two and hoping that the Wizard would work his magic in the dressing room. Perhaps make a couple of changes to refresh the parts which weren't functioning properly, and that the lads would have come out and attacked our end with a vengeance. In fact it was a better half, and Yorkie did have a goal ruled out for a very debatable offside with half an hour to go. And you could see the relief on the hideously contorted Scouse faces as they taunted us for that. They knew — and so did we, that they would have been in grave danger of capitulating had that 'goal' been allowed to stand. Our spirits had improved when Murphy got the red card (not before time), and when Silvestre and Scholes came on we began to look like we could at least pull it back to a draw. But it wasn't to be and you have to give credit to a Liverpool side that deserved their win. "We've only got 10 men," they sang., "You've only got ten pence," we replied, and they couldn't resist rummaging in their pockets to thrust handfuls of change and notes in our direction

Three in a Row

(a dangerous thing to do with so many thieving Scousers around!). We sang it again and again and they did it again and again — sad bastards!

Finally, Poll blew on his whistle and we sang "Get to work you lazy twats" to an emptying Anfield. Ironically, the atmosphere after the final whistle was actually better than during the game itself as the Scousers celebrated and we taunted them by proclaiming ourselves "Champions" and making what was left of the hairs on the back of my neck stand up by singing the "Red Flag". Then it happened, and the sad thing is, I wasn't even surprised. It was as the new breed of Mickies were trooping out, with their bags overflowing with merchandise, that one of their number appeared wearing full Santa Claus regalia and offered up his nether regions for inspection. It was obviously Christmas for them — but not for us. A false reality symptomatic of their decline in recent years.

The atmosphere at Anfield is as poor as OT these days, but when the local urchins can't even be bothered to come out into the streets to take the mickey out of defeated Mancs, then something really has gone out of football forever. We were a quiet bunch heading back down the motorway, but as so often has happened in the past, Manchester City came to our rescue, to remind us that no matter how bad it gets for us, it is always much worse for them. As we listened to the sport on Five Live on the coach, we began to think that the day was going to get even worse — City one-nil up against Villa and playing well. But it only lasted a few minutes and by the time we arrived at OT, City were chasing a draw and struggling. I lost touch at that point as I headed into the centre of Manchester with the son-and-heir. An hour later, however, I turned on my radio on the train on the way home from Piccadilly to find the usual GMR phone-in in session. City had lost again, they needed a miracle to stop them going down and the fans were calling for the head of their manager on a baking tray. All was right with the world after all!

Revenge

Manchester United 0 Bayern Munich 1
Champions' League Tuesday 3rd April 2001

Two defeats on the trot. Crisis looms at the Theatre of Dreams. "Sell the lot of them — they're crap," say the delirious ABUs. Beckham, Giggs, the Nevilles (of course) Cole and Wes too. All apparently absolute rubbish!

Oh really?!

They came for revenge and, to a certain extent, they got it. But at that point it was only half-time. And as it has been pointed out before, and was also said that night, we were 1-0 down at full time too, and we all know what happened then.

It was later than usual when the good doctor finally arrived (not so fresh from work). Not that I would have been able to leave sooner anyway, so Lipstick had to be content with a seat in front of the TV for a while. We were only too well aware it meant we would encounter more traffic than normal as we approached the metropolis they call Birmingham, but even sitting in a traffic jam was preferable to what we had been going through during the previous few days. There was still plenty of time for us to reach our destination despite the predictions from the harbinger in the back who was constantly working out new routes (just in case). And of course we did get there in time and as we walked past Sir Matt's statue, the haunting strains of Freddie's "Barcelona" caressed our eardrums and sent us drifting back to that never to be forgotten night.

Nostalgia was in the air, but those of us who are slightly longer in the tooth, and this includes a certain ex-chair of IMUSA (and his party trick of taking said tooth out) knew that our destiny that night was hardly likely to be so dramatic. It was time for realism.

As I climbed up to my spot, Iggy Pop's "Lust for Life" blasted out over the PA. Had Boylie infiltrated DJ Keegan's booth then? And if he hadn't — then how did that happen? High up in K Stand a portentous banner greeted us. It was held aloft by the Bayern fans in defiance of a hellish night for them, but heaven on earth for us. A dramatic statement which, by the end of the night, had a resonance that hit home rather harder than we'd hoped. "The Revenge is Ours," it stated.

The atmosphere was just like a real European night as we stood in K Stand and sang, "2-1 in your Cup Final" and "Who put the ball in the Germans' Net" over and over, and over again. It was too much for a small band of Munich fans at the front of their section. I never expected to see Munich fans giving us the aeroplane, but they did — if just the once. For the majority of the first half, United dominated as they kicked towards the Stretford End. Solskjaer looked the most likely, although Coley was making a nuisance of himself with Scholes prompting from midfield and Keano snapping and snarling as per usual. But there was no real penetration, and apart from the odd snap shot, Kahn had relatively little to

March madness

do. But there again, neither did Barthez. The two teams had cancelled each other out with United ahead on points.

At half-time we were all fairly relaxed about the outcome. The mood downstairs was upbeat — so much so that I nearly missed the start of the second half. United were attacking our end and everything felt fine. The two lads in front had used the half-time break to top up with their usual beverage and, as usual, amusing everyone within earshot. Their favourite song of the night was sung (at every opportunity) at Kahn in the Bayern goal: "Where were you when Solskjaer scored?" Perhaps in the cold light of day they could have realised the absurdity of that song — but somehow I doubt it! Maybe I'm missing something, but didn't the fact that Kahn was the keeper on that famous night make the answer so obvious that the question was irrelevant? Obviously not to them! And they found it hard to believe that no-one joined in! Mind you, on European nights, they are practically worth the admission price alone!

What with them and the fella behind who referred to Kahn as a 'tart', it probably meant his celebrations were that much sweeter when Bayern substitute Sergio scored with five minutes left on the clock. It could have been far worse had Zickler not missed an absolute sitter right at the end.

The trouble was we didn't seem to have the guile to break the Germans down. Their defence was so well-disciplined and so attentive. The United forwards had nowhere to go and unfortunately lacked the invention to alter the course of a game which, as the half progressed, was being dominated more and more by Bayern. Whenever United attacked, it seemed to break down around the edge of the penalty area with about 20 Germans in the way. There was hardly a hint of a defence-splitting ball fed through to an attacker coming from deep. They just couldn't get close enough. Kahn hardly had anything to do. In fact Silvestre was our best attacker. And it was only his shots that forced the keeper to get his shorts dirty — if you see what I mean.

After the game the mood outside was sombre. It was drizzling. There was not one fanzine seller in sight as I left at the final whistle. But we still lived to fight another day. If they could beat us 1-0 we could do the same to them. And even as we drove south along the river which used to be the M6, there was defiance in the air — or was that the residue of another Roberts rasper. Come back Alan — all is forgiven!

The morning after the Munich game, Ryan Giggs cheered us up by becoming the latest United player to agree a new five-year contract from July 2001.

One down, two to go

Manchester United 2 Charlton Athletic 1
Premier League Tuesday 10th April 2001

It had been a warm, sunny day in Manchester as I sat chained to my computer and gazed longingly through the window towards OT. When I was finally allowed to run whooping down the stairs at the end of the day, I almost left my umbrella behind — after all, the weather men had said I wouldn't need it and the sun was shining brightly! I stopped off for a veggie burger on Oxford Road, and the clouds were gathering ominously. By the time the bus was sitting in the

March madness

usual traffic jam on Chester Road, the rain was pumping down like a City fan's tears on Derby Day, and I was very glad of the umbrella as I sloshed towards a sodden Barney on Sir Matt Busby Way. Thankfully, the rain had returned Barney to his usual mournful self and he was predicting a win against Charlton but a defeat against Coventry at the weekend. After the results of his recent more optimistic predictions, I was much relieved and left him looking a very sad figure indeed as I hurried into the relatively clement atmosphere of the Scoreboard.

Thanks to the return of Le Dieu for the evening, there was an edge of excitement amongst the faithful that would normally not be present for a match against Charlton. There was also an element of nervousness as we looked back at our poor performances over the last couple of weeks — the wheel hadn't really fallen off had it? We wouldn't let such a big lead slip — would we? To those of us with naturally pessimistic natures, at least where United is concerned, recent losses had left us just a little nervous and judging by the determination on the faces of both players and fans of Charlton Athletic, it had left other teams believing that they just might be able to get a result at Old Trafford after all! Thankfully, if the wheel had indeed been loose, it had been firmly re-attached to the wagon in the interim period, and it was business as usual.

But before the game started, there was one little duty that had to be performed and we had the rare sight of the whole stadium in place five minutes before kick-off! Once again we were able to raise our voices to salute the greatest United player of the modern era, as we welcomed Eric back to OT. "Ooh Aah, Cantona," we sang until we were hoarse. Even

Three in a Row

the Charlton fans were clapping — a strange sight at Old Trafford, away fans who actually manage to get over their bitterness long enough to appreciate a great footballer, even if he did happen to wear a United shirt. Sadly, Eric was soon heading up to the Directors' box and our chants were interrupted by that dear Mr Keegan assaulting our ears over the tannoy as he got all giddy announcing the teams. I thought this guy was supposed to be a real United fan? If he was, he would have waited respectfully until Eric was seated and until we had at least got to the end of the bloody chant!

So like good boys and girls, we seated ourselves and prepared to watch United run all over Charlton for the first 20 minutes. Unfortunately, none of the zillion chances presenting themselves in front of us ended up in the net! With the referee on their side, Charlton were living on luck, as United did everything except score! Recent events had obviously thoroughly pissed off Keano because he was everywhere — screaming at any United player who dared to pause long enough to get within earshot. When there was no-one to scream at, he harangued himself and glared at us, much to the amusement of those in the Scoreboard!

I had cheered up immensely. The rainstorm had abated, the lads were playing better than I had seen them in weeks and the atmosphere, thanks to the presence of Le Dieu, was rather better than it had been. Unfortunately, in our little bit of the Scoreboard, we were surrounded by muppets, with many of the usual faces missing. They sat in silence, apart from muttering about Dwight Yorke and missed chances. Up on the shelf, the Charlton fans were quiet as mice — they couldn't even stir themselves to boo Becks

March madness

when he warmed up in front of South Stand — he almost looked disappointed! After half an hour or so, Charlton began to lose their frightened rabbit expressions and started to play — when they weren't hacking down every United player in sight of course, and getting away with it! Johansson almost had two shots within two minutes, but an Irwin tackle and the bar came to our rescue as we breathed a big sigh of relief, grinning nervously at each other! We weren't grinning, of course, when the ref denied us two penalties. One was iffy, but the other was definitely a penalty. Just before half-time, however, we decided he was a nice chap after all. Yorke came steaming towards us from the other half of the pitch, he crossed to Cole whose shot was blocked but rebounded off our (now) friend in black. There was no way that Cole was going to pass up this second opportunity and he buried the ball in the back of the net to our delight. Up on the mantelpiece, the Charlton fans were deflated as we headed off cheerily to the back for our half-time break.

Back in our seats for the second half, the rain had ceased but the pitch was greasy and players were sliding and falling around all over the place. It didn't worry Giggs however, as he tricked his way around Mark Fish. But unfortunately, it wasn't Giggs, but his mate Fish who scored the next goal, right in front of us. Johansson drove the ball into the box and Nev scuffed his clearance. It fell to Fish, who put it past Barthez from close range and the Charlton fans went ballistic. This was the first time they had uttered a sound since we had scored, so we were a mite peeved when they started singing "Shall we sing a song for you?" which must be the most pathetic song of the season, sung by every no-mark fan who turns

Three in a Row

up at Old Trafford with a superiority complex! "Shall we win a cup for you?" we replied, with bored yawns. Twits!

Thankfully, we didn't have to wait long until it was "2-1, in your Cup Final". They were already looking nervous when Ole was seen stripping off his sweatshirt by the touchline and, true to form, it was he who turned in an Irwin cross to put us back in the lead. While we were celebrating, Ilic must have stretched clingfilm across the mouth of his goal because until the end of the game, we did everything but score! The ball came off the bar and off the post. From our end, all we could see was the ball heading for a certain goal, only for it to twang back across the penalty area, or be lobbed into the air!

There was never any feeling that they were likely to equalise again and we were cheerfully singing about our blue friends down the road when Irwin went down and stayed ominously still. The sight of Gary Nev anxiously calling for a stretcher was worrying and Denis was eventually carried off to a standing ovation as Old Trafford sang "There's only one Denis Irwin". The last minutes of the game were spent singing Eric songs, looking forward to Derby Day and laughing at our friends up in the corner who were singing "You've only got 12 men!" Funny how a game can look so different to fans on opposing sides, isn't it?

As we left the stadium, the rain had returned, but no-one was feeling too miserable. One down, two to go — and the third one is the big one!

The portents were not good in the run-up to the vital Champions' League quarter-final game in Munich, with seeming discontent both off and on the pitch. Roy Keane told journalists that he feared

March madness

Manchester United are in danger of being left behind by Real Madrid. He maintained that "heads will roll" at Old Trafford if United crash out of the Champions' League.

On the domestic front the news was brighter, with United moving to within two wins of clinching their seventh Premiership title in nine years, after the win against Charlton. Keane, however, obviously believes that domestic success alone is no longer enough to satisfy supporters and coaches.

Off the pitch, the standing issue was raising its head again, with Trafford Borough Council confirming they would indeed close areas of Old Trafford, specifically the so-called 'fan zone' in the second tier of the Stretty, should United progress in the Champions' League. Not surprisingly, fans reacted angrily to the news, with IMUSA claiming the council was not attacking the real problems.

Seventh Heaven

Three in a row — Champions again

Manchester United 4 Coventry 2
Premier League Saturday 14 April 2001

As we were driving home listening to the radio, the scores started to trickle through from the games that were kicking off at the regular Saturday afternoon time of three o'clock. Arsenal one down. City one up. Then, before we could get over the first salvo, Arsenal went two down and we felt almost let down. Then Leicester pulled a goal back against City and the mood changed. Perhaps there would also be a revival down at Highbury and the Arse would put up a fight — order would be restored. But nothing of the sort happened. Leicester couldn't manage it, and so our dreams of winning the title against Manchester City, while condemning them to relegation, were dashed! We were already Champions by tea-time after our game had finished three hours earlier.

We should have felt elated at the score from north London, but it was all a little anti-climactic if the truth be known. It would have been so much better had we been allowed to play our game against Coventry at the same time as everyone else, so that we could

Seventh Heaven

have all been together at Old Trafford and celebrated properly. Not that it has ultimately detracted from a fantastic achievement of course as this is the Wizard's 14th major honour, which makes him the most successful manager in English football. He has won more Championships than any other manager, and is the first to win three on the bounce. Not bad then?

But it wasn't how we expected the day to unfold as we set off for another early start. We were due to travel up in the Sausageman's fartmobile, but with three of us over six foot, it was deemed too small. So he and Salty piled into mine, and with big Rich also on board, we set off for an easy drive up the M6. I suppose this is the bonus of the earlier kick-off — a distinct lack of traffic. After a brief stop at Knutsford services and a close encounter with a small, but vocal group of green curly wig-wearing Bristolians, who resembled Scousers in reverse, we eventually arrived at OT with plenty of time to spare. As we reached Barney my phone went. It was Lipstick asking where I was. "With Barney," I replied. Then loud guffaws alerted me to the joke — me! And as I turned around there was Lipstick a mere three feet away and grinning all over his face! Bloody smartarse!

Back down at the ground, we had managed to negotiate our way past the rather manky pink rabbit who was accosting anyone who came near, and the usual line of SPS, but got stuck at the turnstiles. The fella in front apparently didn't realise he had to tear out the token from 'his' Season Ticket book and then had to be told to: "Push the bloody turnstile to get through!" If you're going to pass your Season Ticket on, make sure the daft sod knows what to do with it!

Three in a Row

Up top, seven lads carried around a 'Kick Racism Out Of Football' banner before the teams came out. But only one of the seven was black, and he had his head down and half-covered with a woolly hat! Couldn't they have made an effort to find a mix of lads more reflective of what they were advocating?

United kicked towards us in the first half and the game started at a pace, but despite most of the action working its way down to our goal, first blood went to the Sky Blues, and it woke their fans up. Coventrians are habitually apathetic, but after Hartson's first, their mood lifted and they actually thought they had a chance of staying up! "We ARE staying up — we are staying UP," they sang, but not for long! Less than two minutes later their old foe, who used to wear claret and blue, was on hand to drive a wedge through their optimism. Poor Cov — they were doing so well but by this time they were sitting back and suffering in silence as we celebrated. They had given the ball away in midfield and it had found its way to the feet of Yorke who flashed it past Kirkland, who went down like a sack of spuds — a 56lb sack of spuds! "You ARE going down — you are going DOWN!" was the predictable response.

But Coventry weren't about to lie down that easily and with another sack of spuds (but an even bigger one) in the United goal in the shape (and I use the word loosely) of Andy Goram looking decidedly unconvincing, they were in with a chance. Our main threat came from Giggs who, despite a verbal lashing from my next door neighbour Chris, was causing havoc down the United left. And it was from one of his mazy runs that Yorke benefitted when he scored our second.

Now the Cov fans feared the worst and sat back

while we celebrated yet again. But yet again Coventry, and Hartson especially, had different ideas. Johnson had just had a shot cleared away from the line for a throw-in when the Welshman came to their rescue when he caught Wes napping and headed in his, and Coventry's second. Had our newest (if temporary) recruit not been rooted to the spot, unable to lift his lardiness off the ground, he may have saved it, but he's no Barthez, that's for sure!

United were affronted and powered forward, urged by the continuous threats and steely glares from the captain. A long pass out of defence by Nev found Cole on the right. He sent over the perfect ball for his soulmate Yorkie who only had to tap it in at the far post and he would have been leaving with the match ball as a memento of his hat-trick, except he somehow contrived to miss an absolute sitter from two yards. A couple of minutes later, with Silvestre again rescuing the pudding in the United goal, he released the ball to Giggs on the edge of the United area and within seconds he was turning Quinn inside out and then doing it all over again. Telfer ran alongside but thought better of any Intervention, not wanting to suffer the same ignominious fate as his mate who had been left on his arse, flopping on the ground like a flounder — or floundering like a flopper — take your pick. Giggs finally played the perfect ball to the normally reliable Scholes in the area and he bolloxed it completely. It would have been a definite contender for goal of the season had it ended up where it should have done, but it didn't.

United were rampant and the half ended with Keane flashing a shot just over and turning to give young Wes a severe roasting! Only he knows for what, but that's the captain for you! The half-time

Three in a Row

whistle blew — the old fella two rows in front got out his packet of individual pork pies and I disappeared below to meet with the usual bunch of reprobates.

By the time I got back to my seat the game was already under way. The pudding, or as he came to be known, the 'Suet Duff', was between the sticks below us and to complete the picture, he had a pair of gloves on that looked reminiscent of those bloody stupid enormous foam hands people used to wave about in the 80s. Good job he didn't have much to do in the second half — until he had to pull those ridiculous gloves off to make way for Raimondo when he was substituted midway through. It was suggested that it was because he needed to get his bath over with early, as there would be no room for anyone else while he was in it, but I'm not sure that's entirely accurate!

Coventry didn't know what hit them after the break. But to be fair they very nearly survived. Attacking the Stretford End, Goram was left to his own devices and relaxed against the post. The only thing he had to do was to clear a Stam back pass. But instead of booting it clear, he picked it up. He took a chance which resulted in a Coventry free kick in the penalty area and as the Sky Blues shaped to take it, the United wall was all but on the goal line. What a bloody farce. Luckily for Goram, the ball smashed into the wall and rebounded to safety. It was then that we saw the welcome sight of Raimondo warming up.

With half an hour left, the Coventry defence were getting desperate. Giggs and Keane were running them ragged and both should have been awarded free kicks on the edge of the box, except ref Riley decided not to notice either offence. This angered both the team and the crowd and with songster Boyle

Seventh Heaven

at the helm, United cranked up the volume on and off the pitch. With twenty minutes to go, Becks came on for Nicky Butt. Great news for Cov — they get battered to death by Butty and when they are all but exhausted, who should come on but Beckham. It didn't stop the Sky Blue army to our left though. They were up again and singing their song "While we sing together, we will never lose". Well, either they don't sing it often enough or they are sadly deluding themselves, because it plainly isn't working.

Meanwhile, despite the uncharacteristic optimism of the Cov fans, their team's goal was getting a right battering with both Giggs and Cole getting ever closer. It was beginning to look as though they may hang on to the point when Ole started to warm up. That was just what they wanted to see. No sooner had he started to make his way down the steps to the pitch than he was making his way back again as a long cross-field ball from Nev found Giggs who leapt and headed the ball home from all of seventeen yards out. A superb, if astonishing goal from someone who'd threatened with his feet all afternoon and then scored with his head!

The Wizard sent Ole on anyway as a last minute partner for Yorkie and with "We'll win the Football League again and put Man City down" ringing around the ground, the Coventry fans sat resolved to their fate. But it wasn't over yet. What we couldn't understand, at the time, was that the lad in front had come over all jittery, and especially at the introduction of Solskjaer. It came to pass (seasonal reference alert) that he had placed a bet on the game at 350 to 1 that Hartson would score first and the result would be 3-2 to United. For all of five minutes he was in agony as United went close time after time. He was

Three in a Row

£350 the richer for such a short time!

I have never seen a true Red so distraught at a United goal, but when Scholes struck the fourth he was beside himself with despair. Meanwhile the rest of us were having a laugh at his expense. Well, in the end he'd only lost a pound after all. The goal was typical Scholes. Becks had found him 25 yards out and he hit a screamer which dipped and swerved past Kirkland just inside the post. And that was that — United were 16 points ahead and needing only a single victory to clinch the third Championship in a row. Well, they would have done if the Arse had beaten Middlesbrough as everyone had assumed they would.

So where were you when United won the League? After I arrived home, with the Arse already two down, I had been hoping for a revival but when I switched on the TV to get the results as full time approached I learned the Arse were 3-0 down and only a minute away from handing us the Title in rather pathetic fashion. At least I had a minute to savour the achievement then!

Bill Stevens from Winnipeg in Canada mailed me later that day and wrote: "Things are so different here — when I got out of bed just after 8.30 I was surprised to find that everything was white. It had snowed overnight and looked like Christmas outside. I checked my email and realized that the match was already over, and avoided looking at anything so I wouldn't know the score. The broadcast began at 9am here, and I was in total, blissful ignorance of the outcome. At half-time, the announcer said he was going to give the half-time score from the Arsenal match, even though it was going to be shown after the United match. He warned those who did not want to hear it to turn down the volume. I was overjoyed to hear Arsenal were down by two own goals at that point. After the United match, a little sign appeared at the bottom of the screen saying '2001 Champions'. What a great start to the day! April 14th and there I was looking out at the snow feeling as though Santa Claus had arrived. It was only 11am, and the Championship had been won."

After the Coventry game, club and fans slammed Sky over their decision to bring forward the kick-off time to noon, robbing them of a title-winning party, with the Old Trafford crowd already heading home when news of the shock result at Highbury began to filter through.

Standing and threats of closure

The debate, which began with the now infamous announcement at the Arsenal game some years ago, continues to rumble on. We watch with increasing frustration as, again, heavy handed tactics are used to solve what is, after all, a simple problem. Football fans want choice. We don't all want to stand, nor do we all want to sit, we just simply want to be able to choose. With the move to all-seater stadia, that element of choice was taken away from us. At the time it was probably the right thing to do, but with the years has come increasing evidence that it is not standing itself that is dangerous and also that the technology now exists to provide and police safe standing areas for those who wish to take advantage of them.

Of course there are those who will never believe that standing can be safe. They picture the heaving

Three in a Row

terraces of the past and they will never be convinced that it can be different. They equate standing with hooliganism and find it impossible to believe that football fans can stand and get behind the team, can be noisy and rowdy and boisterous, without wanting to beat the crap out of each other or the opposition. Minds like these are set, and debate is a waste of time. Thankfully, it seems that most fans are prepared to debate this issue and listen to sensible arguments.

Unfortunately, when we move beyond the fans then sensible debate goes out the window because those who have other agendas, whether political or financial, don't play fair. One recent example was the seeming ability of a government minister to read a report on safe standing in Germany and publicly come to completely the opposite conclusions as its authors, about the potential of English football grounds to have safe standing areas. It has become increasingly frustrating to listen to the arguments being put forward by those with the power in football, to hear them contradict themselves and sometimes just talk plain nonsense. I would respect them all the more if they would just come straight out and tell us what their real agenda is, because this whole issue certainly isn't about our safety!

We are told that areas of the West Stand tier two will be closed for the possible Euro semi-final game because standing in that area of the ground is 'unsafe'. More than that, persistent standing is seen by the Club and Trafford Borough Council as intrinsically unsafe. As someone who has attended football and rugby league matches, at all levels, for many years, I would argue with the view that persistent standing is, in itself, unsafe, provided that the conditions are controlled — i.e. areas where

Seventh Heaven

people stand are not overcrowded etc. Of course here we are talking about standing in an all-seater ground, but I still fail to see how standing in front of your seat is any more dangerous than jumping up and down when a goal is scored, standing for corners, standing to let the early leavers past or even standing to leave the ground at the end of the game — all activities which the club and council have said again and again, are okay. Indeed, the only accidents I have ever seen in an all-seater stadia have been when fans were celebrating a goal and when fans were leaving at the end of the game. I suppose we will be told not to jump up when we score next, but how are we to leave the ground without standing? Perhaps instead of a standing protest, we should have a sit-down protest. Once we are in our seats, we could perhaps refuse to stand up again, since it is obviously such a dangerous activity. After a couple of days it would get very messy and unpleasant I suppose, but it would get the point across wonderfully!

Trafford Borough Council seem, at the moment at least, to be concentrating on the second tier of West Stand. Ever since the Scoreboard Paddock became all-seater, fans have stood up in there on Euro nights. As a fan who has spent most of the nineties in this area of the ground, I can bear witness to the red-hot atmosphere of the big Euro evenings in the Scoreboard. Even when the Club was cracking down on standing at Premiership games, they left us alone at European games, presumably because they knew that the team needed the extra boost that the atmosphere gave them. I don't remember Trafford Borough Council raising the issue of safety during those years, presumably it wasn't considered a safety issue at the time. But you can't have it both ways — persistent standing can't be dangerous one minute and not dangerous the next! That defies logic. So something must have changed, to change their view.

One thing that has changed is that we now have standing in upper tiers, not just in the lower sections of the ground, and Trafford Borough Council are threatening to close the front section of East Stand tier two because (they say) it is unsafe to stand in those particular sections. What they seemingly fail to see is the total lack of logic in their position. If a stand is so steep that people put themselves in danger by standing up, then that stand is intrinsically unsafe and should not have a safety certificate at all. It has nothing to do with whether people persistently stand or not. If a stand is so steep that getting pushed from behind while standing in front of your seat could lead to you falling down on the punters below, then fans shouldn't be in there without further safety features being installed — barriers in front of each row, for example, as in the Nou Camp.

For one season my son and I had season tickets in the North Stand second tier and leaving the tier at the end of the game was a nightmare. As we came down the steep concrete steps, it was all too obvious that someone slipping behind us could cause a chain reaction that could see bodies hurtling over the barrier at the front, that was only at waist height. When the lights failed in North Stand a couple of seasons ago, some friends of ours who sit in the same row we used to (close to the back), were some of the last fans evacuated — it took one-and-a-half hours! Imagine how disastrous that could be, with a real emergency and a crowd of panicking fans! If

Seventh Heaven

Trafford Borough Council really care about the safety of football fans in Old Trafford, they should forget about the red herring of persistent standing and force Manchester United to sort out these real safety issues, perhaps by providing barriers in front of seats in the upper tiers and ensuring that a realistic and safe plan for the evacuation of these parts of the stadium is in place and is workable. If they can't or won't do so, then all these areas should be closed down until they do.

And if Trafford Borough Council honestly believe that fans persistently standing is unsafe, then why only choose a Euro game? Surely they should be closing the stand, or areas of the stand for all games, just in case fans stand? It is too late afterwards, when half of the second tier have landed in the laps of those in West Lower! But if they did that for Premiership games then MUplc might get sued by those whose seats are not available to them — for the Euro games that can't happen because these people can be accommodated elsewhere. I think the word I am searching for here is hypocrisy!

As someone who has grown cynical over the years about the motives of both the money men and politicians, I wonder just what is on the agenda here. A little more social engineering perhaps? It doesn't take a genius to chart the movement of the 'troublesome' fans from the Scoreboard up into the second tier of West Stand and now out of the stadium altogether. And recent developments re away allocations have led some to believe that United fans are being used to bring all fans to heel, that we are simply part of a Premier League/government campaign to complete the change from active supporter to gullible, megastore bag-carrying

Three in a Row

spectator. Or is it simply about money? About getting as many paying customers into the ground as possible?

Whatever the agenda, this closing of areas of the ground will not improve safety. The upper tiers will remain as unsafe as ever, but I suppose it will be safer to sit in the lower tier as you won't be as likely to have fat lads from the front rows landing in your lap! Indeed it could actually make the situation worse because it will harden attitudes and increase defiance in areas of the ground that are already, in themselves, unsafe. It will put fan against fan as those who don't stand, nonetheless find their seats 'closed' to them and blame those that do.

There is only one solution to this problem and that is the provision of choice to football fans through the introduction of safe standing areas. This can only be achieved if the fans, the Club and the Council work together to put pressure on the only people who have the power to make these decisions — the Government. This cannot happen until the Club and Council stop hiding behind the red herring of standing and take fans' safety and well-being seriously. Whether we get safe standing areas or not, the steep upper tiers of modern football stands must be made safe. I am convinced that if the fans who stand persistently believe that the Club and the Council are seriously behind them in the fight to get safe standing areas, and that if they feel that they were being treated with respect — listened to and taken account of, and their well-being promoted — rather than with hypocrisy and subterfuge, that this problem would evaporate.

Seventh Heaven

Back to the Future

Bayern Munich 2 Manchester United 1
Champions' League
Wednesday 18 April 2001

United take a step back and must now look to the future after another knockout at the quarter-final stage. There is no doubt in my mind that Fergie will use this defeat and build upon it in readiness for his final season in charge. Is our own miracle man destined to take his final bow as manager in Hampden Park at the end of next season while lifting Europe's major trophy? It may be the stuff of dreams at the moment, but it would be uppermost in the Wizard's mind.

The size of the task that faced United in the Olympic Stadium was immense. Not insurmountable, but daunting nevertheless. Bayern had lost only three times at home in European competition. Of course, United's own home record is not dissimilar and Bayern overcame that hurdle, so why not United in Munich?

Ultimately it wasn't to be, United defended badly in the first half and allowed Bayern to cruise into a 2-0 lead through goals from Elber and Mehmet Scholl. Scholl's came five minutes before the break and was the nail in United's coffin. Had they gone in with only the two-goal aggregate deficit I would have fancied their chances of pulling off a great victory but with Effin Stephanburg running the show in midfield it wasn't to be. In effect Giggs did pull a goal back and United could have taken several more, but they didn't and so lost 3-1 on aggregate.

Three in a Row

Just as in Barcelona the two sets of supporters mingled, only this time it was United congratulating Bayern. After the Final of '99, despite their trauma, the Munich fans behaved impeccably, and for that they will always have my respect.

After the game the speculation was not about who Fergie should buy and sell, it was concerning the mystery fan who appeared on the team photo. 'Fat neck' had run onto the pitch and stood alongside Cole at the end of the line and no-one did anything about it! He then ran off, donned a tracksuit and stood next to the photographers at the side of the pitch, sat back and awaited the publicity which duly followed.

The fallout from our exit from the Champions' League continued apace, with Sir Alex Ferguson blaming his defence for extinguishing his joy at winning the Premiership, Ryan Giggs claiming that winning the Champions' League in 1999 will mean nothing unless we do it again, and the seagulls bringing out every Keane quote they could dig up, completely out of context.

The day before the long-awaited Derby game, Teddy Sheringham was named Footballer of the Year by the Football Writers' Association. On the morning of the game, some rather less welcome news began to emerge, however, as fans attending a briefing at OT were told that ticket prices were to rise yet again — for some fans, by as much as ten percent.

Seventh Heaven

Fraternising with the enemy

Manchester United 1 Manchester City 1
Premier League Saturday 21 April 2001

It was a funny old day! Almost surreal in parts and nothing like any Derby Day I can remember. For a start, when I arrived at Old Trafford the tourists were out in their thousands. All around the forecourt, cameras were flashing and prawn sandwiches were being consumed by the bucket-load. Where there used to be tension and edginess and a clued-up crowd who knew exactly what the Derby was about, now there was the sound of first-timers complaining that they couldn't get into the toilets from the outside of the stadium, or the queues were too long in the Megastore. I even heard one fan asking another: "Just why is this game so important to the locals anyway?" The only thing that would tell an observer that this was a Derby game was the hundreds of police officers, in full riot gear, hanging around chatting and calculating their overtime.

I could only take it for so long and soon took myself off into the Scoreboard, where (for most of the time anyway) I could pretend that the new sanitised world of football had never happened! It was almost possible to believe that we were in a time warp as the sound of the Beswick Brass Band came over the tannoy! The conversation before the game was all about Wednesday night of course. Most fans seem to have calmed down a little and are now talking about adding to the squad rather than decimating it. Whatever our view on the reasons and reactions to our early exit from the Champions' League, we were

Three in a Row

all in agreement that our chances of beating Real Madrid in the semi-final had been slim anyway, and that we had to look forward to next year and a May night in Glasgow (doesn't have the same ring as Barcelona, does it — even if it is Fergie's home town!). Not that it would put us off going of course! Funnily enough, there was little talk of the coming game, with most Reds looking decidedly nervous!

The son-and-heir was late but managed to arrive, huffing and puffing from running down Trafford Road, just as we were heading for our seats.

Meanwhile, our other reporter was rueing another early start:

I don't think we will ever get used to these early kick-offs, despite the lack of motorway congestion. I'm not sure they suit United either judging by the football they served up, but at least it was another easy journey and as we parked up at the Throstles Nest we still had an hour to spare before the midday start. We headed for Chester Road for a quick can at the offie to a chorus of trouser trumpets from my two travelling companions. I'd have expected it from fart machine Dobson, but such unpleasant behaviour is not normally forthcoming from big Rich. Mind you, he was still very much the worse for wear after his midweek excesses in Munich. The only advantage to walking in between these two trumpeters was that when we got to the bottom of Seymour Grove even the waiting posse of likely lads parted to allow us through, having heard the warning blasts coming from quite a distance.

Once down at the offie we found, to our surprise, that they had run out of beer! At 11.15am the pavement was littered with an array of empty cans usually associated with much later in the day. Cider

Seventh Heaven

was still on offer, as were miniature spirits, but we all (apart from Duncan) declined. Phil from the Leamington branch came to our rescue and donated a can to the cause which we passed around our group of six! The atmosphere (possibly due to the emptying of the offie) was lively. Any passing Bitters were treated to a loud chorus of "25 years" and various expletives and friendly gestures wished them well on their journeys. After Steve and Eliza had joined us, just in time for the final slurp from the one and only can, we sauntered down to the ground. But where was Barney? Too many bratwurst perhaps?

High Noon at Old Trafford, and expectation filled the air, or maybe it would have done if it could have penetrated the ear-shattering wall of sound emanating from the PA as we arrived. The teams came out — and no guard of honour for the new Premiership Champions from the Bitters either — poor form that! At least we had a strong team out, and one which looked capable of mashing the Potato Heads into a pulp. On the downside, David Elleray was in charge of his first Premiership game at OT since 1997. So the man who has a nasty habit of showing red cards to United personnel (and to Roy Keane in particular — four in all) was back.

With Old Trafford fully charged and belting out "Are you 'avin' a laaarf?", the game got under way with United attacking our end. Perhaps the word 'attacking' is an overuse of artistic licence in this case as it was the laser blues who did more of the attacking in the early stages. And within the first five minutes they could have easily gone one up via the outstretched leg of Wesley Brown, which had diverted the ball on to the underside of the United crossbar.

Three in a Row

The Bitters were even getting ideas about remaining in the Premiership, while several members of the Red fraternity waved their inflatable and caveman-like 'massive clubs' at them. United just couldn't get close and were being kept well away from the City penalty area. I made the mistake of suggesting that perhaps they should score first so that we could then give them a battering. Trouble was, my suggestion coincided with the gangly Wanchope robbing Phil Nev and bursting through the defence to go one-on-one with Barthez. The Costa Rican, who had been a thorn in our side on more than one occasion, rounded Barthez, but thankfully Stam was covering and hoofed the ball away from the goal line. I decided that it would be better to keep my mouth firmly shut from that moment on!

United hadn't looked anything like threatening before a 30-yard free kick from Becks sailed just past the post. And it wasn't until there were only a couple of minutes to go before the break that Nash, in the City goal, had to make a save — a close range shot from Ole. At the break the scores were even. Perhaps it might have made a difference had Elleray noticed that Wanchope had head-butted Phil Nev earlier in the half and then had to brandish one of those red cards he's so fond of waving around at Old Trafford — but he didn't, and neither did his linesman.

During the break Fred the Red and the City mascot (whatever it was supposed to be) squared up to each other down at the Scoreboard End with a certain amount of encouragement from those left in K Stand who were singing "Freddie, Freddie — knock him out!" Order was eventually restored and we welcomed Barthez down to our end for the second half in the hope that Fergie had done the business

Seventh Heaven

and United would be far less benevolent. On the touchline stood one of the very few who has actually requested a transfer from Old Trafford — Andrei Kanchelskis. And as he entered the fray, he was greeted by jeering and the inevitable chorus of "City's going down with a Russian on the wing."

The half-time break had achieved nothing. The game was still scrappy, but at least United showed some intent. On the hour mark, Wes, who had been shifted to right back, was bundled down by Dickov in the box. Without hesitation, Elleray pointed to the spot. With no Denis Irwin on the pitch, Scholesy stepped forward to take the penalty, but it was the Bitters who were celebrating the outcome, as the ball flashed just the wrong side of the post and Scholesy held his head in despair.

Giggs came on immediately afterwards, replacing Chadwick and this introduction, plus the penalty miss, fired United. Nash just managed to gather a Solskjaer shot at the foot of his post and tipped another good effort away. Keano then sent a 25 yarder which fizzed narrowly wide. With 20 minutes to go, the captain sent Ole into the area, but as he turned he was tripped by Dunne. Elleray again pointed to the spot without hesitation, but with repetition. Barthez immediately ran forward in expectation. Urged on by the whole of the Scoreboard, he motioned to the bench and received the necessary encouragement. But when he reached the penalty spot, Sheringham had already decided it was to be his reward. Barthez was gutted and so were we.

As Sheringham stepped up to take the penalty he was booed — in jest, of course, but nevertheless it happened. Sacré bleu — it was the first time I had

Three in a Row

ever experienced a United player stepping up to take a spot kick and getting the bird! Not that we were still booing as he took the kick, and definitely not as the ball hit the back of the net. We were celebrating at last.

The Bitters sat silent as we reminded them of their imminent return to the Nationwide and United were completely dominant without actually looking as though they were going to add to the scoreline. The laser blues were in disarray, but fate was yet to take another turn. We were singing "Stockport, Stockport, give us a wave", "We'll never play you again" and "Shit on the City tonight" when, with seven minutes to go, they won a corner down to our right. Dickov went over to take to a chorus of "Get that dick off!" The ball came over, there was a scramble in the penalty box, and three City players were wheeling away towards a Bitter section that was orgasmic in its joy. "You're not singing anymore," they sang to an Old Trafford that had never really started singing in the first place.

The Russian sub was subbed for the Goat and the final minutes were played out to the accompaniment of Munich chants from the visitors and an increasingly ferocious Roy Keane stamping around the pitch frightening the children. He eventually snapped and a vicious tackle on Haaland (it couldn't have happened to a nicer bloke!) saw him storming down the tunnel to a standing ovation, after a red card from schoolmaster Elleray, who had spent the whole game posturing like he was in his Harrow classroom. Minutes later, the final whistle blew. The Bitters were beside themselves with delirious delight as Steve and I sat in the stadium while it emptied. With just one home game left, and tickets secured for myself and Gina in the Family Stand, I said farewell

Seventh Heaven

to K Stand for the season with City's "Blue Moon" ringing in my ears. Not the scenario I had wished for, or envisaged.

Back at the Throstles Nest, we joined up with the others waiting outside. The doors were shut and the sign said: "Piss off and come back at 4pm" or words to that effect. But a coach load of South Africans (including an ex-United keeper) was due and there was no way we were going to miss it. The post-match mood could have been better, but the game had been massively disappointing. Not to the Bitters of course as we were reminded as a car went past with its blue-shirted passenger leaning out of the window waving his arms about aeroplane-style and screaming "Munichs!" at us as we sat on the steps slurping Duncan's champagne from the bottle.

Eventually we were allowed in to the pub and before the South Africans arrived were approached by the enemy. A blue-shirted Bitter came over to us and we feared the worst. A tirade of embarrassing abuse — no! He started making jokes — about his own team! "One goat and ten donkeys" — that sort of thing! He was actually talking sense! I know — not something you'd expect from a Bitter! It surprised us too, but it was probably due to the fact that the rest of his family (his wife and two kids) were devout Reds, and the result of a massive bout of drinking, having been in the pub since well before the game started!

Eventually, Ethel arrived and what had been a disappointing day turned into a very special one as Gary Bailey walked into the Nest and proceeded to charm everyone, including the City fans in the corner! Gary Bailey is a very special man who seems to be constantly surprised by his legendary status at Old Trafford. He patiently posed for the photos and signed

Three in a Row

the autographs, always with a smile and those of us lucky enough to be there will always remember him, not only for his exploits as a United player, but also for his natural ease and charm. No wonder he left us when he did and went back to the country of his birth though, as judging by the look of him, it has rejuvenating properties. He now looks no different to when he played for us nearly 20 years ago. No-one mentioned 1979 and Alan Sunderland though, or we may have seen him age on the spot!

Between the City game and the next, United signed Ruud Van Nistelrooy from PSV Eindhoven for a reputed 19 million. The deal had fallen through the previous year due to his cruciate problem, so we welcome the Ruud boy and hope he does the business for us.

As the season drew to an end, there was also a sad end for the pub immortalised by United's hardcore fans. The Dog and Partridge was destroyed in an arson attack. For decades, fans gathered before matches at the D and P and many Red terrace anthems had their first airing within its confines. As Pete Boyle said: "It's so sad it should go in this way after all these years. It was a place of noise, song and celebration for the real fan. Now we don't know where we'll go."

Where to now?

An Afternoon on the Marie Celeste

Middlesbrough 0 Manchester United 2
Premier League Saturday 28 April 2001

It was a strange day. I left home in a thunderstorm, with hail pelting down and the heavens flashing and roaring above my head. The temperature felt about minus three. By the time we were halfway to Manchester, the sun had come out and I was pulling off layers of clothing and wilting in the heat of a train full of laser blues from Stockport heading for their nemesis at Maine Road. Well, it would have been their nemesis if my daydreams had worked out right, but hopefully fate is saving that for the last day of the season — it's more fun that way! I arrived in Manchester and saw the football specials waiting in their usual place. "Oh, that's nice," thought I, "the club have arranged transport even though this isn't a normal match day." Thankfully, I realised my mistake before boarding the bus and heading off for the land of the Bitters, and got on the 255 to Old Trafford instead!

It was very odd arriving at the top of Sir Matt Busby Way. Everything seemed as it should be, yet

Three in a Row

Wasn't! Macari's was open, as were the burger bars, but there were very few people about and just one sad looking old fella selling scarves on the corner of Chester Road. It was like the Marie Celeste — everyone had arrived for the game but then been spirited away without warning! As I was very early the gates weren't even open, so I was forced (for the third week running) to eat some chips to pass the time.

Eventually, the ground staff took pity on us and opened up. In we went, to an empty and echoing stadium. After buying a coffee and a packet of Jaffa Cakes (I still have to have my OT match day rituals) I rather forlornly made my way to the back row of the Scoreboard to find a seat. By that point, I would have given anything for a familiar face, but it seemed they were all at the 'real' game, so I turned my attention to the screen set up on the pitch, showing Friday night's MUTV shows. Do people really pay for this rubbish? I suppose it's worth it to watch reserve games etc, but the presenters! Apart from having voices that could be marketed as insomnia cures, they are weird! Especially the one who stares at you like something out of a Night of the Living Dead movie! But it was pleasant enough, sitting in the sunshine watching Alan Keegan making an even bigger prat of himself than he does at live games and listening to the stewards chattering amongst themselves. There was some debate about whether we were allowed to drink alcohol in view of the pitch but apparently we were — providing there were no real footballers running around on it at the time! Gradually the stand filled up and I began to feel less isolated as I spotted a few familiar faces.

Before the game started we had to endure an hour of 'entertainment'. But the kids who made up

Where to now?

most of the crowd seemed to enjoy it, particularly those who won a United 'goodie bag'. One old guy refused to get into the spirit of the thing (letting the kids win) and claimed a bag for himself and yours truly was no better — glaring at the camera everytime my face appeared on the screen and ignoring the pleas to wave and smile — like a rather grumpy Jack Dee. Basically, it was a Fred the Red night, without Fred. What we have to endure to watch a game of football!

By the time the game kicked off, all the grown- ups had had enough and were mightily relieved to see the lads run out onto the pitch. Despite us being a hundred or so miles away, we cheered as if we were there. It was good to see Johnsen and Fortune back and to see another ginger prince making his debut. Despite the annoying commentary (why did we need a commentary? Why couldn't they have just put a microphone in the away section and let us 'be there'?), we could hear the United fans in the background. "We are the Busby Babes" rang out loud and clear.

We'd only just got settled into the game when Phil Nev picked up the ball and curled a stunner into the net! Everyone leapt to their feet and celebrations took place that would not have gone amiss in the Riverside. "City's going down" we could hear from the away section as play went on, and we joined in the roar of derision as Ince's free kick went over the bar. "Pride of all Europe" came over loud and clear as Teddy almost scored with a header, but Schwarzer saved it. "25 years" roared out as Stewart put his shot over the bar. Were there no Boro fans in the ground for the first half? We didn't hear a peep!

A gasp shook the East Stand as Windass looked

Three in a Row

set to equalise, but his shot inched passed the post and the gasp became a sigh of relief. Then there was a groan of disappointment as the City score came on the screen — One-nil up! Still, everyone was looking happy — the sun was shining, we were winning and for the first half-hour or so, the lads were playing the best football I've seen them play since the Arsenal game. At last we seemed to have remembered how to play on the break! It was end- to-end stuff at that point, with Ricard putting another shot wide and then a save by Raimond from Cooper, but nevertheless, United were in charge and not seriously looking as if they were going to do anything other than win the game. A good shot from Ole was saved by Schwarzer and then Raimond made an even better save at the other end, tipping a shot from Windass over the bar.

The half-time break brought me back to the reality of where I was. No nipping behind the seats to pinch a certain IMUSA bigwig's Jaffa Cakes for me! Instead I stayed in my seat and watched the half-time 'entertainment' with my Jack Dee face on once more.

As the second half started, the sun had disappeared and the storm clouds were gathering. Glad that it wasn't a 'real' game, I watched, with a rueful smile, as hundreds vacated the front section of the Scoreboard where I normally sit and climbed up into K Stand to avoid the hailstones!

The second half wasn't as good as the first, with United giving away the ball too often for comfort and the players getting tetchy and swinging their handbags about. Butt was storming around midfield doing his impression of Keano on a bad day and getting cheers in our neck of the woods every time he faced up to Ince. Stewart, unlike Scholesy, seems to be as fiery as his hair — he wasn't too chuffed when

Where to now?

Windass got him booked early in the second half.

There were chances at both ends, with Vickers and Ince wasting good opportunities and Ole taking neither of two chances while the Boro defence panicked and ran round in ever-decreasing circles. There were some odd refereeing decisions — the worst being when Butt won the ball on the edge of our penalty area and was bundled to the ground, but Boro got the free kick! Phil Nev got himself booked for complaining, or kicking the ball or something, and the United players wasted so much time faffing about that the ref moved the ball 10 yards forward, bringing it into the area. The kick was blocked by the wall, came off the bar and was then bundled into the net by Ehiogu. A groan went around Old Trafford as the Boro fans were heard for the first time. But the groan turned to cheers as the goal was disallowed for offside, play resumed, and the Boro fans finally began to get behind their team.

Giggs came on for Fortune and almost immediately made an impact and Cole came on for Ole. In the main the second half was more memorable for the spats than for the football, especially between Becks and Cooper who just didn't seem to be getting on well at all! The Boro crowd, meanwhile, had gone very quiet — indeed had gone home! By the time Giggs cut the ball back to Becks on the edge of the penalty area and Becks put the ball in the back of the net for our second, there were more empty seats than full ones around the Riverside. Chadwick came on for Wilson for the last few minutes and we relaxed and enjoyed the sound of the away end celebrating: "We shall not be moved", "You'll never get a job" and "Champions".

So it was an unusual experience, but I think a

valid one. There were around 3,000 fans (I think) inside OT, most of them not normally able to watch United live. I still think the price was a bit steep, but if unable to go to the game itself, it was certainly better than listening to it on the radio! Man of the match? In my opinion — Nicky Butt. Anyone who wants to sell him must be watching a different player to me.

There followed yet another award for our Teddy as Sheringham secured PFA Player of the Year to add to the Football Writers' award he'd won the previous week. This time it was Keano who came second with the Arse's Henry third.

Dreaming

I had a dream when I was a kid. The initial part of the dream came true when I first stood on the Stretford End and watched the red shirts dance in the floodlights one September evening in 1964. The second part came true at the end of that season as I watched United lift the Championship trophy for the first time. Through the glorious sixties, the trilogy of Best, Law and Charlton majestically strode Europe's finest pitches until the Holy Grail was won in '68 and my dream became reality. As United floundered post-Busby another dream was born. The Doc administered some sweet Scottish elixir — the buccaneers took the football world by storm and the heatwave spread once again. In the 80s under big fat Ron we won FA Cups, gloriously against Everton, somewhat fortuitously against Brighton, but it wasn't until the Wizard rang the changes and brought his particular magic to bear that unparalleled success came to my beloved Manchester United and hence to

Where to now?

me. During the 90s my dreams once again came true and were fully realised in magnificent style accompanied by some of the best football played in the Manchester United way.

And now I have another dream.

I still inhabit the age when football actually meant something special to everyone who passed through the turnstiles. In a time when you had to earn the right to go and watch the lads play. To see a trophy lifted was the greatest moment in our young lives. It was never, ever, the first time we had been to a game — those privileges were reserved for the ones who had paid their dues and deserved to be there. Not so now. There were people at the Derby County game who had never been to Old Trafford before. They had not earned the right to be there, had no idea about the traditions of the club and were taking the places away from those that had earned the right. And how did they manage to get hold of those precious tickets?

As I grew up in the Midlands within a rugby-mad family, I had no-one to teach me about football, let alone somewhere more than a hundred miles north west called Manchester. But I made it my business to find out. I consumed (all too rare) newspaper articles and read books until I understood what Manchester United meant. It was then that I felt I had earned the right to stand on the Stretford End and cheer on the lads with the rest. It felt right. The fact that we had moved north by that time also helped considerably! And since then I have done my best to infect my children with the Red virus. Take them to the dark side and show them the devilish ways of United.

With the advent of rampant commercialism, merchandising madness, over-inflated ticket prices and supposed heaven on earth blasting from our TV screens, football has developed into a monster that is running out of control. My dream is that the monster will be tamed and shackled. That someday the football fat cats will be forced to return the game to its true home that lies deep within the hearts of the real supporters. Only then will we be able to pass it on to our children and feel proud that we have initiated them in the ways of the game and how to support the team that means so much. The game safe and sound in its rightful home and every supporter free to support in the way of their own choosing.

It is surely not too much to ask is it?

Dream on

Manchester United 0 Derby County 1
Premier League Saturday 5 May 2001

It was the start of the Bank Holiday weekend and the world and their dog was out in force. The harbinger doctor had already warned of this when he called in for a quick cuppa while on his way north for the weekend. I was also driving the family up for a weekend in Manchester, so none of the usual crew were with me. Big Rich had offered to drive the Sausageman rather than entrust himself to the delights of the fartmobile and so there were three cars on their way north when there would normally have been one. Luckily, at least two of those cars had left slightly earlier than usual and just managed to slip past the van slumped in the centre lane, smack in the middle of Spaghetti Junction with its hazard lights flashing. The queues that were to build up a

Where to now?

little later warranted a couple of mentions on the radio. The van had suffered a serious malfunction in the front suspension department and had collapsed in a similar fashion to one who had suffered the after effects of a Dobson trouser trumpet.

The motorway was jam-packed with a variety of end-of-season supporters, each with flags and scarves, stickers and mini kits draped ceremoniously over their vehicles and all seemingly celebrating something or other. There were clusters of Rushden and Diamonds, bevvies of Bristols, bin loads of Scousers and one lone Derby fan looking as though he was on the way to the abattoir. If only he had known he would have raised a smile instead of that furrowed brow.

We arrived at Arbuckles in good time despite the motorway procession. The rest of the family were already there. Having passed my Season Ticket over to Eliza, we headed for Old Trafford looking forward to a football display to match the trophy the team were about to receive. Gina munched on her giant hot dog as we approached the ground and had just about finished it by the time we made our way round to the Family Stand. It wasn't an ideal location, but I had been eager to let her witness a trophy being presented and even though we were stationed on the next-to-last row, we were there — and in more or less the same spot as the one I was in when we won the first of our magnificent seven Premiership titles nine short years ago.

How things have changed since that day. On the very last row (and directly behind us) were a family with three kids. Two of these delightful little creatures were intent on splitting my head in two by blasting their referees' whistles as loud as they possibly could

Three in a Row

at every available opportunity (which was all the bloody time). By the time the teams came out I had a headache as hideous as any other experienced. It didn't seem to bother Gina so I tried to ignore the invasion of what was left of my senses and stuck my fingers in my ears to deaden the pain. I remember thinking it was going to be hell when we scored! Why would I have thought that, I wonder?

Denis led the team out in the absence of our outspoken captain and the Derby fans sat silent in their corner — waiting for the inevitable onslaught. Surely the Rams would be put to the slaughter? Unfortunately not! United were suffering a foot and mouth crisis of their own — their feet would not function properly and the only mouth (a certain Mr Keane) was sidelined. There was no real driving force. We may as well have been watching them soaking up the sun on their Caribbean Island retreats, because that is where a few of them seemed to be. The game was a disappointment as massive as the one a certain club from across the City were about to suffer. It can't be that difficult for players to motivate themselves for a game wearing the red shirt can it? Especially as this was a game which had a bearing on relegation. Not that the majority of those who were sat near us seemed at all bothered — they had only come for the glitz.

Maybe it's just me, but I don't care whether the game is a friendly against Flixton — I always want to win. I HATE to lose to anybody. Gina had been looking forward to this game ever since the tickets had flopped through our letterbox and even she was sitting beside me wondering why she had bothered to turn up. At least those whistles remained reasonably subdued, but how I would have gladly paid the price

Where to now?

and suffered for a few goals.

As the sun shone on the far side of the pitch, I slipped easily into a reverie of my own — imagining it beating down on my pate and was instantly transported to my own island retreat. With my eyes closed I could see the multi-coloured sunspots dancing on my eyelids as the heat of the sun soothed my aching temples. As palm fronds rustled gently overhead I was about to order a cool beer when all of a sudden I was brought back to stark reality by a shrill falsetto. "City reject!" cried the lad over to our left as the diminutive ex-Bitter, Kinkladze, dared to attack the United goal. My musings had been shattered and the gentle rustling of palm fronds was, in reality, one of the whistlers opening a huge packet of salt and vinegar.

The football was enlivened only by occasional Barthez trickery, including a couple of superb 50 yard pinpoint passes, a Becks free kick well saved by Poom, the industry of Butt and Stewart in midfield and the class of Ronaldo at the back. Chadders ran and ran but was more reminiscent of a pinball bouncing off defenders than a winger who was going to succeed in a repeat performance of the Derby away game. At least J and K Stands livened things up by staging their own war. They'd tried to wind up the Derby fans without success so turned on each other instead. "Are you City in disguise?" from J was met with "You Scouse bastards!" from K. The banter went back and forth until they both turned on the Stretford with "Can you here the Stretford sing — no-ooh?", which was met with "Who the f**kin' 'ell are you?" "You've only got one song," they replied in unison, but as we got back with "Part-time supporters", Derby went and spoiled all the fun by scoring. As Barthez

Three in a Row

threw himself to the right, Christie's shot flew past him and into the net. The Derby fans went ballistic, but so did many of the Stretford End much to the surprise of the odd few Derby supporters who had managed to secrete themselves away before that moment when they were discovered.

It was all we could do to gain any sort of Satisfaction, so "City's going down with a Russian on the wing" reverberated around Old Trafford with both sets of supporters becoming very strange bedfellows from that moment on. It was a very weird experience and one I have no real desire to repeat. I wish Derby no particular ill will but they should have been hammered out of sight and condemned to suffer a final day of extreme torture. They should not have been allowed to get away with their Premiership survival that easily. Not that the lads didn't step up a gear from then until half-time, but despite a couple of near misses, the score remained Manchester United 0, Derby 1.

Meanwhile back in my usual spot, one of my regular companions obviously wasn't driving back to Blackpool that evening. He had arrived in a sorry state, had carried on consuming beer, fallen asleep during the first half with his head on Steve's shoulder and then disappeared below stairs just before the half-time whistle. The whole of the second half had elapsed by the time he reappeared having spent the entire time fast asleep sitting on the toilet!

Back in the Family Stand, the mass exodus to the bars and kiosks was taking place just as Gina appeared in the nick of time at the top of the steps clutching a large cup of orange pop and looking very pleased with herself that she had managed to beat the rush for once. Paul McGrath did the half-time

Where to now?

draw, Keegan played a birthday request for Boylie, the 'Burnage Bard' and we were informed that over two million visitors had poured through the Old Trafford turnstiles since August. I wonder how many of that two million had known where Old Trafford was before 1993? The teams reappeared and the Family Stand returned to their seats replete with popcorn and pop. Barthez was down at the Scoreboard End playing with a beachball that someone (who had obviously been in the same dream as me) had thrown from the crowd.

Apart from Christie, who missed a completely open goal from six inches, the vast majority of the play was down at our end. The game was gradually prized open, United got closer and closer and the odd intermittent half-volumed 'peep' from the whistle was heard from the row behind. But despite Giggs entering the fray for young Stewart, and Silvestre, who received a rousing welcome (what a difference a year makes) replacing Phil Nev, the Derby defence and Poom somehow managed to keep their goal intact. After several excellent saves and countless goal line clearances later, the Derby fans could celebrate their prolonged stay in the Premiership. They were safe and a certain City were down (Coventry that is). Those from Derby sang "We ARE staying up!" and the rest of us sang "We won the Football League again and City's going down" (Manchester City that is). The Derby players were applauded off the pitch and the majority of their supporters stayed to return the favour — probably still extremely shocked at their good fortune.

As we waited for all the trappings of modern day trophy presentations to be constructed Gina sat bemused. Those of us who have supporter

Three in a Row

credentials that stretch back more than a few years are also bemused — well, perhaps that's not quite the word I would use. Why do we have to have fireworks, elaborate constructions and the deafening bastardised PLC versions of OUR songs blasting at eardrum-splitting volume from the PA when we don't need any of it?

"Forever and ever" brought a tear to my eye and a lump to my throat. It transported me back to another time and, if for only the briefest of seconds, made everything pure again. The trappings of rampant commercialism disappeared and the pitch was unadulterated green. But it didn't last. I could stand my lofty perch no longer so grabbed Gina and moved further down to where there were some who actually seemed to appreciate what was going on. That history had been made. That the Wizard had produced a team which had won three successive Premiership titles and that no other manager had ever done that.

Many had already left, unable to cope with the nonsensical dross that has filtered into the game of football. Even in the Family Stand there were many empty seats. When will those who 'rule' our game ever learn? How that precious hour spent after the final whistle on that balmy night in Barcelona becomes even more and more poignant. The bonding of players and supporters into one huge family. The spirit of football was alive and well that night, but all this dross is killing it stone dead. Why don't they just leave it be?

Anyway, the trophy was presented, the Champagne chucked and the lap of honour completed. It was good to see Fergie beaming proudly. If any man deserves our most fulsome

Where to now?

gratitude it is he. But it was young Brooklyn who stole the show once again. Already showing an aptitude for the beautiful game, he drew cheers from the Stretford End every time he kicked the ball passed to him by his father (a pretty decent footballer himself!) and a request that "Fergie, Fergie, sign him on". As the man himself said as the players were about to take their leave: "This is not the end of this United team."

And my dream still lives of course — that this team will lift many more trophies, playing football in the Manchester United way — but also that we will be allowed to watch and celebrate in our own way. I have an idea the former may be the more likely, but who knows?

Fireworks and a massive shirt

I spent the first 15 minutes of the footballing day trying to make myself as inconspicuous as possible on the station platform — not easy at a station the size of a postage stamp! Why, you may ask. Quite simple really — my local branch of the supporters' club was out in numbers, all decked out in their shirts, scarves and silly hats, showing off like naughty schoolchildren — they were going to Old Trafford for the day, even if they didn't know how to get there! Thankfully, the train arrived before they sussed me out and I was able to sneak into the other carriage of the train, amongst some travelling Derby supporters. Thankfully they were discussing football rather than whether the Megastore would have the new 'gold' kit in yet. Of course they wanted to know whether United might 'do them a favour'. "No chance," I said. "The United lads play to win every game!" Thankfully, I

Three in a Row

didn't have to go through the embarrassment of seeing them again on the way home!

It was early when I arrived at Old Trafford, but the forecourt was packed. In front of me, a drama was being enacted as an old fella was being harassed by three young lads trying to sell him a ticket. "Only 250 quid mate," said one. "Too much," said the old fella. "You'll regret it if you don't buy it," said another. £250! Reports were that touts were buying them for £10 up the road! Eventually, they gave up and wandered off. A few minutes later I saw the same old fella hand over a wad of 20 pound notes to another lad — guess he succumbed in the end. I just hope he thought the poor display on the pitch worth all that money!

Arriving in the Scoreboard, I found the son- and-heir had already arrived and very pleased to see me as he was being bored to death by the moaning old git who sits behind us. Every player was being given his end-of-season rating — most of them poor! We escaped as the teams ran out onto the pitch and arrived in our seats just in time to see the world's ugliest goalkeeper take up his position. I just prayed the rumours about us signing Poom weren't true — I'm not sure I could cope with a close-up of his ugly mug every week!

For the first fifteen minutes or so, the atmosphere was reasonable with plenty of chanting going on around the ground. The front three rows of the Scoreboard, as usual, were filled with the living dead. They sat there, staring straight ahead, so quiet that one of the lads behind us was heard to mutter something about calling an undertaker at one point. Behind us, the moaning old git was getting into his stride as the unfamiliar-looking United team played more like a relegation-threatened side, than

Where to now?

Champions. Ignoring the cemetery in front of us, we joined in with the singing coming from our right and behind us, while the Derby fans sat quietly — presumably waiting, like us, for the United lads to wake up and play like the champions they undoubtedly are. Unfortunately, the lads never did wake up and we were 'treated' to one of the poorest performances I have ever seen.

Irwin was captain for the day, but he's a quiet lad and without Keane to gee 'em up, all the players (apart from a very few notable exceptions) looked as if they had already gone on their summer hols. The young lads were obviously trying to impress, but it was over half an hour before the first real attack of the day, and when it did come, it was at the wrong end and produced a goal for the wrong team! Christie spun away from Wallwork and his shot went past Barthez and into the top corner. The reaction from the crowd, however, was not what the Derby fans had been expecting!

Off the pitch, we were determined to enjoy ourselves even if our enthusiasm for the day wasn't shared by some of the players. Around 20 minutes into the game, fed up with what was happening on the pitch and with the lack of opposition from the Derby fans, the East End of the stadium erupted as J Stand took on K Stand. Back and forth the chants went: "It's just like watching City," J Stand sang. "You're just a bunch of Scousers," replied K Stand. "You're gonna get your f**kin heads kicked in," J warned K. "You fat bastard," they sang together, as Boylie was spotted. No-one was watching the pitch when suddenly, the Derby fans started leaping up and down. At the other end the Derby players were celebrating and the fans in L Stand were standing up

Three in a Row

chanting "Derby, Derby," when the whole of K and J joined in to the amazement of the Derby fans — the irony was lost on them of course, but they got the message all right when the whole stadium joined in a celebratory chorus of "City's going down".

It was a very weird feeling. Very few of us really wanted to lose, but we had got to that point where no-one could see how we were going to win this game, so we might as well make the most of it. After all, it was supposed to be a day of celebration and this particular dark cloud did have a very obvious silver lining!

The second half was not so enjoyable. It was nice to see the chaps from Derby so happy and relieved, but by then the joke had worn off a little and it was a rather forced gaiety that ensued. At one point it looked as if they might even get another, indeed they should have got another as Christie was presented with an empty net from six feet out, and managed to put the ball past the post! Fabien turned to us and joined in with the laughter as we took the mick out of the Derby striker. Eventually, we did bring Giggs on and, as so many times before, we began to look as if we could at least get an equaliser. Only a couple of minutes after coming on the pitch, Giggs had a shot cleared off the line, and for the last ten minutes we bombarded their goal. Only some fine saves by Poom and some last-ditch defending kept us out. Five minutes or so from the end, Fergie brought on Raimond. Instead of taking off Cole and putting Barthez up front, which was what most of the stadium and Barthez himself wanted (he had just spent 10 minutes creeping surreptitiously ever closer to their penalty area!), Fergie swapped a keeper for a keeper and we played through to the end of a disappointing

Where to now?

game with the Derby fans singing "We are staying up" and us singing City songs in an attempt to convince ourselves that we didn't mind the end result!

By this stage, I was finding all this a little hard to take. We were Champions for the third time in a row, the seventh time in nine years and this match was the one at which we were being presented with the trophy. It was also a very important match in terms of the Premiership relegation battle. Normally, I wouldn't give a stuff about the latter and if we had been looking at a Cup Final or two in the coming weeks, I would have been quite happy for Fergie to field a weakened side. But I think we should have gone all out to win, and finish off the season in style and it bloody pissed me off that we didn't! Anything else was short-changing both players and fans.

Once the players went off the pitch we watched the Derby fans and players celebrating as we waited to see what horror the club would come up with this year. To be honest, as these choreographed celebrations go, I suppose it could have been worse. At least it wasn't quite as bad as last year, and despite a lot of people threatening to leave before it started, the ground was still full when the fireworks began and the team came back out onto the pitch. I was aware of almost having to force myself to be excited. All the razzmatazz had very little to do with my experience of football or the way I would want to celebrate. Fireworks banging away, two soldiers (what was all that about?) escorting the trophy onto the pitch, the whole squad lifting the cup in turn with Alan Keegan announcing their names as if we didn't know who they were. The players were being told exactly where to stand and where to go next, jumping up and down for the cameras in a parody of their

Three in a Row

celebrations at Wembley, when we won the first double, and the final insult, Keegan announcing that we would now have a lap of honour. As if we couldn't figure out for ourselves what they were doing!

The worst part of the whole stage-managed event was the presentation of a 'present' to the fans, from 'the team'. They unravelled a truly massive United shirt and the players brought it over to the Scoreboard and gave it to the fans to pass across K Stand. It was embarrassing in the extreme! For them and for us (the only player who looked like he was enjoying himself was Teddy, and he looked pissed!). I suppose Mr and Mrs Megastore and their 2.4 children enjoyed it, but I was cringing! And I was immensely cheered later when I heard that the thing was of such poor quality that the sleeve came off halfway across K Stand and went home in someone's pocket!

But I was determined that I was going to enjoy the occasion — this is OUR team and OUR trophy — and we spent too many years watching them win f**k all to allow the men in suits to take it away from us entirely. And there were some good moments. As the players stood on the rostrum waiting for the trophy, we were able to sing a few of the players' songs: "Yip Jaap Stam" and "Keano" in particular, before the PA shut us up. And once the players had got away from the officials and had picked up the customary gaggle of children, they appeared genuinely pleased to share their success with the fans. Brooklyn was, as last year, the centre of attention. Totally unfazed by the presence of 60,000 people, he dribbled a football around the whole pitch, only pausing in front of the Scoreboard to score his first goal, to a big cheer from the crowd. Finally, Fergie took the mike and thanked

Where to now?

everyone as usual. But his most welcome proclamation was that "This United team is not finished."

As we left the stadium, there was none of the singing and chanting of previous years. Instead, there was an air of anti-climax. Certainly we have been spoiled and for many United fans, these celebrations obviously don't mean as much as they used to. And the club has spoiled what should be a spontaneous outburst of feeling between players and fans (remember Barcelona?) with their choreographed nonsense. Next season — which, let's be honest, could be the last memorable one for a long time — we should be looking at how we can reclaim these celebrations for those who matter — the players and the fans. Here's hoping we have plenty to celebrate!

A couple of days later on the Monday night over at Portman Road the expected happened and our neighbours from Maine Road disappeared down the plughole and into the Nationwide. Ipswich had beaten them 2-1 and the Ipswich fans were singing "you're not massive anymore!" Credit to the tractor boys!

Good Riddance

Southampton 2 Manchester United 1
Premier League Sunday 13 May 2001

It was goodbye and good riddance to the Dell — a place which hasn't always been a happy hunting ground for us Reds. No more trips to the Dell — a tight little ground with the crowd very close to the pitch. Not that we had tickets for this game — we'd both been Chubbed, so maybe, when the new ground at St Mary's is opened for next season, it will herald a change of ticket fortune.

The Saints hadn't won a game for weeks but with United fielding a very young team, including the likes of Wallwork, Fortune, Stewart and Chadwick, they were muscled out and overrun in midfield.

Wes put the Saints ahead with another own goal — this time an absolute cracker of a diving header! Not long afterwards Marian Pahars continued his scoring streak against us with the second goal. 2-0 down after 15 minutes and the omens were looking fairly poor to say the least.

But United rallied, Giggs moved back to the left for the start of the second half and things started to shape up as he almost immediately created and scored the Reds' equaliser. Despite creating countless chances that was the end of the scoring and the curse of the Dell had struck again.

The Battle of Britain

Glasgow Celtic 0 Manchester United 2
Tom Boyd's testimonial 15 May 2001

The English champions against the Scottish champions, on the day that Bobby Murdoch died and not a whisper was heard during the tribute — just as it should be. The same could not be said as Andy Goram, the man they call the 'Flying Pig' came on as second-half sub for Raimond. The Celtic fans were naturally vociferous in their condemnation — hardly a surprise!

This wasn't a match played under competition circumstances of course, but it had its fair share of

Where to now?

passion as both teams went for the win. It was a chance for Fergie to wind up the Celts by giving odds of 4 to 1 that Larsson wouldn't score. In fact it was only the width of the bar which prevented him from having to pay up!

There were chances aplenty at both ends, even one for Tommy Boyd — but he missed! It was David Beckham who lobbed a ball into the Celtic box. A ball which eluded everyone until it reached Mikky Silvestre who stooped to conquer (and head into the net past Douglas).

Eventually the second goal came late on in the second half when substitute Bojan Djordjic spotted the keeper way out off his line and accepted the invitation to scoop the ball over the top and into the vacant net.

The Reds in the crowd were making all the running throughout with much evidence of camaraderie and scarf swapping. The friendly bond that has existed between the two clubs culminated in a joint rendition of "Champions" and the Celts even cheered Giggsy as he collected the trophy.

Full circle

Tottenham Hotspur 3 Manchester United 1
Premier League Saturday 19 May 2001

It was like watching the last decade of your Football-supporting life pass very slowly before your eyes. A magnificent decade of unprecedented success instigated by one man who took hold of our hands and led us to a Catalan heaven and back. And now what does the future hold? Red News had broken the

Three in a Row

story on the Monday night/Tuesday morning that the Wizard had said he would walk away from the club at the end of next season because, in his own words: "United have failed to come up to my expectations." What an indictment — that the club who have become the richest in the world have failed to come up to the expectations of the man who has lined their pockets with gold and our trophy cabinet with silver.

When we all met up before this game there were many rumours. Everyone was talking about the same thing — Alex Ferguson and his rift with the hierarchy at Manchester United. On the train going south, even those who were on their way to the Test Match were talking about it. And the resounding consensus was one of utter disbelief that United hadn't seen fit to acknowledge the man who has turned the club around, from being an underachiever into champions, with at least a seat on the board. Apparently there had been opposition to the appointment. It doesn't take a genius to work out where that opposition came from now does it?

Without Fergie's unquenchable thirst for success, and without his drive and leadership, Manchester United would not be in this position of strength. Despite recent defeats, we have still been untouchable in the Premiership and have enjoyed a consistency in the European Cup which is the envy of 99.9 percent of football. And if you want business speak, have become a club 'brand' that is the strongest in the world. What the PLC don't seem to understand is that you have to be successful on the football pitch to be able to sell shirts, therefore you have to back the manager. When you have a manager who has proved himself the most successful of all time in this country then you have to

Where to now?

keep him at all costs. His experience is invaluable — absolutely priceless. And from our point of view, he has been the one person who has taken notice of the supporters. A true and honest football man, but as marketing and merchandising appear to be taking control, the football manager is answerable to far too many people. In actuality the marketing and merchandising departments are only able to do their jobs (in fact they only HAVE jobs) because of Alex Ferguson and his team. And now he has said he will "Sever all ties" with the club and walk away from Manchester United forever. So as we met up in the pubs before the game, it was no wonder that speculation was rife.

The season, for me, had gone full circle. It had been 7am on Vancouver Island as I sat in Steve Fisher's front room as the season kicked off at an Old Trafford bathed in sunshine. And there I was in a north London pub with Fish, his daft mate Pete and the doctor before the final game. Life as a Manchester United supporter has never been dull. No-one knows what is around the corner, but the one thing that remains constant is the 'family'. I remember years ago people asking me why I went to football on my own. But even though I used to arrive at the ground on my own I was then absorbed into the swaying mass of the Stretford End amongst other members of my adopted family. Now there are friends everywhere and before, during and after this game the family spirit loomed large as we closed ranks.

It should have been a celebration. And to some extent it was, but it was also one of the most arduous and overwhelming experiences ever. We permutated what we knew and tried to make sense of it. We heard rumour upon rumour, theory upon theory.

Three in a Row

Fergie wasn't going to be at the game. He had already left the club. Or, Fergie was going to be at the game, but hadn't travelled with the team, but it was to be his last anyway. It felt like a disaster waiting to happen, but as the afternoon progressed I was so glad I was there to show my support. If the man himself had not been there, word would reach him and let him know what happened.

Down at the ground with 15 minutes to go, all seemed relatively normal until we got inside. We found that the cavernous wasteland behind the stand was strangely empty. Some had stayed far too long in the pubs, but most were already up top, standing ready for whatever was about to unfurl. Fish and I stood, along with Fiona, in the corner of the ground with only a narrow gangway separating us from the home fans. The teams appeared, but no Fergie. We feared the worst. To our surprise ours was a strong line-up despite not having Barthez, Gary Nev, Wes, Stam, Keane or Becks available. As the game kicked off, so did we. "Every single one of us loves Alex Ferguson," we sang. It spread throughout the United section as though it was out of control, and it went on and on and on. For 30 solid minutes we sang "Every single one of us loves Alex Ferguson." A demonstration of commitment and a show of gratitude to the man who has given us so much. It bewildered the locals who were stunned into silence. The game was secondary. I couldn't even tell you whether the lads played well or not.

The singing continued without interruption when they scored their first, broke briefly as we celebrated Scholes scoring ours, and ended on the half-hour with a rasping and aggressive repetition of "U-NI-TED, U-NI-TED". I hadn't experienced anything like it

Where to now?

since the right side and the left side of the Stretford celebrated at the start of the '68-'69 season with "We are the Champions, Champions of Europe." The 45 minutes passed me by in a blur of a decade of glorious memories.

There was the odd dissenter amongst the home support of course. An extremely sad and respectable looking middle-aged man to our left took exception and stood with the middle finger of one hand raised until he was encouraged to shove it by a helpful steward. Occasionally it reappeared but all he got from us were smiling stares which struck home with devastating intensity. He hadn't got a clue what to do about the embarrassing situation. He had trapped himself as we sang and those around him who weren't baffled understood our sentiments. The infectious singing even entranced some of their younger element who were seen to sway to the rhythm whilst mouthing the words — much to the distress of their parents. The massed ranks of United swayed too, and as the singing reached peaks of crescendo the intensity increased and the volume pumped up once more. The memory will stay with me forever. The sight of so many familiar faces in the extended United family singing together with such passion was a magnificent sight and sound.

By half-time our hands were red and swollen and our throats were dry and hoarse, and below stairs we met up with others. Each of us passed on our personal sympathies to Lipstick over his devastating loss — another good Red gone, but not forgotten. Some may be surprised that he was there at all, but we all know it was right and as his father would have wished.

By the start of the second half, the home crowd

Three in a Row

had taken up the challenge and for much of the time they continued where we had left off. It helped their cause that they scored two more goals and we didn't, but we eventually got going again even if the first 45 minutes had taken their toll. Several choruses of "If you want to get to heaven when you die" were all that were required. "If you want to get to heaven when you die, you must keep the Red Flag flying high. You must wear a red bonnet with f**k the Scousers on it..... if you want to get to heaven when you die." Along with "And United said, is that a treble in your cabinet — are you 'avin' a larf, are you 'avin' a larf" sorted us out.

The locals, especially the single digit, naturally revelled in their victory as it probably made their season. A victory against the champions, even if division within the club was bound to affect the football, would be savoured. The game ended as it had begun with several more minutes of "Every single one of us loves Alex Ferguson." It was only at the final whistle that we spotted the Wizard on the touchline, and as he quickly disappeared down the tunnel we hoped it wouldn't be for his final time in charge of the United team. Had he come over to us we™d have known, but thankfully he didn't. Most, but not all, of the players did come over to us with Mikky Silvestre staying longest. And as we left the ground chanting "CHAMPIONS — CHAMPIONS" we said our farewells to the 2000-2001 season.

Several of us walked back to the tube together. At that time none of us were any the wiser whether the status quo would stay or go. Rumours still abounded and uncertainty filled our conversations. Gradually we dispersed, with Fish, Pete and I taking the tube which was to be yet another tedious experience. My train down had been delayed and eventually taken

Where to now?

out of commission, causing a long wait and a change of engine. Our tube journey to the game had been circuitous due to line works and the return was even more so. What a marvellous public transport system — we were glad to be leaving. I said my goodbyes to my two companions when we reached Marylebone. Their destination was Milan via Paddington before returning to the clement summer weather of Vancouver Island.

It wasn't until I was halfway home that my phone rang with a message from the doctor that Fergie had told the press after the game that it was his intention to stay on at United for one last season in charge. That is what he would want. Whether he would be able to carry on was a bone of contention. Only time would tell.

No matter what happens in the future you can be sure that the United family spirit will always remain. As football has become a business it has changed immeasurably for better and for worse. The modern day supporter is vastly different from that when I first went to games and to some extent that is inevitable. Things change but sometimes they change without due consideration of the past. But the way football differs, as a business to any other business, is that it depends on football — the GAME of football. It also depends on true football people and on the interaction and influence between the players and the fans. It depends on you and me — and it depends on people like Alex Ferguson.

So the season ended on a very strange note indeed, but there again, life as a Red is never ever dull is it?